بسم الله الرحمن الرحيم

"The house of al-Arqam is the house of Islām"

Al-Ḥākim (d.403h) in *al-Mustadrak ʿala al-Ṣaḥiḥayn* (6185)

A Critique of the
Ruling of *al-Taqlīd*

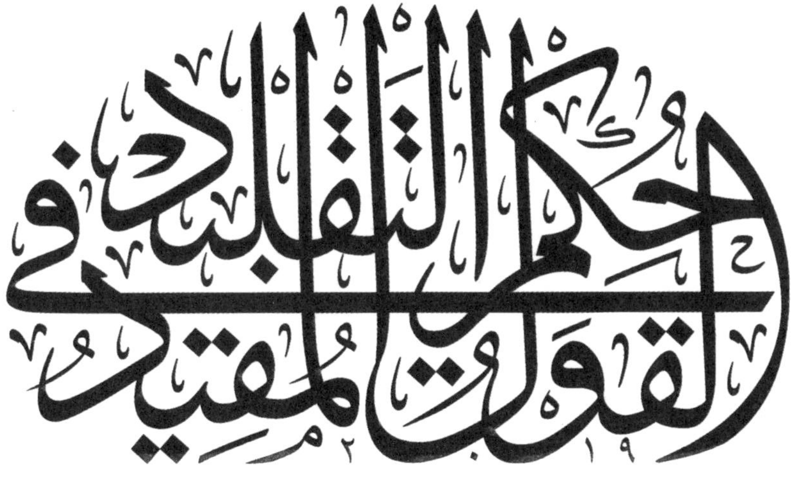

Shaykh al-Islām, the imām of Yemen
Muḥammad ibn ʿAlī al-Shawkānī
(d. 1834/1250)

ISBN: 978-1-9164756-4-9

British Library Cataloguing in Publishing Data
A catalogue record for this book is available from the British Library

Prepared and published by Dar al-Arqam Publishing,
Birmingham, United Kingdom

Translated under the supervision of:

Adnan Karim

Head of translation at Dar al-Arqam. He has translated and edited a number of works for Dar al-Arqam.

www.daral-arqam.co.uk
Email: daralarqam@hotmail.co.uk

Printed in Turkey by Mega | export@mega.com.tr

A CRITIQUE OF

THE RULING OF AL-TAQLĪD

Muḥammad ibn ʿAlī al-Shawkānī (d. 1250H)

الفهرس
Contents

تقديم المترجم

Translator's Foreword

إِنَّ الْحَمْدَ لِلَّهِ نَحْمَدُهُ وَنَسْتَعِينُهُ ونستغفره ونعوذ بالله من شرور أنفسنا ومن سيئات أعمالنا مَنْ يَهْدِهِ اللَّهُ فَلَا مُضِلَّ لَهُ وَمَنْ يُضْلِلْ فَلَا هَادِيَ لَهُ وَأَشْهَدُ أَنْ لَا إِلَهَ إِلَّا اللَّهُ وَحْدَهُ لَا شَرِيكَ لَهُ وَأَنَّ مُحَمَّدًا عَبْدُهُ وَرَسُولُهُ. أَمَّا بَعْدُ:

Due to my personal connection to the past scholars of the Ahl al-Ḥadīth from the Indian Subcontinent (through my grandfather al-Shaykh Faḍal Karīm ʿĀsim, d. 2003 ﵀), I have always intended to translate at least one book of al-Imām al-Shawkānī ﵀. This is because he had a great influence over the Indian subcontinent through al-ʿAllāmah Nawāb Ṣiddīq Ḥasan Khan ﵀. My original intention was to translate his book *al-Darārī al-Muḍiyyah Sharḥ al-Durar al-Bahiyyah*. I commenced this project during 2017, but due to a busy schedule I only reached the mid-point of the book of prayer. In 2019 a translation of this was published. So as not to harm the publisher of this book, I decided not to carry on with my own translation. After consultation with a number of senior colleagues and friends, it was decided to translate this book before you.

Al-Qawlu 'l-Mufīd is a pertinent book to our times, and it provides insight and contextual gems in regards to the methodology and thought process of al-Shawkānī. It also provides short historical insights regarding the political and sectarian landscape of his era.

I will provide some background to al-Shawkānī's life and status below and then give the reader some information in regards to the translation.

About the author:

He was born in 1173/1760 (a Monday, during the month of Dhū 'l-Qaʿdah) in Hijrat Shawkān, a town in Yemen. He grew up in Ṣanʿā, learning the Qur'ān from many teachers of the town and finishing it with al-Faqīh Ḥasan ibn ʿAbdullāh al-Habal. Then he memorised and studied *al-Azhār* (which he later wrote an excellent commentary for, titled *al-Sayl al-Jarrār*) amongst many other works. He consumed himself with learning and became a teacher at a young age.

In Nawāb Ṣiddīq Ḥasan Khan's book *al-Tāj al-Mukallal* (extracts from pp. 443-449), it states:

قال السيد العلامة حسن بن أحمد البهلكي، في كتابه (الديباج الخسرواني في أخبار أعيان المخلاف السليماني)، ما نصه: السنة الخمسون بعد المائتين والألف ، وفيها في شهر جمادى الآخرة كانت وفاة شيخنا محمد بن علي الشوكاني. وهو قاضي الجماعة، شيخ الإسلام، المحقق العلامة الإمام، سلطان العلماء، إمام الدنيا، خاتمة الحفاظ بلا مراء، الحجة النقاد، علي الإسناد، السابق في ميدان الاجتهاد، المطلع على حقائق الشريعة وغوامضها، العارف بمداركها ومقاصدها.

Al-Sayyid al-ʿAllāmah Ḥasan ibn Aḥmad al-Bahlakī wrote in his book *al-Dībaj al-Khusruwānī fī Akhbār Aʿyān al-Mukhālif al-Sulaymānī*: The year 1250: During the month of Jumādā al-Ākhirah our *shaykh* Muḥammad ibn ʿAlī al-Shawkānī passed away. He was the judge of the congregation, the *shaykh* of al-Islam, the *muhaqqiq*, the *ʿallāmah*, the *imām*, the *sulṭān* of the *ʿulamā*, the *imām* of the world, the seal of the *ḥuffāẓ* (i.e. major ḥadīth scholars) without dispute, the proof for debaters, the supreme in *isnād* and the foremost within the domain of *al-ijtihād*. He was cognisant of the obvious aspects of the religion and the subtle, and he was knowledgeable of its purposes and aspects.

وعلى الجملة: فما رأى مثل نفسه، ولا رأى من رآه مثله علماً وورعاً، وقياماً بالحق بقوة جنان وسلاطة لسان.

To summarise: He did not see one similar to himself, and those who saw him did not see his likeness in knowledge and piety, and in standing for the truth with strength of character and preciseness of tongue.

مولده يوم الاثنين الثامن والعشرين من ذي القعدة الحرام سنة اثنتين وسبعين بعد المئة والألف، كما أخبرني بذلك في بلده هجرة شوكان، ونشأ على العفاف والطهارة، وما زال يدرب ويدرج ويجمع النشأت ويحرز المكرمات.

[Al-Shawkānī's student Muḥammad ibn al-Ḥasan al-Shijni authored a biography of him:] He was born on a Monday, the 28th of the blessed month Dhu 'l-Qaʿdah, during the year 1172 (the common date cited is 1173)—as he reported to me—in his town Hijrat Shawkān. He was raised upon virtuosity and pureness, always training himself and attempting to progress in level, and attaining noble stations.

له قراءة على والده، ولازم القاضي إمامَ الفروع في زمانه أحمدَ بنَ محمد الحرازي، وانتفع به في الفقه، وأخذ النحو والصرف عن السيد العلامة إسماعيل بن حسن، والعلامة عبد الله بن إسماعيل النهمي، والعلامة القاسم بن محمد الخولاني، وأخذ علم البيان والمعاني والمنطق والأصلين عن العلامة حسين بن محمد المغربي، والعلامة علي بن الهادي عرهب، ولازم في كثير من العلوم مجددَ زمانه السيد عبدَ القادر بن أحمد الكوكباني، وأخذ في علم الحديث عن الحافظ علي بن إبراهيم بن عامر، وغير هؤلاء من المشايخ الكملة في جميع العلوم العقلية والنقلية، حتى أحرز جميع المعارف، واتفق على تحقيقه المخالف والمؤالف، وصار المشارَ إليه في علوم الاجتهاد بالبنان، والمجلِّي في معرفة غوامض الشريعة عند الرهان.

[Listing his teachers:]

He read works to his father.

He spent time with the judge and *imām* of *al-furū'* (i.e. *al-fiqh*) during his time, Aḥmad ibn Muḥammad al-Ḥārazī. He benefited from him in *al-fiqh*.

He learned grammar and morphology from al-Sayyid al-'Allāmah Ismā'īl ibn Ḥasan, al-'Allāmah 'Abdullāh ibn Ismā'īl al-Nahamī, and al-'Allāmah al-Qāsim ibn Muḥammad al-Khawlānī.

He learned the science of eloquence, expression, logic and *al-aṣlayn* (i.e. *uṣūl al-fiqh* and *uṣūl al-dīn*) from al-'Allāmah Ḥusayn ibn

Muḥammad al-Maghrabī and al-ʿAllāmah ʿAlī ibn al-Hādī ʿUrhab.

He studied many of the sciences with the reviver of his era, al-Sayyid ʿAbd al-Qādir ibn Aḥmad al-Kawkabānī.

He learned the science of ḥadīth from al-Ḥāfiẓ ʿAlī ibn Ibrāhīm ibn ʿĀmir.

He studied from teachers besides these, grasping proficiency within all the rational and textual sciences. This was to the point that he reached the apex of human understanding, his power of examination was acceded to by both friend and foe, his excellence in the sciences of *ijtihād* was acknowledged, and [he became] the one to clarify the matters of subtlety within the religion.

له المؤلفات الجليلة الممتعة المفيدة النافعة في أغلب العلوم، منها (نيل الأوطار شرح منتقى الأخبار) لابن تيمية - رح -، في أربعة مجلدات، لم تكتحل عينُ الزمان بمثله في التحقيق، ولم يسمح الدهر بنحوه في التدقيق، أعطى المسائل حقها في كل بحث على طريق الإنصاف، وعدم التقيد بالتقليد، ومذهب الأخلاف والأسلاف، وتناقله عنه مشايخه الكرام فمن دونهم من الأعلام، وطار في الآفاق في زمان حياته، وقرىء عليه مرارًا، وانتفع به العلماء، وكان يقول: إنه لم يرض، عن شيء من مؤلفاته سواه؛ لما هو عليه من التحرير بأرفع مكان، ومن التمسك بالدليل في أعلى شأن، وكان تأليفه في أيام مشايخه، فنبهوه على مواضع منه حتى تحرر.

He composed many great, interesting and beneficial works within most sciences. From them is *Nayl al-Awṭār Sharḥ Muntaqā al-Akhbār* of Ibn Taymiyyah, in four volumes. The eye of time has not been adorned with its likeness in examination, nor has the entirety of time granted its similitude in attention to the smallest of detail. He gave every issue its due right in his examinations in an impartial manner, absent of any restriction due to *al-taqlīd* or the *madhhabs*, new and old. He transmitted from it to his respected *shaykhs* and those below them from the luminaries, and the book flew within the horizons during his life. It was read to him many times and it was benefited from by the scholars. He used to say that he was not content with any of his works besides it, due to it being composed to the highest grade and its strict adherence to the textual proofs. He authored this whilst his teachers were still present, and they brought his attention to some points contained in his book, so he accommodated their notes and advice until the book became fine-tuned.

[Addition from al-Shawkānī's autobiography in *al-Badr al-Ṭāliʿ* (2/219):

... أرشده إِلَى ذَلِك جمَاعَة من شُيُوخه كالسيد الْعَلامَة عبد الْقَادِر بن أَحْمد والعلامة الْحسن بن إِسْمَاعِيل المغربي وَعرض عَلَيْهِمَا بَعْضًا مِنْهُ وَمَاتَا قبل تَمَامه.

He was guided to authoring it (i.e. a commentary on *Muntaqā al-Akhbār*) by a group of his teachers such as al-Sayyid al-ʿAllāmah ʿAbd al-Qādir ibn Aḥmad and al-ʿAllāmah al-Ḥasan ibn Ismāʿīl al-Maghrabī, both to whom he presented parts. They both passed away before its completion.]

وله التفسير الكبير، المسمى: (فتح القدير) الجامع بين فني الرواية والدراية

من علم التفسير، وقد سبقه إلى التأليف في الجمع بين الرواية والدراية، العلامةُ محمدُ بن يحيى بن بهران، فله تفسير في ذلك عظيم، لكن تفسير شيخنا أبسطُ وأجمعُ وأحسنُ منه ترتيبًا وتصنيفًا، وأحرزُ لمعاني اللغات وشواهدها تحقيقًا وتأليفًا. وقد ذكر الحافظ السيوطي في (الإتقان): أنه جعله مقدمة لتفسير جامع لتحرير الرواية، وتقرير الدراية: وسماه: (مجمع البحرين ومطلع البدرين).

He also has a large *tafsīr* named *Fatḥ al-Qadīr*, which combined between the *riwāyah* (textual/narration based) and *dirāyah* (opinion orientated) forms of *tafsīr*. Al-ʿAllāmah Muḥammad ibn Yaḥyā ibn Bahrān had preceded him in authoring a *tafsīr* work combining between *al-riwāyah* and *al-dirāyah*. Though his contribution to the field through this was great, our *shaykh's* was more simplified, detailed and comprehensive, and better in its ordering and quality of authorship, and its dealing with linguistic meanings and evidences is more encompassing in terms of authorship and verification. Al-Ḥāfiẓ al-Suyūṭī stated in *al-Itqān* that he had also authored a work which combined between citing the *riwāyah* and detailing the *dirāyah*, which he titled *Majmaʿ al-Baḥrayn wa Maṭlaʿ al-Badrayn*.

وله مختصر في الفقه على مقتضى الدليل، سماه: (الدرر البهية)، وشرحه شرحًا نافعًا، (المضية)، أورد فيه الأدلة التي بنى عليها ذلك المؤلف، وله (وَبْل الغمام) حاشية سماه (الدراري شفاء الأوام)، للأمير حسين بن محمد، وله (در السحابة في مناقب القرابة والصحابة)، وله (إرشاد الفحول إلى تحقيق الحق من علم الأصول) يعز نظيره في جمعه وترصيفه، وحسن

ترتيبه وتصنيفه، وله (السيل الجرار المتدفق على حدائق الأزهار)، كان تأليفه في آخر مدته، ولم يؤلف بعده شيئًا - فيما أعلم -.

He has a summarised *fiqh* manual which is based upon proofs, named *al-Durar al-Bahiyyah*, for which he wrote a beneficial commentary called *al-Muḍiyyah*, wherein he provided the proofs upon which he based the manual. He authored *Wabl al-Ghamām* which is a marginal commentary he entitled *al-Darārī Shifā al-Awām* of al-Amīr Ḥusayn ibn Muḥammad. He authored *Darr al-Saḥābat fī Manāqib al-Qarābat wa 'l-Ṣaḥābat*. He authored *Irshād al-Fuḥūl ilā Taḥqīq al-Ḥaq min 'Ilm al-Uṣūl*, which surpasses similar books due its content, structure, order and quality of authorship. He also authored *Sayl al-Jarrār al-Mutadaffiq 'alā Ḥadā'iq al-Azhār*, which he authored in the latter stages of his life, and I do not know a work he authored after this.

وقد تكلم فيه على عيون من المسائل، وصحح من المشروع ما هو مقيد بالدلائل، وزيّف ما لم يكن عليه دليل، وحَسَّن العبارة في الرد والتعليل، والسبب في ذلك أنه نشأ في زمنه جماعة من المقلدة الجامدين على التعصب في الأصول والفروع، ولم تزل المصاولة والمقاولة بينه وبينهم دائرة، ولم يزالوا ينددون عليه في المباحث من غير حجة ولا برهان من سنة وقرآن، فجعل كلامه في ذلك الشرح - في الحقيقة - موجهًا إليهم في التنفير عن التقليد المذموم، وإيقاظهم إلى النظر في الدليل؛ لأنه يرى تحريم التقليد الشوم، وقد ألف في ذلك رسالة سماها: (القول المفيد في حكم التقليد)، وقد تحاماه لما حواه جماعةٌ من علماء الوقت، وأرسل

عليه أهلُ جهته بسببه سهامَ اللوم والمَقْت، وثارت من أجل ذلك فتنة في صنعاء بين مَنْ هو مقلد، وبين من هو متقيد بالدليل.

In his work *al-Sayl al-Jarrār* (which is a commentary on the staple of Zaydi *fiqh* during that time, *al-Azhār*), he spoke about some key issues; asserting the legislation of that which was based upon evidences and repudiating that which had no evidence, penning down exquisite wordings in his critique of [the author's] reasoning. The reason for this was that during his era there arose a group of *muqallids* who were obstinate in being partisan within *al-uṣūl* (fundamental issues in religion) and *al-furūʿ* (subsidiary issues in religion), and tensions and debates between him and them were constant. They did not cease faulting him in the matters he researched whilst not having proof for their arguments from the Sunnah and the Qurʾān. Therefore, he was actually addressing them in this commentary—in reality—so as to turn them away from blameworthy *taqlīd* and encourage them to utilise evidences. This is because he viewed rigid blind following to be impermissible, and in regards to this he authored a treatise he named *al-Qawl al-Mufīd fī Ḥukm al-Taqlīd*. He was shunned by many scholars of his time due to what he wrote in it (i.e. *al-Sayl al-Jarrār*), and he was sent rebuke and extreme hate from the people of his region. Much chaos emerged due to this in Ṣanʿā between the blind followers and those who emphasised the utilisation of evidences.

توهمًا من المقلدين أنه ما أراد إلا هدم مذهب أهل البيت؛ لأن (الأزهار) هو عمدتهم في هذه الأعصار، وعليه في عبادتهم والمعاملة المدار، وحاشاه من التعصب على من أوجب الله تعالى محبتهم، وجعل أجرَ نبينا صلى الله عليه وسلم في تبليغ الرسالة مودتَهم؛ لأن له الولاء التام

لهم، وقد نشر محاسنهم في مؤلفه (در السحابة) بما لم يخالج بعده ريبة لمرتاب، وله العناية التامة بحفظ مذهبهم؛ فإنه أفنى شبابه في الدرس والتدريس في ذلك.

[This was because] the blind followers falsely assumed that he only intended to wipe away the *madhhab* of Ahl al-Bayt, as *al-Azhār* was their mainstay during that era, upon which they based their acts of worship and social transactions. He would never show rigidity towards [the descendants of the Prophet, how could he when] Allah made their love obligatory, and the only return that our Prophet ﷺ asked for delivering the message was to show kindness and goodness to them. He did so because he cared for them extremely. In his book *Darr al-Saḥābah* he presented their merits to an extent which would not leave doubt in one's mind [that he saw them as his enemies.] Furthermore, he gave great service to the preservation of their *madhhab*, having exhausted his youth in studying and teaching it.

وعندي: أن من جملة العناية بهم هذا الشرحَ؛ فإن من تأمله حقَّ التأمل - بعين الإنصاف - عرف أنه بيان لما اقتضاه (متن الأزهار) من الأدلة الصحيحة؛ لأنه جاء فيه بأدلة لم توجد في غيره، وأوضح مأخذها من الكتاب والسنة على أبدع أسلوب، وقد اطلعت على غالب شروح الأزهار، فلم أر في شروحه ما يدانيه في إيراد الأدلة.

In my view, this commentary of his served as a benefit for them. Indeed, if one pondered over it with impartiality, he would conclude that it is an explanation detailing the authentic evidences which the text of *al-Azhār* requires. This is because he provided evidences in his work which are not found in other commentaries, and clarified that its sources are taken from the Qur'ān and Sunnah in the most eloquent of ways. I have read over most of the commentaries upon *al-Azhār* and have not come across one which comes close to it in the presentation of evidences.

[... Page 449:]

ولقد منح رب العالمين سبحانه من بحر فضل كرمه الواسع هذا القاضي الإمام ثلاثة أمور، لا أعلم أنها في هذا الزمان الأخير جُمعت لغيره.

Indeed, the Lord of the worlds, the Most Glorified bestowed this judge and *imām* from the sea of His blessings and generosity with three things, of which I do not believe another in this latter time has encompassed:

الأول: سعة التبحر في العلوم على اختلاف أجناسها وأنواعها وأصنافها.

One. His masterful proficiency in the sciences, despite their different categories, types and variant subjects.

الثاني: سعة التلاميذ المحققين، والنبلاء المدققين، أولي الأفهام الخارقة، والفضائل الفائقة، الحقيق أن يُنشد عند حضور جمعهم الغفير، ولمشاهدة غوصهم على جواهر المعاني التي استخراجُها من بحر الحقائق غير يسير.

Two. The masterful proficiency of his students, who were amongst the *muhaqqiqs* and noble verifiers, were wondrous in intellect and distinguished in virtue. One ought to recite the following lines of poetry when their large number gather to witness how they delve into the subtle meanings that are difficult to extract out of the ocean of facts:

إِنِّي إذا حضرَتْني ألفُ محبرةٍ　　تقولُ أخبرَني هذا وحَدَّثني
صاحَتْ بعقوتها الأقلامُ ناطقةً　　هذي المكارمُ لا قعبانُ من لَبَن

When I am visited, a thousand ink-pots would say so-and-so informed me and narrated to me.
The pens would speak in their place, this is nobility, not serving two pitchers of milk.

الثالث: سعة التصانيف المحررة، والرسائل والجوابات المحبرة، التي تسامى في كثرتها الجهابذة الفحول، وبلغ من تنقيحها وتحقيقها كل غاية وسول.

Three. The vastness of the books he authored, and the letters and responses he penned. High-ranked scholars admired their sheer multitude, and they have been thoroughly scrutinised and verified.

[End from *al-Tāj al-Mukallal*]

'Umar Riḍā al-Kaḥālah said:

مفسر، محدث، فقيه، أصولي، مؤرخ، أديب، نحوي منطقي، متكلم، حكيم.

He was a master scholar in *tafsīr*, ḥadīth, *fiqh*, *uṣūl*, history, literature, grammar, logic, *kalām*, and he was from the wise.[1]

About the translation:

1 *Mu'jam al-Mu'allifīn* (3/541).

The Arabic manuscript we relied upon was the one edited by Maḥfūẓah bint ʿAlī Umm al-Ḥasan found in the larger compilation entitled *Fatḥ al-Rabbānī*, which was overseen by al-Shaykh, al-Muḥaqqiq Muḥammad Ṣubḥī Ḥasan Ḥallāq ﷺ (d. 2017). We typed it according to this version, correcting any typos we noticed and amending punctuation where needed. Also, the footnotes are directly based upon this work. On the rare occasion where I felt it was needed to add a footnote, it is marked with [t]. The *shaykh* gave great efforts towards producing the books of al-Shawkānī in Arabic, and this translation is a fruit of that.

I and the others at Dar al-Arqam may not agree with everything the author states in this book but it has been translated as is. Any points where I felt my own thoughts entered the translation have been marked with square brackets (i.e. [example]).

If the reader notes any typos or mistakes in this work, please contact us via email. Books are nearly always in need of revision and review, as Nawāb Ṣiddīq Ḥasan Khān transmitted in his book *Abjad al-ʿUlūm* (1/71):

وقد كتب أستاذ العلماء البلغاء القاضي الفاضل عبد الرحيم البيساني إلى العماد الأصفهاني معتذرا عن كلام استدركه عليه (إنه قد وقع لي شيء وما أدري أوقع لك أم لا وها أنا أخبرك به وذلك أني رأيت أنه لا يكتب إنسان كتابا في يومه إلا قال في غده: لو غير هذا لكان أحسن، ولو زيد لكان يستحسن، ولو قدم هذا لكان أفضل، ولو ترك هذا لكان أجمل. وهذا من أعظم العبر وهو دليل على استيلاء النقص على جملة البشر) انتهى.

Al-Ustādh al-ʿUlamā, al-Bulaghā, al-Qāḍī, al-Fāḍil ʿAbd al-Raḥīm al-Baysānī wrote to al-ʿImād al-Aṣfahānī apologising for commenting on a matter he discussed, "Something occurred to me but I am not sure if it has occurred to you, so I will inform you of it: I have noted that one does not write something during a day except that he states during the morrow, 'Had I changed such-and-such to such-and-such, it would have been better, if I added such-and-such, it would improve and if I moved such-and-such text to a different place it would be better, and if I left this it would look better.' This is from the greatest of sentiments, and a proof that humans are all overcome by shortcomings."

نَفَعَ اللهُ تَعَالى بِهذه التَرجَمَةِ، كَمَا نَفَعَ بِأَصْلِهَا، في الحَيَاةِ وَبَعْدَ المَمَاتِ.

Adnan Karim
Birmingham, UK

[التمهيد]
[Foreword]

بسم الله الرحمن الرحيم، وبعد حمد لله وصلاته وسلامه على رسول وآله.
فإنه طلب بعض المحققين من أهل العلم أن أجمع له بحثا يشمل على تحقيق الحق في التقليد، أجائز هو أم لا على وجه لا يبقى بعده شك ولا يقبل عنده تشكيل. ولما كان هذا السائل من العلماء المبرزين كان جوابه على نمط علم المناظرة.

In the name of Allah, the Entirely Merciful the Especially Merciful, after praising Allah and seeking His *ṣalāt* and *salām* upon His Messenger and his family: One of the researching scholars amongst the people of knowledge requested me to compile a treatise for him that would contain affirmation of the truth regarding *al-taqlīd* (adopting another person's opinions without seeking proof), as to whether it is permissible or not, in a manner that no doubt would be left after it nor objection to it would be accepted. Since the questioner is one of the eminent scholars, the response will be in the manner of *ʿilm al-munāẓarah* (the science of dialectics).

فنقول وبالله التوفيق: لما كان القائل بعدم جواز التقليد قائما في مقام المنع وكان القائل بالجواز مدعيا كان الدليل على مدعي الجواز وقد جاء المجوزون بأدلة:

So we say—and with Allah lies success: Since the one who upholds that *taqlīd* is not permissible takes the status of the defendant whilst the one who claims that it is permissible is the claimant, the burden of proof is upon the one who claims that it is permissible. Thus, those who permit *taqlīd* presented some evidences:

[أدلة القائلين بجوار التقليد والرد عليها]

[The Evidences of Those Who Permit *al-Taqlīd* and the Response to Them]

[١]: منها قوله تعالى ﴿فَاسْأَلُوا أَهْلَ الذِّكْرِ إِن كُنتُمْ لَا تَعْلَمُونَ﴾ قالوا فأمر الله سبحانه من لا علم له أن يسأل من هو أعلم.

[1] From them is the statement of Allah: **{So ask the people of the message if you do not know.}**[2] They stated that Allah commanded the one who knows not to ask the one who is more learned than him.

(الجواب) أن هذه الآية الشريفة واردة في سؤال خاص خارج عن محل النزاع كما يفيد ذلك السياق المذكور قبل هذا اللفظ الذي استدلوا به وبعده.

The response is that this noble *āyah* was mentioned with regard to a specific question outside of this subject of contention, as indicated to by the context mentioned before and after this excerpt which they utilise as a proof.

قال ابن جرير والبغوي وأكثر المفسرين إنها نزلت ردا على المشركين لما أنكروا كون الرسول بشرا، وقد استوفى ذلك السيوطي في الدر المنثور

2 Al-Naḥl: 43

وهذا هو المعنى الذي يفيده السياق. قال تعالى: ﴿وَمَا أَرْسَلْنَا مِن قَبْلِكَ إِلَّا رِجَالًا نُّوحِي إِلَيْهِمْ ۚ فَاسْأَلُوا أَهْلَ الذِّكْرِ إِن كُنتُمْ لَا تَعْلَمُونَ﴾ وقال [تعالى]: ﴿أَكَانَ لِلنَّاسِ عَجَبًا أَنْ أَوْحَيْنَا إِلَىٰ رَجُلٍ مِّنْهُمْ﴾ وقال [تعالى]: ﴿وَمَا أَرْسَلْنَا مِن قَبْلِكَ إِلَّا رِجَالًا نُّوحِي إِلَيْهِم مِّنْ أَهْلِ الْقُرَىٰ﴾.

Ibn Jarīr,[3] al-Baghawī[4] and most of the commentators of the Qur'ān stated that it was revealed as a refutation against the polytheists when they rejected the fact that the Messenger was a human being (i.e. that the message was given to a human). Al-Suyūṭī recorded this in *al-Durr al-Manthūr*;[5] and this is the meaning which the context indicates. Allah states: **{And We sent not before you except men to whom We revealed [Our message]. So ask the people of the message if you do not know.}**[6] Allah also states: **{Have the people been amazed that We revealed [revelation] to a man from amongst them.}**[7] Also: **{And We sent not before you [as messengers] except men to whom We revealed from among the people of cities.}**[8]

وعلى فرض أن المراد السؤال العام فالمأمور بسؤالهم هم أهل الذكر وهو كتاب الله وسنة رسوله لا غيرهما، ولا أظن مخالفا يخالف في هذا لأن هذه الشريعة المطهرة هي إما من الله عز وجل وذلك هو القرآن الكريم،

3 See *Jāmi' al-Bayān 'an Tàwīl Āyi al-Qur'ān* (8/j 14/108).
4 See *Ma'ālim al-Tanzīl* (3/70).
5 5/132-133.
6 Al-Naḥl: 43
7 Yūnus: 2
8 Yūsuf: 109

أو من رسوله- صلى الله عليه وآله وسلم- وذلك هو السنة المطهرة ولا ثالث لذلك.

Supposing that the intended meaning of the *āyah* is a general question; those whom one is commanded to ask are the people of *dhikr*. *Dhikr* [in this context] is the Book of Allah and the Sunnah of His Messenger ﷺ, and none other than them. I do not think anyone will oppose this today, as this pure *Sharīʿah* is either from Allah—i.e. the Noble Qurʿān—or from the Messenger of Allah ﷺ—i.e. the pure Sunnah, and there is no third source for this.

وإذا كان المأمور بسؤالهم هم أهل القرآن والسنة فالآية المذكورة حجة على المقلدة وليست بحجة لهم لأن المراد أنهم يسألون أهل الذكر ليخبروهم به، فالجواب من المسؤولين أن يقولوا قال الله كذا قال رسوله كذا فيعمل السائلون بذلك وهذا هو غير ما يريده المقلد المستدل بالآية الكريمة فإنه إنما استدل بها على جواز ما هو فيه من الأخذ بأقوال الرجال من دون سؤال عن الدليل فإن هذا هو التقليد، ولهذا رسموه بأنه قبول قول الغير من دون مطالبته بحجة.

Thus, if those whom one is commanded to ask are the people of the Qurʿān and the Sunnah, the mentioned *āyah* is a proof against the *muqallids* (i.e. those who perform *al-taqlīd*) and not a proof in their favour. This is because what is intended is that they should ask the people of knowledge so that they inform them about the matter. Then the response from those being asked (i.e. the people of knowledge) is to say, "Allah said such and such and His Messenger said such and such." Upon this, the questioners should act upon it.

This is contrary to what the *muqallid* intends through the use of this noble *āyah* as a proof. Rather, he only uses it as a proof for what he sees in it in the allowance of taking the opinions of men without asking them for the proof. This is *al-taqlīd*. Consequently, it was defined as accepting the view of others without seeking for a proof.[9]

فحاصل التقليد أن المقلد لا يسأل عن كتاب الله ولا عن سنة رسوله بل يسأل عن مذهب إمامه فقط، فإذا جاوز ذلك إلى السؤال عن الكتاب والسنة فليس بمقلد، وهذا يسلمه كل مقلد ولا ينكره. وإذا تقرر بهذا أن المقلد إذا سأل أهل الذكر عن كتاب الله وسنة رسوله لم يكن مقلد علمت أن هذه الآية الشريفة- على تسليم أن السؤال ليس عن الشيء الخاص الذي يليه السياق بل عن كل شيء من الشريعة كما يزعمه المقلد- تدفع في وجهه وترغم أنفه وتكسر ظهره كما قررناه.

The essence of *al-taqlīd* is that the *muqallid* does not ask about the Book of Allah and the Sunnah of His Messenger ﷺ, rather, he asks about the *madhhab* of his *imām* alone. But if he goes beyond this point by asking [for proof] from the Qur'ān and the Sunnah, then he is not considered to be a *muqallid*. This would be accepted without contestation by the *muqallid*. Thus, if it is established that when a *muqallid* asks the people of *dhikr* about the Book of Allah and the Sunnah of His Messenger ﷺ he is not in fact a *muqallid*, one will realise that this noble *āyah*—if we assume that the question is not about something specific (which the context indicates), but about everything in the *Sharī'ah* as claimed by the *muqallid*—will strike his face, humble him and break his back, as we have established.

9 See *Asās al-Balāghah* (p. 785) and *Mu'jam al-Lughah* (5/19).

[٢]: ومن جملة ما استدلوا به ما ثبت عنه صلى الله عليه وسلم أنه قال في حديث صاحب الشجة ((ألا سالوا إذا لم يعلموا إنما شفاء العي السؤال)) وكذلك حديث العسيف الذي زنى بامرأة مستأجرة فقال أبوه إني سألت أهل العلم فأخبروني أن على ابني جلد مائة وأن على امرأة هذا الرجم، وهو حديث ثابت في الصحيح. قالوا فلم ينكر عليه تقليد من هو أعلم منه.

[2] One of the texts which they cite as proof is the statement established from the Messenger of Allah ﷺ in the ḥadīth of the man with the head injury, "Could they not have asked if they did not know. The cure for ignorance is in asking."[10] [They] likewise [derive proof from] the ḥadīth of the labourer who committed fornication with the wife of his employer. His father said, "I have asked the people of knowledge and they informed me that my son should be given one hundred lashes and the woman should be stoned." It is a ḥadīth that is established in *al-Ṣaḥīḥ*.[11] They argue based upon this that he was not repudiated for performing *taqlīd* of one who was more learned than him.

---

10 It is *ḥasān bi shawāhidhu* (*ḥasan* with its witnessing reports). Reported by Abu Dāwūd (336), al-Bayhaqī (1/228), and al-Dāraquṭnī. Its *shāhid* are two reports on the authority of Ibn ʿAbbās: (i) Reported by Abu Dāwūd (337) and Ibn Mājah (572), which is *ḥasan*, and (ii) reported by al-Ḥākim (1/178) and al-Dāraquṭnī (1/190).

11 Reported by al-Bukhārī (6859), Muslim (1698, 1697), Mālik in *al-Muwaṭṭa* (2/822 no. 6), al-Tirmidhī (1433)—who said that it is *ḥasan ṣaḥīḥ*, Abu Dāwūd (4445), al-Nāsāʾī (8/240 no. 5410) and al-Shāfiʿ in *al-Risālah* (p. 248 no. 691).

(الجواب): أنه لم يرشدهم صلى الله عليه وآله وسلم في حديث صاحب الشجة إلى السؤال عن آراء الرجال بل أرشدهم إلى السؤال عن الحكم الشرعي الثابت عن الله ورسوله، ولهذا دعا عليهم لما أفتوا بغير علم فقال [صلى الله عليه وآله وسلم]: ((قتلوه قتلهم الله)) مع أنهم قد أفتوا بآرائهم فكان الحديث حجة عليهم لا لهم، فإنه اشتمل على أمرين. أحدهما: الإرشاد لهم إلى السؤال عن الحكم الثابت بالدليل. والآخر الذم لهم على اعتماد الرأي والإفتاء به، وهذا معلوم لكل عالم فإن المرشد إلى السؤال هو رسول الله صلى الله عليه وآله وسلم وهو باق بين أظهرهم فالإرشاد منه إلى السؤال وإن كان مطلقا ليس المراد به إلا سؤاله صلى الله عليه وآله وسلم أو سؤال من يسأله أو سؤال من قد علم هذا الحكم منه.

The response is that the Prophet ﷺ did not direct them in the ḥadīth of the man with the head injury to ask in regards to the opinions of men, rather, he directed them to ask in regards to a legislative ruling that is established from Allah and His Messenger. As such, he supplicated against them when they issued a verdict without knowledge. He ﷺ then said, "They killed him, may Allah kill them," despite the fact that they issued the verdict based upon their personal opinions, and thus the ḥadīth serves as a proof against their argument and not for it. This is because it comprises of two issues. The first of them is that it directs them to ask in regards to a ruling that is established with evidence. The second is the disparagement directed towards them for relying on personal opinion and issuing verdicts with it. This is well known to every scholar, and the guide to direct questions towards is the Messenger of Allah ﷺ—and he was present in their midst. So the directive from him to ask—even if it was unrestricted [in its wording]—does not mean anything other than to ask him ﷺ, one who asked him or one who has learnt this ruling from him.

والمقلد كما عرفت سابقا لا يكون مقلدا إلا إذا لم يسأل عن الدليل أما إذا سأل عنه فليس بمقلد فكيبف يتم الاحتجاج بذلك على جواز التقليد وهل يحتج عاقل على ثبوت شيء بما ينفيه وعلى صحة أمر بما يفيد فساده فإنا لا نطلب منكم معشر المقلدة إلا ما دل عليه ما جئتم به فنقول لكم اسألوا أهل الذكر عن الذكر وهو كتاب الله وسنة رسوله واعملوا عليه واتركوا آراء الرجال والقيل والقال. ونقول لكم كما قال رسول الله [صلى الله عليه وآله وسلم] ألا تسألون فإنما شفاء العي السؤال عن كتاب الله وسنة رسوله لا عن رأي فلان ومذهب فلان فإنكم إذا سألتم عن محض الرأي فقد قتلكم من أفتاكم به كما قال رسول الله صلى الله عليه وآله وسلم في حديث صاحب الشجة ((قتلوه قتلهم الله)).

A *muqallid*—as you have come to know—cannot be called a *muqallid* except when he does not ask for proof. If he asks regarding the proof, he is not a *muqallid*. So, how can [this narration] be used as a proof for the permissibility of *taqlīd*? Does a rational person cite as proof for something that which negates it, or for the validity of something that which indicates its nullity? So, we do not demand from you O assembly of *muqallids* except that which is dictated by the evidences you bring forth. So we say to you: Ask the people of *dhikr* in regards to the *dhikr,* which is the Book of Allah and the Sunnah of His Messenger ﷺ. Act upon it and leave the personal views of men and pointless discussion. We state to you as the Messenger of Allah ﷺ stated: Would you not have asked, for the cure to ignorance is to ask from the Book of Allah and the Sunnah of His Messenger ﷺ and not the personal opinion of so-and-so and the *madhhab* of so-and-so. Indeed if you ask in regards to pure opinion then the one giving you the ruling based upon it would [figuratively] kill you, as stated by the Messenger of Allah ﷺ in the ḥadīth of the man with the head injury, "They killed him, may Allah kill them."

وأما السؤال الواقع من والد العسيف فهو إنما سأل علماء الصحابة عن حكم مسألته من كتاب الله وسنة رسوله ولم يسألهم عن آرائهم ومذاهبهم، وهذا يعلمه كل عالم، ونحن لا نطلب من المقلد إلا أن يسأل كما سأل والد العسيف ويعمل على ما قام عليه الدليل الذي رواه له العالم المسؤول ولكنه قد أقر على نفسه أنه لا يسأل إلا عن رأي إمامه لا عن روايته، فكان استدلاله بما استدل به هاهنا حجة عليه لا له والله المستعان.

With regard to the question that emanated from the father of the labourer, he only asked the scholars amongst the Companions concerning the ruling on the issue from the Book of Allah and the Sunnah of His Messenger, and he did not ask them about their personal views and *madhhabs*. This is known to every scholar. And we do not seek from the *muqallid* except that he ask—just as the father of the labourer asked—and act upon whatever is established by the proof narrated to him by the scholars he posed the question to. However, he has resolved himself to only ask regarding the personal view of his *imām* and not regarding his narration (i.e. transmission of proofs). So, his attempt at deriving support for his view through this has in fact served as a proof against him and not in his favour. And Allah is the source of help.

[٣]: ومن جملة ما استدلوا به ما ثبت أن أبا بكر قال في الكلالة: أقضي فيها برأيي فإن يكن صوابا فمن الله وإن يكن خطأ فمني ومن الشيطان، والله بريء منه وهو ما دون الولد والوالد. فقال عمر بن الخطاب: إني لأستحي من الله أن أخالف أبا بكر. وصح عنه أنه قال لأبي بكر رأينا تبع لرأيك. وصح عن ابن مسعود أنه كان يأخذ بقول عمر. وصح أن الشعبي قال كان ستة من أصحاب رسول الله صلى الله عليه وآله وسلم يفتون الناس: ابن مسعود، وعمر بن الخطاب، وعلي بن أبي طالب، وزيد بن ثابت، وأبي بن كعب، وأبو موسى [رضي الله عنهم] وكان ثلاثة منهم يدعون قولهم لقول ثلاثة كان عبد الله يدع قوله لقول عمر وكان أبو موسى يدع قوله لقول علي وكان زيد يدع قوله لقول أبي بن كعب.

[3] Amongst the evidences from which they deduce the permissibility of *taqlīd* is the narration established from Abu Bakr that he said concerning *al-kalālah*,[12] "I will judge according to my opinion about it, and if it is correct, then this correctness is from Allah, and if it is wrong, then it is from me and from the devil and Allah is absolved from it. [*Al-kalālah*] refers to one who leaves behind neither child nor parents."[13] 'Umar ibn al-Khaṭṭāb said, "I feel shyness from Allah that I differ in opinion with Abu Bakr." And it was authentically reported that he said to Abu Bakr, "Our opinion follows

12 [T] See: **{They request from you a [legal] ruling. Say: Allah gives you a ruling concerning *al-kalālah*.}** [Sūrat al-Nisā: 176]

13 Reported by 'Abd al-Razzāq in his *Muṣannaf* (10/304 no 19191), al-Dārimī (2/365-366) and al-Bayhaqī (6/224). Its narrators are *thiqāt* but al-Sha'bī did not hear from Abu Bakr, thus the ḥadīth is *munqaṭi'*.

yours." It was authentically reported from Ibn Mas'ūd[14] that he used to hold to the view of 'Umar. It was authentically narrated that al-Sha'bī said, "Six companions of the Messenger of Allah ﷺ used to issue verdicts to the people: Ibn Mas'ūd, 'Umar ibn al-Khaṭṭāb, 'Alī ibn Abī Ṭālib, Zayd ibn Thābit, 'Ubayy ibn Ka'b and Abu Mūsā. Three of them would dismiss their own view for the view of the other three. 'Abdullāh would dismiss his view for that of 'Umar, Abu Mūsā would dismiss his view for that of 'Alī and Zayd would dismiss his view for that of 'Ubayy ibn Ka'b."

(وَالْجَوَاب): عَن قَول عمر أَنه قد قيل إِنه يستحي عمر من مُخَالفَة أبي بكر فِي اعترافه بِجَوَاز الْخَطَأ عَلَيْهِ وَأن كَلَامه لَيْسَ كُله صَوَابا مَأْمُونا عَلَيْهِ الْخَطَأ، وَهَذَا وَإِن لم يكن ظَاهر لكنه يدل عَلَيْهِ مَا وَقع من مُخَالفَة عمر لأبي بكر فِي غير مَسْأَلَة، كمخالفته لَهُ فِي سبي أهل الرِّدَّة، وَفِي الأَرْض المغنومة فَقَسمهَا أَبُو بكر ووقفها عمر. وَفِي الْعَطاء فقد كَانَ أَبُو بكر يرى التَّسْوِيَة وَعمر يرى المفاضلة. وَفِي الِاسْتِخْلَاف فقد اسْتخْلف أَبُو بكر وَلم يسْتَخْلف عمر بل جعل الْأَمر شُورَى. وَقَالَ إِن أستخْلف فقد اسْتخْلف أَبُو بكر، وَإِن لم أستخْلف فَإِن رَسُول الله صلى الله عَلَيْهِ وَآله وَسلم لم يسْتَخْلف.

Response: With regard to the statement of 'Umar that he was shy of contradicting Abu Bakr, it contains acknowledgement that he could err and that all of his statements are not correct and free from mistakes. Though this may not be apparent, it is supported by the instances of variance which occurred between 'Umar and Abu Bakr

14 This was mentioned by Ibn al-Qayyim within *I'lām al-Muwaqqi'īn*.

in other issues. Examples include his differing with him regarding prisoners of war of those who apostatised and in conquered land. Abu Bakr divided them whilst 'Umar endowed them. In addition, in regards to gifts, Abu Bakr held that they should be equal in distribution whilst 'Umar held that preference should be given. With regard to succession, Abu Bakr appointed a successor whilst 'Umar did not, instead delegating the matter to a *shūrā* (council) stating, "If I choose to appoint a successor, Abu Bakr had appointed a successor, and if I choose not to appoint a successor, the Messenger of Allah ﷺ did not appoint a successor."[15]

قَالَ ابْن عمر فوَاللَّه مَا هُوَ إِلَّا أَن ذكره رَسُول الله صلى الله عَلَيْهِ وَآله وَسلم فَعلمت أَنه لَا يعدل برَسُول الله صلى الله عَلَيْهِ وَآله وَسلم أحدا وَأَنهُ غير مستخلف. وَخَالفهُ أَيْضا فِي الْجد والأخوة فَلَو كَانَ المُرَاد بقوله إِنه يستحي من مُخَالفَة أبي بكر فِي مسألة الْكَلَالَة وهُوَ مَا قَالُوهُ لَكَانَ منقوضا عَلَيْهِم بِهَذِهِ المخالفات فَإِن صَحَّ خِلَافه لَهُ، وَلم يستح مِنْهُ فَمَا أجابوا بِهِ فِي هَذِه المخالفات فَهُوَ جَوَابنَا عَلَيْهِم فِي تِلْكَ الْمُوَافقَة.

Ibn 'Umar said, "I swear by Allah that he did not mention anyone but the Messenger of Allah ﷺ. I learnt that he would not equate anyone with the Messenger of Allah ﷺ for he did not appoint any successor." He also differed with him regarding [the inheritance case of] the grandfather and brothers. If the intended meaning of his statement that he is shy of contradicting Abu Bakr concerning *al-kalālah* is as they stated, these contradictions would be a refutation

15 Recorded by al-Bukhārī as contained in *al-Fatḥ* (13/205) from the ḥadīth of 'Abdullāh ibn 'Umar which is close to the mentioned version. *Istikhlāf* refers to a *khalīfah* appointing another *khalīfah* to succeed him upon his death.

against them, because these variances have been authentically transmitted and he was not shy of doing so. Whatever their response is in regards to their (i.e. 'Umar and Abu Bakr) variances would be our response against them with regard to that [aforementioned] concurrence.

وَبَيَانه أنهُم إِذا قَالُوا خَالفه فِي هَذِه الْمسَائِل لِأَن اجْتِهَاده كَانَ على خلاف اجْتِهَاد أبي بكر. قُلْنَا وَوَافقَهُ فِي تِلْكَ الْمَسْأَلَة لِأَن اجْتِهَاده كَانَ مُوَافقا لاجتهاده وَلَيْسَ من التَّقْلِيد فِي شَيْء.

If they say that 'Umar disagreed with him in these issues because his *ijtihād* was contrary to the *ijtihād* of Abu Bakr, we would say that he agreed with him in that issue because his *ijtihād* conformed to the *ijtihād* of Abu Bakr and it is not *taqlīd* in any way.

وَأَيْضًا قد ثَبت أَن عمر بن الْخطاب أقرّ عِنْد مَوته بِأَنَّهُ لم يقْض فِي الْكَلَالَة بِشَيْء واعترف أَنه لم يفهمها فَلَو كَانَ قد قَالَ بِمَا قَالَ بِهِ أَبُو بكر تقليدا لَهُ لما أقرّ بِأَنَّهُ لم يقْض فِيهَا بِشَيْء وَلَا قَالَ إِنه لم يفهمها. وَلَو سلمنَا أَن عمر قلد أَبَا بكر فِي هَذِه الْمَسْأَلَة لم تقم بذلك حجَّة، لما تقرر من عدم حجَّة أَقْوَال الصَّحَابَة، وَأَيْضًا غَايَة مَا فِي ذَلِك تَقْلِيد عُلَمَاء الصَّحَابَة فِي مَسْأَلَة من الْمسَائِل الَّتِي يخفى فِيهَا الصَّوَاب على الْمُجْتَهد مَعَ تَسْوِيغ الْمُخَالفَة فِيمَا عدا تِلْكَ الْمَسْأَلَة، وَأَيْنَ هَذَا مِمَّا يَفْعَله المقلدون من تَقْلِيد الْعَالم فِي جَمِيع أُمُور الشَّرِيعَة من غير الْتِفَات إِلَى دَلِيل وَلَا تعريج على تَصْحِيح أَو تَعْلِيل.

In addition, it is established from 'Umar that he acknowledged at the time of his death to not judging regarding *al-kalālah* and he admitted that he did not understand it. Had it been that he held the view of Abu Bakr out of *taqlīd* to him, he would not have affirmed that he did not perform a judgement regarding it nor say that he did not understand it. And if we assume that 'Umar did *taqlīd* of Abu Bakr in this issue, this would not serve as proof due to what is established that the statements of the companions are not proof.[16] The utmost of what it contains is *taqlīd* of the scholars amongst the companions in one of the issues wherein the correct position is hidden to the *mujtahid,* whilst variance between them is displayed in other issues besides it. How does this correlate with the actions of the *muqallidūn*, wherein they blindly follow a scholar in all religious issues without giving heed to the evidences nor turning to the authentication or reasoning [for the ruling]?

16 This statement is not unrestricted, rather there are details to the discussion: (i) The statement of the companion in that which cannot be attained through personal reasoning or *ijtihād* is a proof according to the scholars. This is because they would have attained it via the Prophet ﷺ, thus it is like the Sunnah, and the Sunnah is a source of the religion. (ii) The statement of the companion upon which agreement occurs is considered to be a proof, as it is a point of *ijmā'* (consensus). Likewise is the case for the statement of a companion upon which there was no variance after it spread widely, as this is a form of *al-ijmā' al-sukūtī*, which is also a religious proof. (iii) The statement of a companion derived from his own interpretation and *ijtihād*. This is not binding upon the companion of his like nor those who come after him, rather it is given consideration to in the instance where there is no evidence from the Book, Sunnah or consensus. (iv) The statement of the companion which contradicts *ṣaḥīḥ marfū'* reports is not a proof, rather it is rejected. (v) The statement of the companion which is varied upon by another companion is not a proof. See *al-Baḥr al-Muḥīṭ* (6/53-56).

وَبِالْجُمْلَةِ فَلَو سلمنَا أَن ذَلِك تَقْلِيد من عمر كَانَ دَلِيلا للمجتهد إِذا لم يُمكنهُ الِاجْتِهَاد فِي مَسْأَلَة، وَأمكن غَيره من الْمُجْتَهدين الِاجْتِهَاد فِيهَا أَنه يجوز لذَلِك الْمُجْتَهد أَن يُقَلّد الْمُجْتَهد الآخر مَا دَامَ غير مُتَمَكن من الِاجْتِهَاد فِيهَا إِذا تضيقت عَلَيْهِ الْحَادِثَة. وَهَذِه مَسْأَلَة أُخْرَى غير المسالة الَّتِي يريدها الْمُقَلّد، وَهِي تَقْلِيد عَالم من الْعلمَاء فِي جَمِيع مسَائِل الدّين وَقبُول رَأيه دون رِوَايَته وَعدم مُطَالبَته بِالدَّلِيلِ، وَترك النّظر فِي الْكتاب وَالسّنة، والتعويل على مَا يرَاهُ من هُوَ أَحْقَر الآخذين بهما، فَإِن هَذَا هُوَ عين اتِّخَاذ الْأَحْبَار والرهبان أَرْبَابًا كَمَا سيأتيك بَيَانه.

In short, if we assume that this was *taqlīd* from ʿUmar, it serves as an evidence to the *mujtahid* that if he is unable to perform *ijtihād* in an issue whilst another *mujtahid* other than him is able to do so, it is permissible for the former to make *taqlīd* of the latter so long as it is not feasible for him to exercise *ijtihād* in it, i.e. in a scenario wherein a case is proving difficult for him. This is an issue different to the issue which is intended by the *muqallid* (i.e. which they cite it as proof for); which is to adopt the opinion of a scholar in all matters of the religion and to accept his personal view instead of his narration, not seeking evidence from him and leaving off analysing the Qurʾān and Sunnah, rather depending upon the personal view of one who is lower in standing that those who hold fast to them. This is similar to taking rabbis and monks as lords besides Allah, which will be explained later.

وَأَيْضًا لَو فرض مَا زعموه من الدلَالَة لَكَانَ ذَلِك خَاصّا بتقليد عُلَمَاء الصَّحَابَة فِي مَسْأَلَة من الْمسَائِل فَلَا يَصح إِلْحَاق غَيرهم بهم لما تقرر من

المزايا الَّتِي للصحابة الْبَالِغَة إِلَى حد يقصر عَنهُ الْوَصْف حَتَّى صَار مثل جبل أحد من متأخري الصَّحَابَة لَا يعدل الْمَدّ من متقدميهم وَلَا نصيفه. وَصَحَّ أَنهم خير الْقُرُون فَكيف يلحق بهم غَيرهم! وَبعد اللتيا وَالَّتِي فمَا أوجدتمونا نصا فِي كتاب الله وَلَا فِي سنة رَسُوله صلى الله عَلَيْهِ وَآله وَسلم وَلَيْسَت الْحجَّة إِلَّا فيهمَا، وَمن لَيْسَ بمعصوم لَا حجَّة لنا وَلَا لكم فِي قَوْله وَلَا فِي فعله فَمَا جعل الله الْحجَّة إِلَّا فِي كِتَابه وعَلى لِسَان نبيه، عرف هَذَا من عرفه وجهله من جَهله وَالسَّلَام.

In addition, if we accept what they cite as proof, it would be specific to performing *taqlīd* of the scholars amongst the Companions on an issue. And it is not correct to attach others to them, due to the establishment of virtues for the companions which reach a level transcendent of a suitable description, to the point that [charity] equivalent of Mount Uhud from a later companion does not equal to a *mudd* of an earlier companion, nor even half a *mudd*.[17] It was also authentically reported that they are the best of generations.[18] So how can others be attached to them? After much argumentation

17 He is referring to what al-Bukhārī (2541) reported as contained in *al-Fatḥ* (7/21) from the ḥadīth of Abu Saʿīd al-Khudrī that the Prophet ﷺ said: "Do not abuse my companions for if any one of you spent gold equal to Uhud, it would not be equal to a *mudd* or even half of it spent by one of them." Muslim reported it (2541) from the ḥadīth of Abu Hurayrah and Abu Saʿīd al-Khudrī which is close to the wording of al-Bukhārī. It was also reported by Abu Dāwūd (4658) and al-Tirmidhī (3861).

18 He is referring to what al-Bukhārī (2652) reported as contained in *al-Fatḥ* (7/3) that the Prophet ﷺ said: 'The best of my Ummah is my generation; then those who will come after; then those who will come after them." It was also reported by Muslim (2533).

and commotion, they did not find for us a textual citation from the Book of Allah nor the Sunnah of His Messenger ﷺ and there is no religious proof except through them. Whoever is not infallible does not serve as a proof for us nor for you, neither in his speech nor his actions. Allah has not placed religious proof except in His Book and upon the tongue of his Prophet ﷺ. The one who knows this, knows it and the one who is ignorant of this, is ignorant of it.

وَأما مَا استدلوا بِهِ من قَول عمر لأبي بكر رَأينَا لرأيك تبع فَمَا هَذِه أول قَضِيَّة جَاءُوا بهَا على غير وَجههَا فَإِنَّهُم لَو نظرُوا فِي الْقِصَّة بكمالها لكَانَتْ حجَّة عَلَيْهِم لَا لَهُم، وسياقها فِي صَحِيح البُخَارِيّ هَكَذَا:

As for the evidence they derive from the statement of 'Umar to Abu Bakr, "Our view follows yours." This is not the beginning of the matter, and they did not present it properly. If they had examined the story completely, it would have been a proof against them and not in their favour. The text as contained in *Ṣaḥīḥ al-Bukhārī* is as follows:

عَن طَارق بن شهَاب قَالَ جَاءَ [بزاخة] وَفد من أَسد وغَطَفَان إِلَى أبي بكر يسألونه الصلح فَخَيرهمْ بَين الْحَرْب المجلية وَالسّلم المخزية، فَقَالُوا هَذِه المجلية قد عرفناها فَمَا المخزية. قَال: ننزع مِنْكُم الْحلقَة والكراع ونغنم مَا أصبْنَا مِنْكُم وتردون علينا مَا أصبتُم منا، وتدون لنا قَتْلَانَا وَيكون قَتْلَاكُمْ فِي النَّار، وتتركون أَقْوَامًا يتبعُون أَذْنَاب الْإِبِل حَتَّى يري الله خَليفَة رَسُوله صلى الله عَلَيْهِ وَآله وَسلم والمهاجرين أمرا يعذرونكم بِهِ.

Tāriq ibn Shihāb narrated, "A delegation from Asad and Ghaṭafān came to Abu Bakr seeking a truce. He presented them with a choice between a drastic war and an ignominious peace. They said, 'We understand the drastic war, but what is ignominious peace?' He said, 'We shall take your weapons, fighting horses and possessions as booty, and you shall return to us our possessions that you took from us. You must also pay us blood money for our dead whilst your fallen are in the fire. You will also be left to follow the tails of camels until Allah displays something to the successor of his Prophet ﷺ and the Muhājirūn that will cause them to forgive you.'

فَعرض أَبُو بكر مَا قَالَ على الْقَوْم فَقَامَ عمر بن الْخطاب فَقَالَ: قد رَأَيْت
رَأيا وسنشير عَلَيْك، أما مَا ذكرت من الْحَرْب المجلية والسّلم المخزية
فَنعم مَا ذكرت وَأما مَا ذكرت أن تغنم ما أصبنا منكم وتردون ما أصبتم
منا فنعم ما ذكرت، وأما ما ذكرت تدون قَتْلَانَا وَيكون قَتْلَاكُمْ فِي النَّار
فَإِن قَتْلَانَا قَاتَلت فقتلت على أَمر الله، أجورها على الله لَيْسَ لَهَا ديات
فتتابع الْقَوْم على مَا قَالَ عمر.

Then, Abu Bakr presented his decision to the people. 'Umar ibn al-Khaṭṭāb rose and said, 'I see an opinion, and we shall advise you about it: As for what you have stated about the drastic war and the truce of ignominy, this is well said. With regard to what you have said about us taking what we attained from them whilst they are to return what they attained from us, this too is well said. As for what you said about them giving blood money for our dead and their own dead being in the fire, as our fallen fought and were killed in obedience to Allah their reward is with Allah and there is no blood money for them.' The people then agreed with what 'Umar stated."[19]

---

19 Recorded by al-Bukhārī as contained in *al-Fatḥ* (13/206) from the ḥadīth

فَفِي هَذَا الحَدِيث مَا يرد عَلَيْهِم فَإِنَّهُ قرر بعض مَا رَآهُ أَبُو بكر [رَضِي الله عَنهُ] ورد بعضه، وَفِي بعض أَلْفَاظ هَذَا الحَدِيث: قد رَأَيْت رَأيا ورأينا لرأيك تبع فَلَا شكّ أَن الْمُتَابَعَة فِي بعض مَا رَآهُ أَو فِي كُله لَيْسَ من التَّقْلِيد فِي شَيْء، بل الاستصواب مَا جَاءَ بِهِ فِي الآراء والحروب وَلَيْسَ ذَلِك بتقليد، وَأَيْضًا قد يكون السُّكُوت عَن اعْتِرَاض بعض مَا فِيهِ مُخَالفَة من آراء الْأُمَرَاء لقصد إخلاص الطَّاعَة لِلْأُمَرَاءِ الَّتِي ثَبت الْأَمر بهَا وَكَرَاهَة الْخلاف الَّذِي أرشد صلى الله عَلَيْهِ وَآله وَسلم إِلَى تَركه. ثم هَذِه الآراء إِنَّمَا هِيَ فِي تدبير الحروب وَلَيْسَت فِي مسَائِل الدّين وَإِن تعلق بَعْضهَا بِشَيْء من ذَلِك فَإِنَّمَا هو على طَرِيق الاستتباع.

This ḥadīth contains a refutation against them because 'Umar affirmed some of the views of Abu Bakr and rejected some of them. In some wordings of this ḥadīth the following is mentioned, "You have an opinion and our opinion follows yours." There is no doubt that following him in some of his views or in all of them is not considered *taqlīd* in any way. Rather it is a form of approval or assent to his opinions and military strategy, and this is not *taqlīd*. In addition, it could be a form of silence from objecting to some of the opinions of the leaders that contain contradiction with an intent of obedience to the leaders—of which the command to has been established, and the dislike of differing which the Messenger of Allah ﷺ directed to the abandonment of. These opinions are with regard to military stratagem and are not related to issues of the religion. If some of them are related to the religion, it just happens that they coincide with it.

---

of Ṭāriq bin Shihāb.

وَبِالْجُمْلَةِ فاستدلال من اسْتدلَّ بِمثل هَذَا على جَوَاز التَّقْلِيد تَسْلِيَة لهَؤُلَاء الْمَسَاكِين من المقلدة بِمَا لَا يسمن وَلَا يُغني من جوع، وعَلى كل حَال فَهَذِهِ الْحجَّة الَّتِي استدلوا بهَا عَلَيْهِم لَا لَهُم لِأَن عمر [رَضِي الله عَنهُ] قرر من قَول أبي بكر مَا وَافق اجْتِهَاده ورد مَا خَالفه.

In short, the deduction of one who cites the like of this as a proof for the permissibility of *al-taqlīd* is like entertaining these needy *muqallids* with what cannot make one fleshy nor suffice one's hunger. Nevertheless, this proof from which they make deduction from is against them and not in their favour. This is because 'Umar assented to the statement of Abu Bakr that agreed with his *ijtihād* and rejected what disagreed with it.

وَأما مَا ذكروه من مُوَافقَة ابْن مَسْعُود لعمر وَأَخذه بقوله، وَكَذَلِكَ رُجُوع بعض السِّتَّة الْمَذْكُورين من الصَّحَابَة إِلَى بعض فلَيْسَ هذا إلا من باب موافقة العالم المجتهد للعالم المجتهد، وليس هذا ببدع وَلَا مستنكر فالعالم يُوَافق الْعَالم فِي أَكثر مِمَّا يُخَالِفهُ فيه من الْمسَائِل، ولاسيما إِذا كَانَا قد بلغا إلى أَعلَى مَرَاتِب الِاجْتِهَاد فَإِن الْمُخَالفَة بَينهمَا قَليلَة جدا، وَأَيْضًا قد ذكر أهل الْعلم أن ابْن مَسْعُود خَالف عمر فِي نَحْو مائَة مَسْأَلَة، وَمَا وَافقه إِلَّا فِي نَحْو أَربع مسَائِل فَأَيْنَ التَّقْلِيد من هَذَا وَكَيف صلح مثل مَا ذكر للاستدلال بِهِ على جَوَاز التَّقْلِيد؟ وَهَكَذَا رُجُوع بعض السِّتَّة الْمَذْكُورين إِلَى أَقْوَال بعض فَإِن هَذَا مُوَافقَة لَا تَقْلِيد، وَقد كَانُوا جَمِيعًا هم وَسَائِر الصَّحَابَة إِذا ظَهرت لَهُم السّنة لم يتركوها لقَوْل أحد كَائِنا من

كَانَ بل كَانُوا يعضون عَلَيْهَا بالنواجذ، ويرمون بآرائهم وَرَاء الْحَائِط فَأَيْنَ هَذَا من صنيع المقلدين الَّذين لَا يعدلُونَ بقول من قلد كتابا وَلَا سنة وَلَا يخالفونه قطّ. وَإِن تَوَاتر لَهُم مَا يُخَالِفهُ من السّنة.

As regards to what is mentioned concerning the concurrence of Ibn Masʿūd with ʿUmar and his adoption of his view in this, and likewise that some of the six mentioned Companions resorted to others, this is naught but the case of *mujtahid* scholars being in concordance, which is not a novelty nor disapproved of. A scholar agrees with other scholars in more issues than vice versa, especially if they have attained the highest level of *ijtihād*; disagreement between them will be very minute. Also, the people of knowledge have stated that Ibn Masʿūd differed with ʿUmar in one hundred issues and only agreed with him in four issues. So where is the *taqlīd* in this? How is the like of what has been mentioned suitable to deduce the permissibility of *al-taqlīd*? The same applies to the resorting of some of the six mentioned companions to the views of others, this is concurrence and not *al-taqlīd*. In fact, their manner and that of the other companions when a Sunnah was made apparent to them was to not ignore it for the statement of anyone—regardless who he was, rather, they would cling to it "with their molars" (i.e. strongly) and throw their opinions behind a wall. There is no comparison between this and the practice of *muqallidūn*, who do not leave off the view of the one they make *taqlīd* of for [a text from] the Qur'ān and Sunnah, and they do not differ with him ever, even if the report from the Sunnah which opposes his view is *mutawātir*.

وَمَعَ هَذَا فَإِن الرُّجُوع الَّذِي كَانَ يَقع من بعض الصَّحَابَة إِلَى قَول بعض إِنَّمَا هُوَ فِي الْغَالِب رُجُوع إِلَى رِوَايَته لَا إِلَى رَأْيه، لكَونه أخص بِمَعْرِفَة ذَلِك

المروى مِنْهُ بِوَجْه من الْوُجُوه كَمَا يعرف هَذَا من عرف أَحْوَال الصَّحَابَة.

Despite this, the resorting that occurred from some of the Companions to the opinion of others is mostly a resorting to the other's narration and not to his personal view. This is because he would be more competent to understand what he narrated from a particular aspect, as is known by those who understand the characteristics of the Companions.

وَأما مُجَرّد الآراء المحضة فقد ثَبت عَن أكابرهم النَّهْي عَنْهَا والتنفير مِنْهَا كَمَا سَيَأْتِي بَيَان طرف من ذَلِك إِن شَاءَ الله وَإِنَّمَا كَانُوا يرجعُونَ إِلَى الرَّأْي إِذا أعوزهم الدَّلِيل وَضَاقَتْ عَلَيْهِم الْحَادِثَة، ثمَّ لَا يبرمون أمرا إِلَّا بعد التراود والمفاوضة، وَمَعَ ذَلِك فهم على وَجل، وَلِهَذَا كَانُوا يكْرهُونَ تفرد بَعضهم بِرَأْي يُخَالف جَمَاعَتهمْ حَتَّى قَالَ أَبُو عُبَيْدَة السَّلمَانِي لعَلي بن أبي طَالب: لرأيك مَعَ الْجَمَاعَة أحب إِلَيْنَا من رَأْيك وَحدك.

As for pure and unadulterated assumption, its prohibition has been established from the major companions and that it be refrained from, as will be explained later, Allah willing. They would only resort to [pure] opinion when they were bereft of evidence and the matter was difficult to them; but they would not conclude upon the issue except after analysis and brainstorming. Despite this, they would remain fearful [of doing so.] It is due to this that they detested having a lone view that contradicted the majority of them. Abu ʿUbaydah al-Salmānī said to ʿAlī ibn Abī Ṭālib, "For your opinion to concord with the Jamāʿah (main body/congregation) is dearer to us than your opinion being isolated."

[٤]: احْتَجُّوا أَيْضا بقوله صلى الله عَلَيْهِ وَآله وَسلم: ((عَلَيْكُم بِسنتي وَسنة الْخُلَفَاء الرَّاشِدين المهديين من بعدِي)) وَهُوَ طرف من حَدِيث الْعِرْبَاض بن سَارِيَة وَهُوَ حَدِيث صَحِيح وَقَوله صلى الله عَلَيْهِ وَآله وَسلم: ((اقتدوا باللذين من بعدِي أبي بكر وَعمر)) وَهُوَ حَدِيث مَعْرُوف مَشْهُور ثَابت فِي السّنة وَغَيرهَا.

[4] Further, they used as proof the statement of the Prophet ﷺ, "Adhere to my Sunnah and the Sunnah of the Rightly Guided Caliphs after me." This is part of the ḥadīth of al-'Irbāḍ ibn Sāriyah and it is a *saḥīh* ḥadīth.[20] And [they also utilise as proof] his ﷺ statement: "Imitate the two men who will come after me: Abu Bakr and 'Umar."[21] This is a well-known ḥadīth which is established in the *Sunan* and other ḥadīth collections.

(وَالْجَوَاب): أن مَا سنه الْخُلَفَاء الراشدون من بعده فالأخذ بِهِ لَيْسَ إِلَّا لأَمره صلى الله عَلَيْهِ وَآله وَسلم بِالْأَخْذِ بِهِ فَالْعَمَل بِمَا سنوه والاقتداء بِمَا فَعَلُوهُ هُوَ لأَمره صلى الله عَلَيْهِ وَآله وَسلم لنا بِالْعَمَلِ بِسنة الْخُلَفَاء الرَّاشِدين والاقتداء بِأبي بكر وَعمر وَلم يَأْمُرنَا بالاستنان بِسنة عَالم من عُلَمَاء الْأمة وَلَا أرشدنا إِلَى الاقتداء بِمَا يرَاهُ مُجْتَهد من الْمُجْتَهدين.

Response: Taking the prescriptions of the Rightly Guided Caliphs

---

20 Reported by al-Tirmidhī (5/44).

21 Reported by al-Tirmidhī (3662), who stated that it was *ḥasan*. It was also reported by Aḥmad (5/382, 385 and 302), Ibn Mājah (97), al-Ḥākim in *al-Mustadrak* (3/75) and others from the route of 'Abdul Malik ibn 'Umayr, which is a *ṣaḥīḥ* ḥadīth.

after him is only due to his ﷺ order to do so. So acting upon their dictates and following them in their actions is due to the command of the Prophet ﷺ to act upon the *sunnah* of the Rightly Guided Caliphs and to follow Abu Bakr and ʿUmar. He did not command us to stick to the *sunnah* of a scholar among the scholars of the Ummah, nor did he direct us to adopt whatever a *mujtahid* holds.

فَالْحَاصِل أَنَّا لم نَأْخُذ بِسنة الْخُلَفَاء وَلَا اقتدينا بِأبي بكر وَعمر إِلَّا امتثالا لقَوْله صلى الله عَلَيْهِ وَآله وَسلم: ((عَلَيْكُم بِسنتي وَسنة الْخُلَفَاء الرَّاشِدين المهديين من بعدِي)) وَبِقَوْلِهِ: ((اقتدوا باللذين من بعدِي أبي بكر وَعمر)) فَكيف سَاغ لكم أَن تستدلوا بِهَذَا الَّذِي ورد فِيهِ النَّص على مَا لم يرد فِيهِ! فَهَل تَزْعُمُونَ أَن رَسُول الله صلى الله عَلَيْهِ وَآله وَسلم قَالَ عَلَيْكُم بِسنة أبي حنيفَة وَمَالك وَالشَّافِعِيّ وَابْن حَنْبَل حَتَّى يتم لكم مَا تُرِيدُونَ.

In short, we do not take the *sunnah* of the Caliphs nor imitate Abu Bakr and ʿUmar except out of compliance to the statement of the Prophet ﷺ, "Adhere to my Sunnah and the *sunnah* of the Rightly Guided Caliphs after me." And his statement, "Imitate the two who will come after me: Abu Bakr and ʿUmar." So how is it justified for you to deduce from this reported text that which it does not contain? Do you delude yourselves that the Messenger of Allah ﷺ said: "Adhere to the Sunnah of Abu Ḥanīfah, Mālik, al-Shāfiʿī and Ibn Ḥanbal" so that you attain what you need for your viewpoint?

فَإِذا قُلْتُمْ نَحن نقيس أَئِمَّة الْمذَاهب على هَؤُلَاءِ الْخُلَفَاء الرَّاشِدين فيا عجبا لكم كَيفَ ترتقون إِلَى هَذَا المرتقى الصعب وتقدمون هَذَا الْإِقْدَام فِي مقَام الإحجام فَإِن رَسُول الله صلى الله عَلَيْهِ وَآله وَسلم إِنَّمَا خص

الْخُلَفَاء الرَّاشِدين وَجعل سُنتهمْ كسنته فِي اتباعها لأمر يخْتَص بهم وَلَا يتعداهم إِلَى غَيرهم وَلَو كَانَ الْإِلْحَاق بالخلفاء الرَّاشِدين سائغا لَكَانَ إِلْحَاق المشاركين لَهُم فِي الصُّحْبَة وَالْعلم مقدما على من لم يشاركهم فِي مزية من المزايا، بل النِّسْبَة بَينه وَبينهمْ كالنسبة بَين الثرى والثريا، فلولا أَن هَذِه المزية خَاصَّة بهم مَقْصُورَة عَلَيْهِم لم يخصهم بهَا رَسُول الله صلى الله عَلَيْهِ وَآله وَسلم دون سَائِر الصَّحَابَة فدعونا من هَذِه التمحلات الَّتِي يأباها الْإِنْصَاف.

If you state that you are using analogy to equate the *imāms* of the *madhhabs* to these Rightly Guided Caliphs, then one derives wonderment from how you rise to this steep vantage point and advance forward to this blockaded location. Indeed the Messenger of Allah ﷺ specified the Rightly Guided Caliphs and made their *sunnah* similar to his Sunnah in terms of being followed, which is due to an issue that is specific to them and not extended to others. Had it been justified to attach others with the Rightly Guided Caliphs, then those who share in companionship and knowledge with them would have taken precedence over the one who does not share any excellence with them. However, the comparison between him and them is like the comparison between the earth and the stars. Were it not that this excellence was specific to them, the Messenger of Allah ﷺ would not have distinguished them with it whilst excluding the rest of the companions. So, leave us out of these petty arguments that fairness rejects.

وليتكُمْ قلدتم الْخُلَفَاء الرَّاشِدين لهَذَا الدَّلِيل أَو قلدتم مَا صَحَّ عَنْهُم على مَا يَقُوله أئمتكم، وَلَكِنَّكُمْ لم تَفعلُوا بل رميتم بِمَا جَاءَ عَنْهُم وَرَاء الْحَائِط

إذا خَالف مَا قَالَه من أَنْتُم أَتبَاع لَهُ، وَهَذَا لَا يُنكره إِلَّا مكابر معاند بل رميتم بِصَرِيح الْكتاب ومتواتر السّنة إِذا جَاءَ بِمَا يُخَالف من أَنْتُم متبعون لهم، فَإِن أنكرتم هَذَا فَهَذِهِ كتبكم أَيهَا المقلدة على ظهر البسيطة عرفونا من تتبعون من الْعلمَاء حَتَّى نعرفكم بِمَا ذكرْنَاهُ.

Would that you had made *taqlīd* of the Rightly Guided Caliphs due to this evidence or given preference to what is authentically reported from them over what your *imāms* say, but you do not do so. Rather, you throw away what is reported from them behind the wall if it disagrees with the view of the one you follow. None reject this except a proud and obstinate person. In fact, you would cast off a clear text from the Qur'ān and *mutawātir* Sunnah if it opposes that which the one you are following is upon. If you deny this, these are your books upon the surface of the earth O *muqallids*, tell us who you are following amongst the scholars so that we can show you what we have stated (i.e. from their books).

[٥]: ومن جملَة مَا استدلوا بِهِ حَدِيث: ((أَصْحَابِي كَالنُّجُومِ بِأَيِّهِمْ اقْتَدَيْتُمْ اهْتَدَيْتُمْ)).

[5] Amongst that which they cite as proof is the ḥadīth: "My Companions are like stars, whichever of them you use as a guide, you will be rightly guided."[22]

(وَالْجَوَاب): أن هَذَا الحَدِيث قد روى من طَرِيق عَن جَابر وَابْن عمر

22 It is a *mawḍū'* (fabricated) ḥadīth. This ḥadīth was reported from Abu Hurayrah, Ibn 'Abbās, 'Umar ibn al-Khaṭṭāb and his son 'Abdullāh. See *Silsilah al-Ḍa'īfah* (1/78, 1/439).

وَصرح أَئِمَّة الْجرْح وَالتَّعْدِيل بِأَنَّهُ لا يَصح مِنْها شَيْء، وَأَن هَذَا الحَدِيث لم يثبت عَن رَسُول الله صلى الله عَلَيْهِ وَآله وَسلم وَقد تكلم عَلَيْهِ الْحفاظ بِمَا يشفي وَيَكْفِي، فَمن رام الْبَحْث عَن طرقه وَعَن تضعيفها فَهُوَ مُمكن بِالنّظرِ فِي كتاب من كتب هَذَا الشَّأْن وَبِالْجُمْلَةِ فَالْحَدِيث لَا تقوم بِهِ حجَّة ثمَّ لَو كَانَ مِمَّا تقوم بِهِ الْحجَّة فما لكم أَيهَا المقلدون وَله، فَإِنَّهُ تضمن منقبة للصحابة ومزية لَا تُوجد لغيرهم فَمَاذَا تُرِيدُونَ مِنْهُ؟ فَإِن كَانَ مَا تقلدونه مِنْهُم احتجنا إِلَى الْكَلَام مَعكُمْ، وَإِن كَانَ من تقلدونه من غيرهم فاتركوا مَا لَيْسَ لكم لهم، ودعوا الْكَلَام على مَنَاقِب خير الْقُرُون، وهاتوا مَا أَنْتُم بصدد الِاسْتِدْلَال عَلَيْهِ.

Response: This ḥadīth has been reported through chains from Jābir and Ibn 'Umar, and the *imāms* of *al-jarh wa 'l-ta'dīl* have explicitly declared that it is not authentic at all, and that it is not established from the Messenger of Allah ﷺ. The scholars of ḥadīth have spoken about it to an extent which would gratify one's desire and suffice. So, whoever seeks to study its chains and its weakness should consult the books on this issue. In short, the ḥadīth cannot be cited as a proof, and even if it could be cited so, what is your business with it, O *muqallid*? Its purport is concerning the merit and excellence of the Companions that do not relate to those besides them, so what do you derive from it? If the ones you make *taqlīd* of fall within them then this necessitates us to discuss with you, but if they are not, leave the citation of that which does not concern them. Leave the narrations regarding the merits of the best of generations and bring forth something pertinent to what you are attempting to prove.

فَإِن هَذَا الْحَدِيث لَو صَحَّ لَكَانَ الْأَخْذ بِأقوال الصَّحَابَة لَيْسَ إِلَّا لِكَوْنِه صلى الله عَلَيْهِ وَآله وَسلم أَرشدنا إِلَى أَن الاقتداء بِأَحدهم اهتداء فَنَحْن إِنَّمَا امتثلنا إِرشاد رَسُول الله [صلى الله عَلَيْهِ وَآله وَسلم] وعملنا على قَوْله وتبعنا سنته، فَإِن مَا جعله محلا للاقتداء يكون ثُبُوت ذَلِك لَهُ بِالسنةِ وَهِي قَول رَسُول الله صلى الله عَلَيْهِ وَآله وَسلم فَلم نخرج عَن الْعَمَل بِسنة رَسُول الله [صلى الله عَلَيْهِ وَآله وَسلم] وَلَا قلدنا غَيره بل سمعنَا الله يَقُول: ﴿ وَمَا آتَاكُمُ الرَّسُولُ فَخُذُوهُ وَمَا نَهَاكُمْ عَنْهُ فَانتَهُوا﴾ وسمعناه يَقُول: ﴿قُلْ إِن كُنتُمْ تُحِبُّونَ اللَّهَ فَاتَّبِعُونِي﴾ وَكَانَ هَذَا الْقَوْل من جملة مَا أَتَانَا بِه فَأخذناه واتبعناه فِيهِ، وَلم نتبع غَيره وَلَا عولنا على سواهُ. فَإِن كُنْتُم تثبتون لأئمتكم هَذِه الْمزية قِيَاسا فَلَا أَعجبَ مِمَّا افتريتموه وتقولتموه، وَقد سبق الْجَواب عَنْكم فِي الْبَحْث الَّذِي قبل هَذَا.

And if this ḥadīth were to be authentic, it would simply mean that the views of the Companions are adopted purely due to the Prophet ﷺ informing us that following one of them contains guidance. So, we would only be complying with the directive of the Messenger of Allah ﷺ, acting upon his statement and following his Sunnah. It would be the case that he made it a form of following established through his Sunnah—i.e. through a statement of the Messenger of Allah ﷺ—so, [in acting in accordance to the ḥadīth] we would not go outside of acting upon the Sunnah of the Messenger ﷺ nor be blindly following other than him. Rather we heard Allah's statement: {And whatever the Messenger has given you - take; and what he has forbidden you - refrain from.}[23] And: {Say [O Mu-

23 Al-Hashr: 7

hammad]: "If you love Allah then follow me."}[24] This statement is from that which he delivered to us and we assent to it and follow him in it without following other than him, and we do not rely on other than him. If you affirm this merit to your *imām* through analogy, I would not be surprised regarding what you have invented and concocted. And the reply to you has preceded in the discussion that preceded this one.

وبمثل هَذَا الْجَواب يُجَاب عَن احتجاجهم بقوله صلى الله عَلَيْهِ وَآله وَسلم ((إِن معَاذًا قد سنّ لكم سنة)) وَذَلِكَ فِي شَأْن الصَّلَاة حَيْثُ أخر قَضَاءِ مَا فَاتَهُ مَعَ الإِمَام وَلَا يخفى عَلَيْك أَن فعل معَاذ هَذَا إِنَّمَا صَار سنة بقول رَسُول الله صلى الله عَلَيْهِ وَآله وَسلم لَا بِمُجَرَّد فعله، فَهُوَ إِنَّمَا كَانَ السَّبَب لثُبُوت السّنة وَلم تكن تِلْكَ السنة سنةً إِلَّا بقول رَسُول الله صلى الله عَلَيْهِ وَآله وَسلم وَهَذَا وَاضح لَا يخفى. وبمثل هَذَا الْجَواب على حَدِيث ((أَصْحَابِي كَالنُّجُوم)) يُجَاب عَن قَول ابْن مَسْعُود فِي وصف الصَّحَابَة فاعرفوا لَهُم حَقهم وتمسكوا بهديهم فَإِنَّهُم كَانُوا على الْهدى الْمُسْتَقيم.

This type of response is likewise appropriate to be given to their citing of proof from the statement of the Prophet ﷺ, "Indeed, Muʿādh has introduced a *sunnah* for you."[25] This was with regard to the issue of the *ṣalāt* (prayer), whereby he delayed making up what he missed

24 Āli 'Imrān: 31

25 Reported by Aḥmad in *al-Musnad* (5/246), Abu Dāwūd in *al-Sunan* (506, 507) and Ibn Khuzaymah in *al-Ṣaḥīḥ* (381, 383) from the route of 'Abd al-Raḥmān ibn Abī Laylā. It is *ṣaḥīḥ*.

with the *imām*, and it should be evident to the reader that this action of Muʿādh became a Sunnah on account of the statement of the Messenger of Allah ﷺ and not through its mere actioning. The reason for it becoming established as a Sunnah was the statement of the Messenger of Allah ﷺ. This is clear and not hidden. The like of this reply can also be given to the ḥadīth of, "My Companions are like stars," and the statement of Ibn Masʿūd in describing the Companions thus, "Know their right and adhere to their guidance, for indeed they are upon the straight path."[26]

26 It was mentioned by Ibn al-Qayyim in *Iʿlām al-Muwaqqiʿīn* (2/302-303).

[خلاصة ما تقدم]
[A Conclusion of What Has Been Covered]

ثم هَاهُنَا جَوَاب يشمل مَا تقدم من حَدِيث ((عَلَيْكُم بِسنتي وَسنة الْخُلَفَاء)) وَحَدِيث ((اقتدوا باللذين من بعدِي)) وَحَدِيث ((أَصْحَابِي كَالنُّجُوم)) وَقَول ابْن مَسْعُود وَهُوَ أَن المُرَاد بالاستنان بهم والاقتداء هُوَ أَن يَأْتِي المستن والمقتدي بِمثل مَا أَتَوا بِهِ وَيفْعل كَمَا فعلوا، وهم لَا يَفْعَلُونَ فعلا وَلَا يَقُولُونَ قولا إِلا على وفْق فعل رَسُول الله صلى الله عَلَيْهِ وَآله وَسلم وَقَوله.

Furthermore, here we provide a response which comprises what has preceded, i.e. the ḥadīth, "Adhere to my Sunnah and the *sunnah* of the Rightly Guided Caliphs," the ḥadīth, "Follow the two men who will come after me", and the ḥadīth, "My companions are like stars" and the aforementioned statement of Ibn Masʿūd: The intended meaning of adopting their way and following them is that the person adopting their way and following them should come with the like of what they came with and do as they did, and they did not perform an action nor utter a statement except that it conformed to the actions and words of the Messenger of Allah ﷺ.

فالاقتداء بهم هُوَ اقتداء برَسُول الله صلى الله عَلَيْهِ وَآله وَسلم والاستنان بسنتهم هُوَ استنان بِسنة رَسُول الله صلى الله عَلَيْهِ وَآله وَسلم وَإِنَّمَا أرشد

النَّاس إِلَى ذَلِك لأَنهم المبلغون عَنهُ الناقلون شَرِيعَته إِلَى من بعده من أمته فالفعل وَإِن كَانَ لَهُم فَهُوَ على طَرِيق الْحِكَايَة لفعل رَسُول الله صلى الله عَلَيْهِ وَآله وَسلم، كأفعال الطَّهَارَة وَالصَّلَاة وَالْحج وَنَحْو ذَلِك فهم رُوَاة لَهُ وَإِنَّمَا كَانَ مَنْسُوبا إِلَيْهِم لكَونه قَائِما بهم، وَفِي التَّحْقِيق هُوَ رَاجع إِلَى مَا سنه رَسُول الله صلى الله عَلَيْهِ وَآله وَسلم، فالاقتداء بهم اقتداء بِهِ، والاستنان بسنتهم استنان بِسنة رَسُول الله صلى الله عَلَيْهِ وَآله وَسلم وَإِذا خَفِي عَلَيْك هَذَا فَانْظُر مَا كَانَ يَفْعَله الْخُلَفَاء الراشدون وأكابر الصَّحَابَة فِي عباداتهم فإنك تَجدهُ حِكَايَة لما كَانَ يَفْعَله رَسُول الله صلى الله عَلَيْهِ وَآله وَسلم وَإِذا اخْتلفُوا فِي شَيْء من ذَلِك فَهُوَ لاختلافهم فِي الرِّوَايَة لَا فِي الرَّأْي، وَقل أَن جاء فعل من تِلْكَ الْأَفْعَال صادر عَن أحد مِنْهُم لمحض رَأْي رَآهُ، بل قد لَا تَجِد ذَلِك لَا سِيمَا فِي أَفعَال الْعِبَادَات وَهَذَا يعرفهُ كل من لَهُ خبْرَة بأحوالهم.

So following them is [actually a form of] following the Messenger of Allah and emulating their way is emulating the way of the Messenger of Allah ﷺ. [The Prophet] only directed people to this because the companions are the ones who conveyed from him and transmitted the religion to his later followers. Even though the action emanates from them, it is a means of transmitting the action of the Messenger of Allah ﷺ, such as the actions of purification, prayer, Ḥajj etc. Thus they are his narrators, and the action is only attributed to them due to it being displayed from them, whilst in reality, it emanates from the Prophetic Sunnah. Therefore, following them is akin to following the Prophet, and adopting their way is adopting the way of the Messenger of Allah ﷺ. If this is hidden from you, analyse the actions of the Rightly Guided Caliphs and the major companions in their worship; you will realise that they are [akin to] narrations of the Messenger of Allah's ﷺ actions. And if they differed in anything in this, it was due to their differences in narration and not in personal opinion. It is rare for you to find an action from the aforementioned actions (i.e. rites) that emanated from one of them due to pure personal opinion. Rather, you will not find this, especially in actions related to acts of worship. This fact is known by all who possesses knowledge about their (i.e. the companions) state.

وعَلى هَذَا فَمَعْنَى الحَدِيث أَن رَسُول الله صلى الله عَلَيْهِ وَآله وَسلم خَاطب أَصْحَابه أَن يقتدوا بِمَا يشاهدونه بِفِعْلِهِ من سنَنه، وَبِمَا يشاهدون من أفعَال الْخُلَفَاء الرَّاشِدين فَإِنَّهُم المبلغون عَنهُ العارفون بسنته المقتدون بهَا، فَكل مَا يصدر عَنْهُم فِي ذَلِك صادر عَنهُ وَلِهَذَا صَحَّ عَن جمَاعَة من أكَابِر الصَّحَابَة ذمّ الرَّأْي وَأَهله وَكَانُوا لَا يرشدون أحدا إِلَّا إِلَى سنة رَسُول الله صلى الله عَلَيْهِ وَآله وَسلم لَا إِلَى شَيْء من آرائهم وَهَذَا مَعْلُوم لَا يخفى على عَارِف.

On the basis of this, the meaning of the ḥadīth is that the Messenger of Allah ﷺ addressed his companions to imitate whatever action of his Sunnah they saw, and likewise what they saw from the actions of the Rightly Guided Caliphs. Thus, they are the ones who transmitted from him and are well acquainted with his Sunnah and steadfast to following it. So, everything that emanated from them in this respect emanated from him. As such, condemnations of personal opinion and its people have been authentically reported from a group amongst the major companions. They did not direct anyone to anything except the Sunnah of the Messenger of Allah ﷺ, and not to their personal opinions. This is well known and not hidden to one who is learned.

وَمَا نسب إِلَيْهِم من الاجتهادات وَجعله أهل الْعلم رَأيا لَهُم فَهُوَ لَا يخرج عَن الْكتاب وَالسّنة إما بتصريح أَو بتلويح، وَقد يظنّ خُرُوج شَيْء من ذَلِك وَهُوَ ظن مَدْفُوع لمن تَأمل حق التَّأَمُّل، وَإِذا وجد نَادرا رَأَيْت الصَّحَابِيّ يتحرج أَبلغ تحرج وَيُصَرح بِأَنَّهُ رَأْيه وَأن الله بَرِيء من خطئه وينسب الْخَطَأ إِلَى نَفسه وَإِلَى الشَّيْطَان، وَالصَّوَاب إِلَى الله كَمَا تقدم عَن الصّديق فِي تَفْسِير الْكَلَالَة وكما روي عَنهُ وَعَن غَيره فِي فَرَائض الْجد، وكما كَانَ يَقُول عمر فِي تَفْسِير قَوْله تَعَالَى: ﴿وَفَاكِهَةً وَأَبا﴾ وَهَذَا الْبَحْث نَفِيس فتَأَمّله حق تَأمله تنْتَفع بِهِ.

The independent reasonings (*ijtihād*) that are attributed to them—which the people of knowledge consider to be their personal opinions—do not fall outside of the Qur'ān and Sunnah, either explicitly or implicitly. One may assume that some of it may fall outside of these two sources but this is a faulty assumption, made clear after considering the matter correctly. One will come across on rare instances a companion traversing the depths of distress whilst declaring something to be his personal view and that Allah is free from his error; and he would attribute the error to himself and the devil, whilst attributing the correct view to Allah—as preceded from Abu Bakr al-Ṣiddīq with regard to the explanation of [the inheritance issue known as] *al-kalālah*. Likewise [this statement] was reported from him and other than him concerning the inheritance of the grandfather, and 'Umar used to state it concerning the explanation of the statement of Allah: **{And fruit and herbage.}**[27] This is an invaluable discourse; so brood over it to the level it deserves, and one will benefit.

[٦] وَمن جملَة مَا استدلوا بِهِ قَوْل الله تَعَالَى: ﴿أَطِيعُوا اللَّهَ وَأَطِيعُوا الرَّسُولَ وَأُولِي الْأَمْرِ مِنكُمْ﴾ قَالُوا أولي الْأَمر هم الْعلمَاء وطاعتهم تقليدهم فِيمَا يفتون بِهِ.

[6] Amongst the evidences they derive proof from is the statement of Allah: **{Obey Allah and obey the Messenger, and those of you who are in authority.}** They argued that those who are in authority are the scholars and obedience to them means making *taqlīd* of them in their verdicts.

(وَالْجَوَاب): أَن لِلْمُفَسِّرِينَ فِي تَفْسِير أولي الْأَمر قَوْلَيْنِ: أَحدهمَا أَنهم الْأُمَرَاء وَالثَّانِي الْعلمَاء. وَلَا تمْتَنع إِرَادَة الطَّائِفَتَيْنِ من الْآيَة الْكَرِيمَة، وَلَكِن أَيْن هَذَا من الدّلَالَة على مُرَاد المقلدين فَإِنَّهُ لَا طَاعَة لِلْعُلَمَاء وَلَا لِلْأُمَرَاءِ إِلَّا إِذا أمروا بِطَاعَة الله على وفْق شَرِيعَته وَإِلَّا فقد ثَبت عَنهُ صلى الله عَلَيْهِ وَآله وَسلم: ((أنه لَا طَاعَة لمخلوق فِي مَعْصِيَة الْخَالِق))، وَأَيْضًا الْعلمَاء إِنَّمَا أرشدوا غَيرهم إِلَى ترك تقليدهم ونهوهم عَن ذَلِك كَمَا سَيَأْتِي بَيَان طرف مِنْهُ عَن الْأَئِمَّة الْأَرْبَعَة وَغَيرهم فطاعتهم ترك تقليدهم.

Response: There are two views amongst the exegetes of the Qurʾān regarding the meaning of those in authority: (i) it refers to leaders and (ii) it refers to the scholars, and both parties could be intended

---

27 ʿAbasa: 31

by this noble *āyah*. However, where is the proof in this to indicate the intent of the *muqallid*? For there is no obedience to the scholars or rulers except if they command obedience to Allah in conformity with His legislation. It is established from the Prophet ﷺ that he said, "There is no obedience to any human being if it involves disobedience to the Creator."[28] Furthermore, the scholars have guided others to leave off making *taqlīd* of them and forbade this, and we will detail later some statements from the four *imāms* and other than them. Thus, obedience to them is to abandon making *taqlīd* of them.

وَلَو فَرضنَا أَن فِي الْعلمَاء من يرشد النَّاس إِلَى التَّقْلِيد ويرغبهم فِيهِ لَكَانَ مرشدا إِلَى مَعْصِيّة الله، وَلَا طَاعَة لَهُ بِنَص حَدِيث رَسُول الله [صلى الله عَلَيْهِ وَآله وَسلم] وَإِنَّمَا قُلْنَا إِنه مرشد إِلَى مَعْصِيّة الله لِأَنَّه من أرشد هَؤُلَاءِ الْعَامَّة الَّذين لَا يعْقلُونَ الْحجَج وَلَا يعْرفُونَ الصَّوَاب من الْخَطَأ إِلَى التَّمَسُّك بالتقليد كَانَ هَذَا الْإِرْشَاد مِنْهُ مستلزما لإرشادهم إِلَى ترك الْعَمَل بِالْكتاب وَالسّنة إِلَّا بِوَاسِطَة آراء الْعلمَاء الَّذين يقلدونهم فَمَا عمِلُوا بِهِ عمِلُوا وَمَا لم يعملوا بِهِ لم يعملوا بِهِ، وَلَا يلتفتون إِلَى كتاب وَلَا سنة، بل من شَرط التَّقْلِيد الَّذين أصيبوا بِهِ أَن يقبل من إِمَامه رَأْيه وَلَا يعول على رِوَايَته، وَلَا يسْأَله عَن كتاب وَلَا سنة، فَإِن سَأَلَهُ عَنْهُمَا خرج عَن التَّقْلِيد لِأَنَّهُ قد صَار مطالبا بِالْحجَّةِ.

28 Reported by al-Baghawī in *Sharḥ al-Sunnah* (2455) from the ḥadīth of al-Nawās ibn Sam'ān with a *ḍa'īf isnād*. However, it has witnessing reports including the ḥadīths of al-Hakam ibn 'Amr al-Ghafārī and 'Imrān ibn al-Ḥuṣayn reported by Aḥmad (5/66) and al-Ṭayālisī with a *ṣaḥīḥ isnād*.

And if we assume that there is one amongst the scholars who urges people to perform *taqlīd* and encourages them towards it, he would be considered a guide to the disobedience of Allah and not obedience to Him, on the basis of the text of the ḥadīth of the Messenger of Allah ﷺ. We stated that he is a guide to the disobedience of Allah because whomsoever guides these laymen who do not possess understanding of the proofs or know the correct from the incorrect to cling firmly to *al-taqlīd*; this directive from him implies directing them to abandon acting upon the Qur'ān and Sunnah except through the medium of the personal views of the scholars whom they blindly follow. Whatever their scholars act upon, they will act upon and whatever their scholars do not act upon, they will not act upon it nor turn to the Qur'ān and Sunnah. In fact, one of the conditions of *al-taqlīd* which they have been afflicted with is to accept the personal view of their *imām* and shun his narration. They neglect to ask him about the Qur'ān or Sunnah, whereas if they do ask regarding them, they would have removed themselves from the confines of *al-taqlīd* due to this seeking of proof.

وَمن جملَة مَا تجب فِيهِ طَاعَة أولي الْأَمر تَدْبِير الحروب الَّتِي تدهم النَّاس وَالِانْتِفَاع بآرائهم فِيهَا وَفِي غَيرهَا من تَدْبِير أَمر المعاش وجلب الْمصَالح وَدفع الْمَفَاسِد الدُّنْيَوِيَّة، وَلَا يبعد أَن تكون هَذِه الطَّاعَة فِي هَذِه الْأُمُور الَّتِي لَيست من الشَّرِيعَة هي المرادة بِالْأَمر بطاعتهم، لِأَنَّهُ لَو كَانَ المُرَاد طاعتهم فِي الْأُمُور الَّتِي شرعها الله وَرَسُوله لَكَانَ ذَلِك دَاخِلا تَحت طَاعَة الله وَطَاعَة الرَّسُول، وَلَا يبعد أَيْضا أَن تكون الطَّاعَة لَهُم فِي الْأُمُور الشَّرْعِيَّة فِي مثل الْوَاجِبَات المخيرة وواجبات الْكِفَايَة، فإذا أمروا بواجب من الواجبات المخيرة أَو ألزموا بعض الْأَشْخَاص بِالدُّخُولِ فِي وَاجِبَات

الْكِفَايَة لزم ذَلِك فَهَذَا أَمر شَرْعِي وَجبت فِيهِ الطَّاعَة.

From that which is obligatory in terms of obedience to the leaders is the stratagem for wars that take people unaware; benefiting from their personal opinions concerning it and other than it such as managing the economy, bringing benefits and repelling worldly harms. It is not far-fetched that obedience to them is with regard to issues that are not from the religion, and this is the intended meaning of the command to obey them. This is because if the intended meaning of their obedience is in affairs that Allah and His Messenger have ordained, this would fall under obedience to Allah and His Messenger ﷺ. It is also not far-fetched that obedience to them could be in religious affairs, e.g. voluntary obligations or collective obligations. Thus if they order people to partake in either of these then it is binding, and it would be a religious order wherein obedience is an obligation.

وَبِالْجُمْلَةِ فَهَذِهِ الطَّاعَة لأولي الْأَمر الْمَذْكُورَة فِي الْآيَة هَذِه هِيَ الطَّاعَة الَّتِي ثبتت فِي الْأَحَادِيث المتواترة فِي طَاعَة الْأُمَرَاء مَا لم يأمروا بِمَعْصِيَة الله أَو يرى الْمَأْمُور كفرا بواحا، فَهَذِهِ الْأَحَادِيث مفسرة لما فِي الْكتاب الْعَزِيز وَلَيْسَ ذلك من التَّقْلِيد فِي شَيْء بل هُوَ فِي طَاعَة الْأُمَرَاء الَّذين غالبهم الْجَهْل والبعد عَن الْعلم فِي تَدْبِير الحروب وسياسة الأجناد وجلب مصَالح الْعباد وَأما الْأُمُور الشَّرْعِيَّة الْمَحْضَة فقد أغْنى عَنْهَا كتاب الله وَسنة رَسُوله.

In brief, the obedience to those in authority mentioned in the *āyah* is the obligation that is established in *mutawātir aḥādīth* regarding obedience to the rulers as long as they do not command to the disobedience of Allah, or if the one ordered views it to be clear disbelief. These *aḥādīth* serve as explanation to that which is in the Qur'ān and as such, it is not *taqlīd* in any manner. Rather, it is with respect to the obedience of rulers—who are most often ignorant and far from knowledge—in the management of wars, military policy, and bringing benefits to the slaves. As for pure legislative issues, the Book of Allah and the Sunnah of the Messenger of Allah ﷺ suffice.

[٧] وَأعلم أَن هَذَا الَّذِي سقناه هُوَ عُمْدَة أَدِلَّة المجوزين للتقليد، وَقد أبطلنا ذَلِك كُله كَمَا عرفت. وَلَهُم شبهة غير مَا سقناه وَهِي دون مَا حررناه كَقَوْلِهِم إِن الصَّحَابَة قلدوا عمر فِي الْمَنْع من بيع الْأُمَّهَات الْأَوْلَاد، وَفِي أَن الطَّلَاق يتبع الطَّلَاق، وَهَذِه فِرْيَة لَيْسَ فِيهَا مرية، فَإِن الصَّحَابَة مُخْتَلفُونَ فِي كلا الْمَسْأَلَتَيْنِ فَمنهمْ من وَافق عمر اجْتِهَادًا لَا تقليدا وَمِنْهُم من خَالفه، وَقد كَانَ الموافقون لَهُ يسألونه عَن الدَّلِيل ويستروونه النُّصُوص، وشأن الْمُقَلّد أَن لَا يبْحَث عَن دَلِيل بل يقبل الرَّأْي وَيتْرك الرِّوَايَة، وَمن لم يكن هَكَذَا فَلَيْسَ بمقلد.

[7] Know that what we have cited above forms the foundation of proofs for those who permit *al-taqlīd*, and we have repudiated it all, as you have seen. They have doubts other than what we have cited but they are less than what we have written about, e.g. their saying that the Companions did *taqlīd* of 'Umar in the prohibition of selling *umahāt al-awlād* (pl. of *umm al-walad*, i.e. bondmaidens who have borne their masters' children) and that divorce follows divorce. This is a form of falsity wherein there is no doubt. The companions differed in these two issues, some of them agreed with 'Umar due to *ijtihād* and not *taqlīd*, whilst others disagreed with him. Those who

agreed with him asked for evidences and sought the narration of textual proof, which is contrary to the manner of the *muqallid* who does not seek for proof, rather, he accepts the opinion whilst leaving the narration. Whoever is not like this is not a *muqallid*.

[٨]: وَمن جملَة مَا تمسكوا بِهِ أَن الصَّحَابَة كَانُوا يفتون وَالرَّسُول صلى الله عَلَيْهِ وَآله وَسلم حي بَين أظهرهم وَهَذَا تَقْلِيد لَهُم.

[8] Amongst that which they cling to is that the Companions used to issue verdicts whilst the Messenger of Allah ﷺ was in their midst, and this is *taqlīd* of them.

وَيُجَاب عَن ذَلِك بِأَنَّهُم كَانُوا يفتون بالنصوص من الْكتاب وَالسّنة وَذَلِك رِوَايَة مِنْهُم، وَلَا يشك من يفهم أَن قبُول الرِّوَايَة لَيْسَ بتقليد فَإِن قبُول الرِّوَايَة هُوَ قبُول للحجة، والتقليد إِنَّمَا هُوَ قبُول الرَّأْي، وَفرق بَين قبُول الرِّوَايَة وَقبُول الرَّأْي، فَإِن قبُول الرِّوَايَة لَيْسَ من التَّقْلِيد فِي شَيْء بل هُوَ عكس رسم الْمُقَلّد فاحفظ هَذَا فَإِن مجوزة التَّقْلِيد يغالطون بِمثل ذَلِك كثيرا فَيَقُولُونَ مثلا إِن الْمُجْتَهد هُوَ مقلد لمن روى لَهُ السّنة وَيَقُولُونَ إِن من التَّقْلِيد قبُول قَول الْمَرْأَة أَنَّهَا قد طهرت وَقبُول قَول الْمُؤَذّن أَن الْوَقْت قد دخل، وَقبُول الْأَعْمَى لقَوْل من أخبرهُ بالقبلة. بل وَجعلُوا من التَّقْلِيد قبُول شَهَادَة الشَّاهِد وتعديل المعدل وجرح الْجَارِح.

The response to this is that they used to issue verdicts based upon the text of the Qur'ān and Sunnah, and so this is [akin to] narration from them. Whoever can understand will not doubt the fact that accepting narration is not considered *taqlīd*, as acceptance of a narration is acceptance of proof, while *al-taqlīd* is acceptance of an opinion. There is a stark distinction between acceptance of narration and acceptance of personal opinions, because acceptance of narration is not *taqlīd* at all. Rather, it fundamentally opposes the description of a *muqallid*. The reader should hold onto this, as those who permit *al-taqlīd* err greatly in similar matters. They say, for example, a *mujtahid* is a *muqallid* to the one who narrated the Sunnah to him. And they say that part of *taqlīd* is the acceptance of a woman's statement that she is pure, acceptance of the statement of the *mu'adhin* regarding prayer times and the blind person accepting the statement of one who informs him about the *qiblah* (direction of prayer). In fact, they consider acceptance of the testimony of a witness, praise by the praiser and criticism by the critic as *al-taqlīd*.

وَلَا يخفى عَلَيْك أَن هَذَا لَيْسَ من التَّقْلِيد فِي شَيْء بل هُوَ من قبُول الرِّوَايَة لَا من قبُول الرَّأْي، إِذْ قبُول الرَّاوِي للدليل والمخبر بِدُخُول الْوَقْت وبالطهارة وبالقبلة وَالشَّاهِد والجارح والمزكي هُوَ من قبُول الرِّوَايَة إِذْ الرَّاوِي إِنَّمَا أخبر المروى لَهُ بِالدَّلِيلِ الَّذِي رَوَاهُ وَلم يُخبرهُ بِمَا يرَاهُ من الرَّأْي، وَكَذَلِكَ الْمخبر بِدُخُول الْوَقْت إِنَّمَا أخبر بِأَنَّهُ شَاهد عَلامَة من عَلَامَات الْوَقْت، وَلم يخبر بِأَنَّهُ قد دخل الْوَقْت بِرَأْيِهِ وَكَذَلِكَ الْمخبر بِالطَّهَارَةِ فَإِن الْمَرْأَة مثلا أخْبرت أَنَّهَا قد شاهدت عَلَامَات الطُّهْر من الْقِصَّة الْبَيْضَاء وَنَحْوهَا، وَلم تخبر بِأَن ذَلِك رَأْي رَأَتْهُ، وَهَكَذَا الْمخبر بالقبلة أخبر أَن جِهَتهَا أَو عينهَا هَاهُنَا حَسبمَا تَقْتَضِيه الْمُشَاهدَة بالحاسة وَلم يخبر عَن رَأْيه، وَهَكَذَا الشَّاهِد فَإِنَّهُ أخبر عَن أَمر يُعلمهُ بِأحد الْحَواس وَلم يخبر عَن رَأْيه فِي ذَلِك الْأَمر.

It will not be hidden to the reader that this is not *taqlīd* at all. Rather, it is acceptance of narration and not acceptance of personal opinion, since acceptance of a narrator is for an evidence. When being informed about the time of prayer, purity, the *qiblah*, and hearing witness testimony, criticism and praise, this is all a form of acceptance of narration. This is because the narrator only informs the one receiving the narration of the proof he narrates, without informing him of his personal opinion. Likewise is the case for one informing about the time of prayer; he only informs that he has seen one of the signs of the time; he does not inform that the prayer time has commenced based upon his personal opinion. Likewise if a woman—for example—informs that she has seen a sign of purity such as white discharge and the like; she did not inform that it is her personal opinion. The same applies to the person who informs about the *qiblah*, he informed regarding its direction or position based on the dictates of the senses, he did not inform about his personal opinion. The same applies to the witness; he informs of an issue he knows through one of the senses, he does not inform about his personal opinion on the issue.

وَبِالْجُمْلَةِ فَهَذَا أوضح من أَن يخفى، وَالْفرق بَين الرِّوَايَة والرأي أبين من الشَّمْس، وَمن الْتبس عَلَيْهِ الْفرق بَينهمَا فَلَا يشغل نَفسه بالمعارف العلمية فَإِنَّهُ بهيمي الْفَهم وَإِن كَانَ فِي مسلاخ إِنْسَان.

In brief, this matter is too clear for it to be obscure to anyone, and the difference between narration and personal opinion is clearer than the sun. One who is confused about the distinction between them should not preoccupy himself with scholastic matters, for he is akin to an animal in understanding, despite him bearing the skin of a human being.

قَالَ ابْن خويز منداد الْبَصْرِيّ الْمَالِكِي: (التَّقْلِيد): مَعْنَاهُ فِي الشَّرْع الرُّجُوع إِلى قَوله لَا حجَّة لقائله عَلَيْهِ، وَذَلِكَ مَمْنُوع مِنْهُ فِي الشَّرِيعَة، (والإتباع): مَا ثَبت عَلَيْهِ الْحجَّة.. إِلَى أَن قَالَ: والإتباع فِي الدّين متبوع والتقليد مَمْنُوع، وَسَيَأْتِي مثل هَذَا الْكَلَام لِابْن عبد الْبر وَغَيره.

Ibn Khuwayz Mandād al-Baṣrī al-Mālikī said, "The technical meaning of *al-taqlīd* is to rely upon a statement, for which the utterer has no proof and such is prohibited in the Legislation. *Al-ittibāʿ* is that which is established upon proof. [...] *Al-ittibāʿ* in the religion is allowed whilst *al-taqlīd* is prohibited." The statements similar to this from Ibn ʿAbd al-Barr and others will come later.

وَقد أورد بعض أسراء التَّقْلِيد كلَاما يُؤَيّد بِهِ دَعْوَاهُ الْجَوَاز فَقَالَ مَا مَعْنَاهُ لَو كَانَ التَّقْلِيد غير جَائِز لَكَانَ الِاجْتِهَاد وَاجِبا على كل فَرد من أَفْرَاد الْعباد، وَهُوَ تَكْلِيف مَا لَا يُطَاق، فَإِن الطباع البشرية مُتَفَاوِتَة فَمِنْهَا مَا هُوَ قَابل للعلوم الاجتهادية وَمِنْهَا مَا هُوَ قَاصِر عَن ذَلِك، وَهُوَ غَالب الطباع، وعَلى فرض إِنَّهَا قَابِلَة لَهُ جَمِيعهَا فوجوب تَحْصِيله على كل فَرد يُؤَدِّي إِلَى تبطيل المعايش الَّتِي لَا يتم بَقَاء النَّوْع بِدُونِهَا، فَإِنَّهُ لَا يظفر برتبة الِاجْتِهَاد إِلَّا من جرد نَفسه للْعلم فِي جَمِيع أوقاته على وَجه لَا يشْتَغل بِغَيْرِهِ، فَحِينَئِذٍ يشْتَغل الحراث والزراع والنساج والعمار وَنَحْوهم بِالْعلمِ، وَتبقى هَذِه الْأَعْمَال شاغرة معطلة فَتبْطل المعايش بأسرها ويفضي ذَلِك إِلَى إنخرام نظام الْحَيَاة وَذَهَاب نوع الْإِنْسَان، وَفِي هَذَا من الضَّرَر وَالْمَشَقَّة وَمُخَالفَة

مَقْصُود الشَّارِع مَا لَا يخفى على أحد.

[9] One of the patrons of *al-taqlīd* has mentioned some words so as to support his claim of the permissibility of *taqlīd*. He said words to the meaning of: Had it been that *taqlīd* is not permissible, *ijtihād* would have been obligated upon every individual. This would impose upon people something beyond their capability, because human nature differs; some are capable of absorbing the knowledge of *ijtihād* whilst others are incapable, and this is the nature of most people. Supposing that all human beings were capable of absorbing the knowledge of *ijtihād*, the obligation of attaining it by everyone would lead to disruption of livelihood, without which life cannot be maintained. None are able to attain the level of *ijtihād* except one who dedicates his life to knowledge, engrossing his time with it in a manner where nothing else preoccupies him. Then the plowman, farmer, weaver, architect etc. would be preoccupied with knowledge and these jobs would be left vacant and idle, thereby rendering industries inactive and leading to the disruption of the system of life and extinction of the human race. This contains harm, difficulty and opposition to the goal of the Legislator, which is not hidden to anyone. [End]

وَيُجَاب عَن هَذَا التشكيك الْفَاسِد بِأَنا لَا نطلب من كل فَرد من أَفْرَاد الْعباد أَن يبلغ رُتْبَة الِاجْتِهَاد بل الْمَطْلُوب هُوَ أَمر دون التَّقْلِيد وَذَلِكَ بِأَن يكون القائمون بِهَذِهِ المعايش والقاصرون إدراكا وفهما كَمَا كَانَ عَلَيْهِ أمثالهم فِي أَيَّام الصَّحَابَة وَالتَّابِعِينَ وتابعيهم وهم خير الْقُرُون ثم الَّذين يَلُونَهُمْ، ثمَّ الَّذين يَلُونَهُمْ، وَقد علم كل عَالم أَنهم لم يَكُونُوا مقلدين وَلَا منتسبين إِلَى فَرد من أَفْرَاد الْعلمَاء بل كَانَ الْجَاهِل يسْأَل الْعَالم عَن

الحكم الشَّرْعِيّ الثَّابِت فِي كتاب الله أَو بِسنة رَسُوله فيفتيه بِهِ وَيَرْوِيه لَهُ لفظا أَو معنى فَيعْمل بذلك من بَاب الْعَمَل بالرواية لَا بِالرَّأْيِ، وَهَذَا أسهل من التَّقْلِيد فَإِن تفهم دقائق علم الرَّأْي أصعب من تفهم الرِّوَايَة بمراحل كَثِيرَة.

The response to this baseless doubt is that we do not seek from every individual that he should attain the level of performing *ijtihād*. Rather, what is demanded is something other than *taqlīd*. This is so that those who carry out these jobs and the incapable ones would have knowledge and understanding, as was the case with their likes during the era of the companions, the successors and their successors—whom are the best generations—followed by those who followed them then those who followed them. All scholars know that they were not blind followers nor did they attribute themselves to the way of an individual amongst the scholars. Rather the ignorant would ask the learned for a legislative ruling that is established from the Book of Allah or the Sunnah of His Messenger ﷺ. He would give a verdict based upon them, and narrate it to him in wording or in meaning, thus the one who sought the verdict acted upon it as a way of acting concordant to a narration and not a personal opinion. This is easier than *al-taqlīd*, as understanding the intricacies of a personal opinion is more difficult in many grades than understanding a narration.

فَمَا طلبنا من هَؤُلَاءِ الْعَوام إِلَّا مَا هُوَ أخف عَلَيْهِم مِمَّا طلبه مِنْهُم الملزمون لَهُم بالتقليد، وَهَذَا هُوَ الْهدى الَّذِي درج عَلَيْهِ خير الْقُرُون ثمَّ الَّذين يَلُونَهُمْ ثمَّ الَّذين يَلُونَهُمْ حَتَّى استدرج الشَّيْطَان بذريعة التَّقْلِيد من استدرج وَلم يكتف بذلك حَتَّى سَوَّلَ لَهُم الِاقْتِصَار على تَقْلِيد فَرد من أَفْرَاد الْعلمَاء

وَعدم جَوَاز تَقْلِيد غَيره ثمَّ توسع فِي ذَلِك فخيل لكل طَائِفَة أَن الْحق مَقْصُور على مَا قَالَه إمامها وَمَا عداهُ بَاطِل، ثمَّ أوقع فِي قُلُوبهم الْعَدَاوَة والبغضاء حَتَّى إِنَّك تَجِد من الْعَدَاوَة بَين أهل الْمذَاهب الْمُخْتَلفَة مَا لَا تَجدهُ بَين أهل الْملَل الْمُخْتَلفَة وَهَذَا يعرفهُ كل من عرف أَحْوَالهم.

Thus, we do not seek from the laity except that which is lighter upon them than what those who enjoin *al-taqlīd* seek. This is the guidance upon which the best of generations traversed; followed by those who followed them, then those who followed them until the devil allured those whom he allured through the means of *al-taqlīd*. He was not satisfied with this until he beautified for them restricting *al-taqlīd* to an individual amongst the scholars, and [deeming] impermissible the *taqlīd* of other than him. Then he expanded this by making every group imagine that the truth is limited to what their *imām* said, and that anything other than it is baseless. Then he placed in their hearts enmity and hatred, so much so that a level of enmity was witnessed amongst the people of different *madhhabs* that one would not witness between the people of different religions. This is known by everyone who knows of their affair.

فَانْظُر إِلَى هَذِه الْبِدْعَة الشيطانية الَّتِي فرقت أهل هَذِه الْملَّة الشَّرِيفَة وصيرتهم على مَا ترَاهُ من التباين والتقاطع والتخالف، فَلَو لم يكن من شُؤْم هَذِه التقليدات والمذاهب المبتدعات إِلَّا مُجَرّد هَذِه الْفرْقَة بَين أهل الْإِسْلَام مَعَ كَونهم أهل مِلَّة وَاحِدَة وَنَبِي [وَاحِد] وَكتاب وَاحِد لَكَانَ ذَلِك كَافِيا كَونهَا غير جَائِزَة فَإِن النَّبِي صلى الله عَلَيْهِ وَآله وَسلم كَانَ ينْهَى عَن الْفرْقَة ويرشد إِلَى الِاجْتِمَاع ويذم المتفرقين فِي الدّين حَتَّى إنه قَالَ فِي

تِلَاوَة الْقُرْآن وَهُوَ من أعظم الطَّاعَات أنهُم إِذا اخْتلفُوا تركُوا التِّلَاوَة وَإِنَّهُمْ يَتلون مَا دَامَت قُلُوبهم مؤتلفة.

Look at this devilish innovation that has caused division amongst the people of this noble religion and caused them to engage in what you see of differing, severing of relations and opposing one another. If there were no other evils brought forth by this innovated *taqlīd* and these innovated schools of *fiqh* except this division amongst the people of Islam—in spite of the fact that they belong to one religion, have one Prophet and one Book—it would suffice [as proof] for its impermissible nature. Indeed, the Prophet ﷺ would forbid division whilst guiding to unity. He condemned those who cause division in the religion to the extent that he mentioned as regards to recitation of the Qur'ān—which is one of the greatest acts of righteousness—that if they differ, they should leave reciting it and that they should recite so long as their hearts are in harmony.[29]

وَثَبت ذمّ التَّفَرُّق وَالِاخْتِلَاف فِي مَوَاضِع من الْكتاب الْعَزِيز مَعْرُوفَة فَكيف يحل لعالم أَن يَقُول بِجَوَاز التَّقْلِيد الَّذِي كَانَ سَبَب فرقة أهل الْإِسْلَام وانتشار[٣٠] مَا كَانَ عَلَيْهِ من النظام والتقاطع بَين أَهله وَإِن كَانُوا ذَوي أَرْحَام.

Condemnation of differing and division has been established in several places within the Qur'ān. This is well known, so how is it per-

29 He is referring to the ḥadīth reported by al-Bukhārī (5060) and Muslim (3/2667) upon the authority of Jundab ibn 'Abdullāh al-Bajali, "Recite the Qur'ān whilst your hearts are united, and if you differ in it then cease."

30 [T] This appears to be a typo, and Allah knows best. We have translated this sentence by substituting it with the following word:

(انتثار) i.e. with a (ث) instead of a (ش).

missible for a scholar to declare the permissibility of *al-taqlīd*, a concept which has led to the division of the people of Islam, breaking of the structured system it has established and severing of relations amongst its people—even amongst close relatives?

[١٠]: وَقد احْتج بعض أسراء التَّقْلِيد وَمن لم يخرج عَن أَهله وَإِن كَانَ عِنْد نَفسه قد خرج مِنْهُ - بِالْإِجْمَاع - على جَوَازه، وَهَذِه دَعْوَى لَا تصدر من ذِي قدم راسخة فِي علم الشَّرِيعَة، بل لَا تصدر من عَارِف بأقوال أهل الْعلم بل لَا تصدر من عَارِف بأقوال أَئِمَّة الْمذَاهب الْأَرْبَعَة فَإِنَّهُ قد صَحَّ عَنْهُم الْمَنْع من التَّقْلِيد.

[10] Some patrons of *al-taqlīd* and one who is not excluded from its people—though he considers himself not from them—may use consensus as a proof for its permissibility. This claim cannot emanate from someone who is firmly grounded in knowledge of the Legislation. In fact, it cannot emanate from someone who is familiar with the statements of the people of knowledge. Rather, it cannot emanate from one who is familiar with the statements of the *imāms* of the four *madhhabs*, because the prohibition of *al-taqlīd* has been authentically reported from them.

[أَقْوَال الْعلمَاء فِي النَّهْي عَن التَّقْلِيد]

[Statements of the Scholars Regarding the Prohibition of *al-Taqlīd*]

قَالَ ابْن عبد الْبر: إنه لَا خلاف بَين أَئِمَّة الْأَمْصَار فِي فَسَاد التَّقْلِيد وَأورد فصلا طَويلا فِي محاجة من قَالَ بالتقليد وإلزامه بطلَان مَا يزعمه من جَوَازه فَقَالَ:

Ibn ʿAbd al-Barr stated that there is no difference of opinion amongst the scholars of various cities [of Islam] concerning the invalidity of *al-taqlīd*. He mentioned a long discourse in debating with the one who holds that *al-taqlīd* is permissible and using his own evidence to nullify the claim of its permissibility. So, he said:

يُقَال لمن قَالَ بالتقليد لما قلت بِهِ وخالفت السّلف فِي ذَلِك فَإِنَّهُم لم يقلدوا فَإِن قال قلدت لِأَن كتاب الله تَعَالَى لَا علم لي بتأويله، وَسنة رَسُوله صلى الله عَلَيْهِ وَآله وَسلم لم أحصها وَالَّذِي قلدته قد علم ذَلِك فقلدت من هُوَ أعلم مني قيل لَهُ أما الْعلمَاء إِذا أَجمعُوا على شَيْء من تَأْوِيل الكتاب أَو حِكَايَة سنة رَسُول الله صلى الله عَلَيْهِ وَآله وَسلم أَو اجْتمع رَأْيهمْ على شَيْء فَهُوَ الْحق لَا شكّ فِيهِ وَلَكِن قد اخْتلفُوا فِيمَا قلدت فِيهِ بَعضهم دون بعض فَمَا حجتك فِي تَقْلِيد بعض دون بعض وَكلهمْ عَالم

وَلَعَلَّ الَّذِي رغبت عَن قَوْله أعلم من الَّذِي ذهبت إِلَى مذْهبه.

It should be said to the one who holds that *al-taqlīd* is permissible: For holding this view, you have opposed the pious predecessors in that, because they did not perform *taqlīd*. If he says, "I perform *taqlīd* because I do not understand the meanings of Allah's Book and am not aware of all of the Sunnah of His Messenger ﷺ. But the one I have made *taqlīd* of knows this. As such, I have made *taqlīd* of one who is more knowledgeable than me." It should be said to him, "If the scholars have come to a consensus upon something from the explanation of the Qur'ān or narration of the Sunnah of the Messenger of Allah ﷺ, or they are unanimous in their view of something, it is undoubtedly correct. However, they differed as to you doing *taqlīd* of some of them over others. So, what is your proof for performing *taqlīd* of some of them over others, whilst all of them are scholars? It may be that the one you are averse to is more learned than the one whom you have followed."

فَإِن قَالَ قلدته لِأَنِّي علمت أَنه صَوَاب قيل لَهُ علمت ذَلِك بِدَلِيل من كتاب الله أَو سنة أَو إِجْمَاع، فَإِن قَالَ نعم فقد أبطل التَّقْلِيد وطولب بِمَا ادَّعَاهُ من الدَّلِيل، وَإِن قَالَ قلدته لِأَنَّهُ أعلم مني قيل لَهُ فقلدْ كل من هُوَ أعلم مِنْك فَإِنَّك تَجِد من ذَلِك خلقا كثيرا وَلَا تخص من قلدته، إِذْ علتك فِيهِ أَنه أعلم مِنْك.

If he says, "I adopted his view because I knew he is correct." It should be said to him, "Did you come to know this through a proof from the Book of Allah, Sunnah or consensus?" If he says yes, then he has invalidated *al-taqlīd* and sought proof for the view. If he says, "I adopted his view because he is more learned than me." It should be said to him, "Then make *taqlīd* of everyone who is more knowledgeable than you, for you will find multitudes of people in this respect and would not be able to restrict yourself to the one you chose to blindly follow, for your reason is that he is more knowledgeable than you."

فَإِن قَالَ قلدته لِأَنَّهُ أعلم النَّاس قيل لَهُ فَهُوَ إِذا أعلم من الصَّحَابَة وَكفى بقوله مثل هَذَا قبحا... انتهى مَا أردْت نَقله من كَلَامه وَهُوَ طَوِيل وَقد حكى فِي أَدِلَّة الْإِجْمَاع على فَسَاد التَّقْلِيد فَدخل فِيهِ الْأَئِمَّة الْأَرْبَعَة دُخُولا أوليا.

If he says, "I adopted his view because he is the most learned of mankind." It should be said to him, "In that case he is more learned than the companions, and this type of statement is repulsive enough."[31] This is the end of what I wanted to cite from his words on this matter, which are lengthy.[32] He narrated the evidence of *ijmāʿ* (consensus) upon the invalidity of *al-taqlīd* and the four *imāms* were the first he mentioned regarding it.

وَحكى ابْن الْقيم عَن أبي حنيفَة وَأبي يُوسُف أَنَّهُمَا قَالَا: لَا يحل لأحد أَن يَقُول بقولنا حَتَّى يعلم من أَيْن قُلْنَاهُ انتهى. وَهَذَا هُوَ تَصْرِيح يمْنَع التَّقْلِيد لِأَن من علم بِالدَّلِيلِ فَهُوَ مُجْتَهد مطَالب بِالْحجَّةِ لَا مقلد والمقلد فَإِنَّهُ الَّذِي يقبل القَوْل وَلَا يُطَالب بِحجَّة.

Ibn al-Qayyim reported from Abu Ḥanīfah and Abu Yūsuf that both of them stated, "It is not permissible for anyone to hold our

31 In his book, *Jāmiʿ Bayān al-ʿIlm* (2/994-995).

32 That is, the words of Ibn ʿAbd al-Barr.

view until he knows from where we have derived it."[33] This is a clear prohibition of *al-taqlīd*, because the one who knows the evidence is a *mujtahid* who is called upon for proof and it is not the *muqallid*. A *muqallid* is one who accepts a view and does not seek the proof.

وَحَكَى ابْنُ عبدِ البَرِّ أَيْضًا عَن معنِ بن عِيسَى بِإِسْنَادٍ مُتَّصِلٍ بِهِ قَالَ سَمِعت مَالِكًا يَقُولُ إِنَّمَا أَنا بشرٌ أَخطِئُ وَأُصِيبُ فَانظروا فِي رَأْيِي فَكل مَا وَافق الْكتاب وَالسّنة فَخُذُوهُ وكل مَا لم يُوَافق الْكتاب وَالسّنة فاتركوه.

انتهى .

Ibn 'Abd al-Barr reported from Ma'n ibn 'Īsā—with a connected chain of narration to him—that he said, "I heard Mālik say. 'I am only a human being. Sometimes I err and sometimes I am correct. Therefore, look into my opinions; all that concords with the Book and the Sunnah, accept it; and all that does not concord with the Book and the Sunnah, leave it."[34]

وَلَا يخفى عَلَيْك أَنْ هَذَا تَصْرِيحٌ مِنْهُ بِالْمَنْعِ من تَقْلِيده لِأَنّ الْعَمَل بِمَا وَافق الْكتاب وَالسّنة من كَلَامه هُوَ عمل بِالْكتاب وَالسّنة وَلَيْسَ بمنسوب إِلَيْهِ، وَقد أَمر أَتْبَاعه بترك مَا كَانَ من رَأْيه غير مُوَافق للْكتاب وَالسّنة.

It should not be hidden from you that this is a declaration from him prohibiting anyone from adopting *taqlīd* of his view, because acting upon what concords with the Book and the Sunnah from his speech is acting upon the Book and the Sunnah; and it is not attributed to him. Thus, he ordered his followers to ignore any of his personal

---

33 *I'lām al-Muwaqqi'īn* (2/211).
34 *Jāmi' Bayān al-'Ilm* (1/775, no. 1435) with a *ḥasan* chain.

opinions which do not agree with the Book and the Sunnah.

وَقَالَ سَنَد بن عنان الْمَالِكِي فِي شَرحه على مدونة سَحْنُون الْمَعْرُوفَة بِالْأُمِّ مَا لَفظه: أما مُجَرّد الِاقْتِصَار على مَحْض التَّقْلِيد فَلَا يرضى بِهِ رجل رشيد. وَقَالَ أَيْضا: نفس الْمُقَلّد لَيْسَت على بَصِيرَة وَلَا يَتَّصِف من الْعلم بِحَقِيقَة، إِذْ لَيْسَ التَّقْلِيد بطرِيق إِلَى الْعلم بوفاق أهل الْآفَاق، وَإِن نوزعنا فِي ذَلِك أبدينا برهانه فَنَقُول قَالَ تَعَالَى: ﴿فَاحْكُم بَيْنَ النَّاسِ بِالْحَقِّ﴾ وَقَالَ: ﴿بِمَا أَرَاكَ اللَّهُ﴾ وَقَالَ: ﴿وَلَا تَقْفُ مَا لَيْسَ لَكَ بِهِ عِلْمٌ﴾ وَقَالَ: ﴿وَأَن تَقُولُوا عَلَى اللهِ مَا لَا تَعْلَمُونَ﴾. وَمَعْلُوم أَن الْعلم هُوَ معرفَة الْمَعْلُوم على مَا هُوَ بِهِ، فَنَقُول للمقلد إِذا اخْتلفت الْأَقْوَال وتشعبت من أَيْن تعلم صِحَة قَول من قلدته دون غَيره أَو صِحَة قولة على قولة أُخْرَى، وَلَا يبدي كلَاما فِي ذَلِك إِلَّا انعكس عَلَيْهِ فِي نقيضه، سِيمَا إِذا عرض لَهُ ذَلِك فِي قولة لإِمَام مذْهبه الَّذِي قَلّدهُ وقولة تُخَالِفهَا لبَعض أَئِمَّة الصَّحَابَة إِلَى أَن قَالَ أما التَّقْلِيد فَهُوَ قبُول قَول الْغَيْر من غير حجَّة فَمن أَيْن يحصل بِهِ علم وَلَيْسَ لَهُ مُسْتَند إِلَى قطع، وَهُوَ أَيْضا فِي نَفسه بِدعَة محدثة لأَنا نعلم بِالْقطعِ أَن الصَّحَابَة رضوَان الله عَلَيْهِم لم يكن فِي زمانهم وعصرهم مَذْهَب لرجل معِين يدْرس ويقلد.

Sanad ibn 'Anān al-Mālikī stated in his commentary on the *Mudawwanah* of Sahnūn, referred to famously as *al-Umm*, "As for limiting oneself to absolute *taqlīd*, no sensible person would be pleased with it." He also said, 'A *muqallid* is not upon sure knowledge and he cannot be described as having knowledge in reality, since *al-taqlīd* is not the means of attaining knowledge according to the agreement of the scholars. If they disagree with us in this, we will show them the proof and state, Allah the Most High states: **{So judge between the people in truth.}**[35] And: **{By that which Allah has shown you.}**[36] And: **{And follow not that of which you have no knowledge.}**[37] And: **{And saying things about Allah of which you have no knowledge.}**[38] It is known that knowledge denotes knowing a fact according to its reality. Therefore, we say to the *muqallid*: If opinions differ and diverge, how will you come to know the correctness of the opinion of the one you blindly follow excluding others, or the correctness of his view over those of others? To this, he will not bring forth an argument except that it counteracts what he intended to prove, especially if he is presented with a statement of the *imām* of the *madhhab* he blindly follows with a view contrary to it which is held by some *imāms* of the companions. As regards to *al-taqlīd*, it is to accept the view of others without proof. So where will he attain knowledge whilst he is not depending upon the explicit [texts]? It is also an innovation in of itself because we know for sure that during the time and era of the companions there was no school of *fiqh* of a specific person whose view was taught and adopted.

وَإِنَّمَا كَانُوا يرجعُونَ فِي النَّوَازِل إِلَى الْكتاب وَالسّنة أَو إِلَى مَا يتمخض

---

35 Ṣād: 26. The *āyah* further reads: **{"... And do not follow [your own] desire, as it will lead you astray from the way of Allah." Indeed, those who go astray from the way of Allah will have a severe punishment for having forgotten the Day of Account.}**

36 Al-Nisā: 105. Allah states: **{Indeed, We have revealed to you, [O Muhammad], the Book in truth so you may judge between the people by that which Allah has shown you.}**

37 Al-Isrā: 36

38 Al-Aʿrāf: 33

بَينهم من النّظر عِنْد فقد الدَّلِيل وَكَذَلِكَ تابعوهم أَيْضا يرجعُونَ إِلَى الْكتاب وَالسّنة فَإِن لم يَجدوا نظرُوا إِلَى مَا أجمع عَلَيْهِ الصَّحَابَة فَإِن لم يَجدوا اجتهدوا وَاخْتَارَ بَعضهم قَول صَحَابِيّ فَرَآهُ الْأَقْوَى فِي دين الله تَعَالَى. ثمَّ كَانَ الْقرن الثَّالِث وَفِيه كَانَ أَبُو حنيفَة وَمَالك وَالشَّافِعِيّ وَابْن حَنْبَل فَإِن مَالِكًا توفّي سنة تسع وَسبعين وَمِائَة وَتُوفِّي أَبُو حنيفَة سنة خمسين وَمِائَة، وَفِي هَذِه السّنة ولد الإِمَام الشَّافِعِي وَولد ابْن حَنْبَل سنة أَربع وَسِتِّينَ وَمِائَة وَكَانُوا على منهاج من مضى لم يكن فِي عصرهم مَذْهَب رجل معِين يتدارسونه وعَلى قريب مِنْهُم كَانَ أتباعهم فكم من قَوْلة لمَالِك ونظرائه خَالفه فِيهَا أَصْحَابه، وَلَو نقلنا ذَلِك لخرجنا عَن مَقْصُود هذا الْكتاب، مَا ذَاك إِلَّا لجمعهم آلَات الِاجْتِهَاد وقدرتهم على ضروب الاستنباطات، وَلَقَد صدق الله نبيه فِي قَوْله: ((خير النَّاس قَرْني ثمَّ الَّذين يَلُونَهُمْ ثمَّ الَّذين يَلُونَهُمْ)) ذكر بعد قرنه قرنين والْحَدِيث فِي صَحِيح البُخَارِيّ.

Rather, they used to refer new instances to the Book and the Sunnah or to what they derived amongst themselves through study, in the absence of proof. The same is the case for those who succeeded them, they would refer to the Book and Sunnah, but if they could not find what they required, they would look into what the companions unanimously agreed upon, and if they could not find this, they would resort to *ijtihād* and some would adopt the view of the companion they deemed to be more firmly grounded in Allah's religion. Then the third generation included Abu Ḥanīfah, Mālik, al-Shāfiʿī and Ibn Ḥanbal. Mālik died in the year 179 and Abu Ḥanīfah died in the year 150. It was in this year that al-Imām al-Shāfiʿī was born, and Ibn Ḥanbal was born in the year 164. They were upon the methodology of those who preceded them. In their era, there was no *madhhab* of a specific person which was adopted and their followers were close to them. How many were the views and opinions of Mālik that his companions disagreed with. If we were to transmit them, we would exit from the aim of this book. This was due to nothing but their proficiency in the tools of *ijtihād* and their ability to derive rulings. Indeed, Allah affirmed the truth of his Prophet in his saying: "The best of mankind is my generation; then those who will come after them, followed by those who will come after them." He mentioned two generations after his generation, and the *ḥadīth* is found in *Ṣaḥīḥ al-Bukhārī*.[39]

فالعجب لأهل التَّقْلِيد كَيفَ يَقُولُونَ هَذَا هُوَ الْأَمر الْقَدِيم وَعَلِيهِ أدركنا الشُّيُوخ، وَهُوَ إِنَّمَا حدث بعد مِائَتي سنة من الْهِجْرَة، وَبعد فنَاء الْقُرُون الَّذين أثنى عَلَيْهِم الرَّسُول ... انتهي.

It is amazing that the people of *al-taqlīd* would say that this is an ancient issue and upon it they align with the scholars. Rather, it was innovated after the year two hundred *hijri*, and after the passing away of the generations that the Messenger of Allah ﷺ praised." [End quote.]

39 In his *Ṣaḥīḥ* (2602). I say: It was recorded by Muslim in his *Ṣaḥīḥ* (2533), al-Tirmidhī (3859); all of them are from the ḥadīth of ʿAbdullāh ibn Masʿūd.

[تاريخ التقليد]
[The History of *al-Taqlīd*]

وَقد عرفت بِهَذَا أَن التَّقْلِيد لم يحدث إِلَّا بعد انْقِرَاض خير الْقُرُون ثمَّ الَّذين يَلُونَهُمْ ثمَّ الَّذين يَلُونَهُمْ، وَأَن حُدُوث التمذهب بمذاهب الْأَئِمَّة الْأَرْبَعَة إِنَّمَا كَانَ بعد انْقِرَاض الْأَئِمَّة الْأَرْبَعَة وَإِنَّهُم كَانُوا على نمط من تقدمهم من السّلف فِي هجر التَّقْلِيد وَعدم الِاعْتِدَاد بِهِ وَأَن هَذِه الْمذَاهب إِنَّمَا أحدثها عوام المقلدة لأَنْفُسِهِمْ من دون أَن يَأْذَن بهَا إِمَام من الْأَئِمَّة الْمُجْتَهدين، وَقد تَوَاتَرَتْ الرِّوَايَة عَن الإِمَام مَالك أَنه قَالَ لَهُ الرشيد أَنه يُرِيد أَن يحمل النَّاس على مذْهبه، فَنَهَاهُ عَن ذَلِك وَهَذَا مَوْجُود فِي كل كتاب فِيهِ تَرْجَمَة الإِمَام مَالك وَلَا يَخْلُو من ذَلِك إِلَّا النَّادِر.

Upon this, you now know that *al-taqlīd* was not invented except after the demise of the best generation, those after them and those after them; and that the emergence of adopting the four *madhhabs* was only after the passing away of the four *imāms*. They were upon the way of those who preceded them amongst the pious predecessors in abandonment of *al-taqlīd* and not giving it any consideration. Furthermore, these *madhhabs* were invented by the *muqallid* masses for themselves without any authority from any of the *mujtahid imāms*. There is a mass-transmitted report from al-Imām Mālik that Rashīd informed him of his desire to encourage the people to follow his *madhhab*, but he forbade him from doing so. This is found in every book that contains the biography of al-Imām Mālik, and only a few of them are devoid of it.

وَإِذا تقرر أَن الْمُحدث لهَذِهِ الْمذَاهب والمبتدع لهَذِهِ التقليدات هم جهلَة المقلدة فَقَط، فقد عرفت مِمَّا تقرر فِي الْأُصُول أَنه لَا اعْتِدَاد بهم فِي الْإِجْمَاع وَأَن الْمُعْتَبر فِي الْإِجْمَاع إِنَّمَا هم المجتهدون، وَحِينَئِذٍ لم يقل بِهَذِهِ التقليدات عَالم من الْعلمَاء الْمُجْتَهدين أما قبل حدوثها فَظَاهر، وَأما بعد حدوثها فَمَا سمعنَا عَن مُجْتَهد من الْمُجْتَهدين أَنه يسوغ صَنِيع هَؤُلَاءِ المقلدة الَّذين فرقوا دين الله وخالفوا بَين الْمُسلمين بل أكَابِر الْعلمَاء بَين مُنكر لَهَا وَسَاكِت عَنْهَا سكُوت تقية لمخافة ضَرَر أَو لمخافة فَوَات نفع كَمَا يكون مثل ذَلِك كثيرا لَا سِيمَا من عُلَمَاء السوء.

So, as it is established that the ones who innovated these *madhhabs* and [forms of] *al-taqlīd* were the ignorant *muqallids*; the reader should be aware that it is entrenched within the principles of jurisprudence that no consideration is given to the laity in the forming of a consensus, rather, those who are to be given consideration in the forming of consensus are the *mujtahids*. As such, none of the *mujtahid* scholars held the view of the permissibility of adopting such [forms of] *taqlīd*. As for before their emergence, this is clear. As for after their emergence, we have not heard of any *mujtahid* permitting the acts of these *muqallids* who have divided the religion of Allah and caused division amongst the Muslims. In fact, major scholars have explained its evils, while those who did not speak kept silent out of caution, due to fear of harm or of losing some benefits—as done by many, especially the evil scholars.

وكل عَاقل يعلم أَنه لَو صرح عَالم من عُلَمَاء الْإِسْلَام الْمُجْتَهدين فِي مَدِينَة من مَدَائِن الْإِسْلَام فِي أَي مَحل كَانَ بِأَن التَّقْلِيد بِدعَة مُحدثة لَا يجوز الِاسْتِمْرَار عَلَيْهِ وَلَا الِاعْتِدَاد بِهِ لقام عَلَيْهِ أَكثر أَهلهَا إِن لم يقم عَلَيْهِ كلهم وأنزلوا بِهِ من الإهانة والإضرار بِمَالِه وبدنه وَعرضه مَا لَا يَلِيق بِمن هُوَ دونه، هذا إِذا سلم من الْقَتْل على يَد أول جَاهِل من هَؤُلَاءِ المقلدة وَمن يعضدهم من جَهله الْمُلُوك والأجناد فَإِن طبائع الْجَاهِلين بِعلم الشَّرِيعَة مُتَقَارِبَة وهم لكَلَام من يجانسهم فِي الْجَهْل أقبل من كَلَام من يخالفهم فِي ذَلِك من أهل الْعلم.

Every rational person knows that if an individual from the *mujtahid* scholars of Islam publicly declared in an Islamic city in any place that *al-taqlīd* is an innovation and that it is not permissible to persist in it nor give consideration to it, many—if not all—of the people of *al-taqlīd* would stand up against him and cause him humiliation and harm in his property, body and honour that does not befit the one lower than him [in status]. And this would only be the case if he was safe from murder at the hands of the ignoramuses amongst these *muqallids*, and those who aid them from the ignorant kings and soldiers. This is because the nature of those who are ignorant of the knowledge of the religion is similar; they accept the speech of anyone who is concordant with them in ignorance over the speech of someone who differs with them from amongst the people of knowledge.

وَلِهَذَا طبقت هَذِه الْبِدْعَة جَمِيع الْبِلَاد الإسلامية، وَصَارَت شَامِلَة لكل فَرد من أَفْرَاد الْمُسلمين فالجاهل يعْتَقد أَن الدّين مَا زَالَ هَكَذَا وَلنْ يزَال إِلَى

الْمحَشْر، وَلَا يعرف مَعْرُوفا وَلَا يُنكر مُنْكرا وَهَكَذَا من كَانَ من المشتغلين بِعلم التَّقْلِيد فَإِنَّهُ كالجاهل بل أقبح مِنْهُ لِأَنَّهُ يضم إِلَى جَهله وإصراره على بِدعَة وتحسينها فِي عُيُون أهل الْجَهْل الازدراء بالعلماء الْمُحَقِّقين والعارفين بِكِتَاب الله وسنة رَسُوله ويصول عَلَيْهِم ويجول وينسبهم إِلَى الابتداع وَمُخَالفَة الْأَئِمَّة والتنقص بشأنهم فيسمع ذَلِك مِنْهُم الْمُلُوك وَمن يتَصَرَّف بالنيابة عَنْهُم من أعوانهم فيصدقونه ويذعنون لقَوْله إِذْ هُوَ مجانس لَهُم فِي كَونه جَاهِلا وَإِن كَانَ يعرف مسَائِل قد قلد فِيهَا غَيره لَا يدْرِي أهي حق أم بَاطِل لَا سِيمَا إِذا كَانَ قَاضِيا أَو مفتيا فَإِن الْعَاميّ لَا ينظر إِلَى أهل الْعلم بِعَين مُمَيزَة بَين من هُوَ عَالم على الْحَقِيقَة وَمن هُوَ جَاهِل وَبَين من هُوَ مقصر وَمن هُوَ كَامِل لِأَنَّهُ لَا يعرف الْفضل لأهل الفضل إِلَّا أَهله.

Consequently, this innovation became widespread in all of the Islamic lands and every individual amongst the Muslims became involved in it. The ignorant one believes that the religion has always been like this and that it will not cease being like this until the Day of Resurrection. He does not recognise good nor forbid evil. And this is the case for one who is amongst those engrossed with the knowledge of *al-taqlīd*, for he is like an ignorant person. In fact, he is viler than an ignorant person because in addition to his ignorance, he persists in the innovation of *al-taqlīd*, and makes it appear alluring to the eyes of ignorant people; and he bears contempt for the researching scholars who are acquainted with the Book of Allah and the Sunnah of His Messenger ﷺ, attacks them, obsesses with them and accuses them of innovation and opposition to the *imāms*, as well as lowering their status. Then the kings and those who deputise for them amongst their aides would hear this and believe him, acquiescing to his statement since he is similar to them in ignorance. Even if he knows [the ruling] of some issues in which he makes *taqlīd* of others, he in actuality does not know whether they are correct or wrong, which is especially pertinent if he is a judge or a *muftī*. This is because the layman does not look at the people of knowledge with the eye that distinguishes between the one who is a scholar in reality and the one who is ignorant; and between the one who is incapable and the one who is capable, as none know the virtue of the people of virtue except its people.

وَأما الْجَاهِل فَإِنَّما يسْتَدلّ على الْعلم بالمناصب والقرب من الْمُلُوك واجتماع المتدرسين من المقلدين وتحرير الْفَتَاوَى للمتخاصمين وَهَذِه الْأُمُور إِنَّمَا يقوم بهَا رُؤُوس هَؤُلَاءِ المقلدة فِي الْغَالِب كَمَا يعلم ذَلِك كل عَالم بأحوال النَّاس فِي قديم الزَّمن وَحَدِيثه، وَهَذَا يعرفهُ الْإِنْسَان بِالْمُشَاهَدَةِ لأهل عصره وبمطالعة كتب التَّارِيخ الحاكية لما كَانَ عَلَيْهِ من قبله.

As for an ignorant person, he bases the knowledge of an individual upon his rank, closeness to the kings, the congregating of students from the *muqallids* [around him] and his issuing of verdicts to contending parties. These affairs are normally undertaken by the heads of these *muqallids* in most cases, as is known by every scholar who knows the conditions of the people of the past and present. A person can recognise this by looking at his contemporaries and reading books of history which detail the affairs of those before him.

وَأما الْعلمَاء الْمُحَقِّقُونَ المجتهدون فالغالب على أَكْثَرهم الخمول لِأَنَّهُ لما كثر التَّفَاوُت بَينهم وَبَين أهل الْجَهْل كَانُوا متباعدين لَا يرغب هَذَا فِي

هَذَا وَلَا هَذَا فِي هَذَا.

As for the researching and *mujtahid* scholars, most of them are idle, because when differences became excessive between them and the ignorant people, they became distant; this one does not want that one nor does that one desire this one.

ومنزلة الْفَقِيه من السَّفِيه   كمنزلة السَّفِيه من الْفَقِيه

فَهَذَا زاهد فِي حق هَذَا   وَهَذَا أزهد مِنْهُ فِيهِ

The status of a scholar to a fool is like the status of a fool to a scholar.

This one lacks interest in him and that one is more indifferent to him than him.

وَمِمَّا يَدْعُو الْعلمَاء إِلَى مهاجرة أكَابِر الْعلمَاء ومقاطعتهم أَنَّهُم يجدونهم غير راغبين فِي علم التَّقْلِيد الَّذِي هُوَ رَأس مَال فقهائهم وقضاتهم والمفتين مِنْهُم بل يجدونهم مشتغلين بعلوم الِاجْتِهَاد وَهِي عِنْد هَؤُلَاءِ المقلدة لَيست من الْعُلُوم النافعة بل الْعُلُوم النافعة عِنْدهم هِيَ الَّتِي يتعجلون نَفعهَا بِقَبض جرابات التدريس وَأُجْرَة الْفَتَاوَى ومقررات الْقَضَاء وَمَعَ هَذَا فَمن كَانَ من هَؤُلَاءِ المقلدة مُتَمَكنًا من تدريسهم فِي علم التَّقْلِيد إِذا درسهم فِي مَسْجِد من الْمَسَاجِد أَو فِي مدرسة من الْمدَارِس اجْتمع عَلَيْهِ مِنْهُم جمع جم يُقَارب الْمِائَة أَو يجاوزها من قوم قد ترشحوا لِلْقَضَاءِ والفتيا وطمعوا فِي نيل الرياسة الدُّنْيَوِيَّة أَو أَرَادوا حفظ مَا قد ناله سلفهم

من الرياسة وَبَقَاء مناصبهم والمحافظة على التَّمَسُّك بهَا كَمَا كَانَ عَلَيْهِ أسلافهم فهم لهَذَا الْمَقْصد يلبسُونَ الثِّيَاب الرفيعة ويديرون على رُؤُوسهمْ عمائم كالروابي.

One of the things that made the masses abandon the major scholars and sever relationships with them is that they found them not interested in the science of *al-taqlīd*, which is the primary capital of their jurists, judges and *muftis* who are amongst them. Rather, they found them preoccupying themselves with the sciences of *ijtihād*, and according to these *muqallids*, this is not counted within beneficial knowledge. According to them, beneficial knowledge is that which reaps benefits like collecting salaries for teaching, wages for issuing verdicts and giving judicial decisions. In light of this, if one amongst these *muqallids* is well established in teaching them the science of *taqlīd*, when he teaches them in any of the *masājid* or schools, multitudes of them—close to a hundred or more—will gather around him, amongst whom are people who seek to stand for judgeship, issuing verdicts and who crave for the attainment of worldly leadership, or they intend to preserve what their predecessors had attained of leadership and for their prestige to remain intact and to persevere in clinging to it as their predecessors did. Due to this aim, they don fine clothes and tie turbans upon their heads like mounds.

فَإِذا نظر الْعَاميّ أَو السُّلْطَان أَو بعض أعوانه إِلَى تِلْكَ الْحلقَة البهية الْمُشْتَملَة على الْعدَد الْكثير والملبوس الشهير والدفاتر الضخمة لم يبْق عِنْده شكّ أَن شيخ تِلْكَ الْحلقَة ومدرسها أعلم النَّاس فَيقبل قَوْله فِي كل أَمر يتَعَلَّق بِالدّينِ ويؤهله لكل مشكلة ويرجو مِنْهُ الْقيام بالشريعة مَا لَا يرجوه

من الْعَالم على الْحَقِيقَة المبرز فِي علم الْكتاب وَالسّنة وَسَائِر الْعُلُوم الَّتِي يتَوَقَّف فهم المعلمين عَلَيْهَا وَلَا سِيمَا وغَالب المبرزين من الْعلمَاء تَحْت ذيل الخمول إِذا درسوا فِي علم من عُلُوم الِاجْتِهَاد فَلَا يجْتَمع عَلَيْهِم فِي الْغَالِب إِلَّا الرجل وَالرجلَانِ وَالثَّلَاثَة لِأَن الْبَالِغين من الطّلبَة إِلَى هَذِه الرُّتْبَة المستعدين لعلم الِاجْتِهَاد هم أقل قَلِيل لِأَنَّهُ لَا يرغب فِي علم الِاجْتِهَاد إِلَّا من أخْلص النِّيَّة وَطلب الْعلم لله عز وَجل وَرغب عَن المناصب الدُّنْيَوِيَّة وربط نَفسه برباط الزّهْد وألجم نَفسه بلجام القنوع.

If the layman, the ruler or one of his aides would witness these dazzling gatherings—which comprise of droves of people, ostentatious clothing and enormous books—no doubt would be left in him that the scholar or teacher of the gathering is the most learned of people. Thus, he will accept his view in every religious matter and he will direct every problem to him, placing hope in him to implement the Legislation contrary to the trust he places in a true scholar who is outstanding in the knowledge of the Qur'ān, Sunnah and other sciences which depend upon the understanding of teachers (i.e. the learner's understanding is based upon the knowledge of the teacher). This is more so the case due to the especially outstanding scholars falling under the tail of inactivity. If they teach people regarding the sciences of *ijtihād*, in most cases the people will not gather around them except one, two or three men. This is because the students who have reached this level and are ready for the knowledge of *ijtihād* are very few, as none would be interested in the science of *ijtihād* except one whose intention is sincere and who is seeking knowledge for the sake of Allah, becoming averse to worldly prestige whilst fastening himself with the rope of *zuhd* and harnessing himself with the bridle of contentment.

فَلْيَنْظُرِ الْعَاقِلُ أَيْنَ يكون مَحلُّ هَذَا الْعَالِمِ على التَّحْقِيقِ عِنْد أهل الدُّنْيَا إذا شاهدوه فِي زَاوِيَة من زَوَايَا الْمَسْجِدِ وَقد قعد بَين يَدَيْهِ رجل أَو رجلان من مَحل ذَلِك الْمُقَلِّد الَّذِي اجْتمع عَلَيْهِ المقلدون فَإِنَّهُم رُبَمَا يَعْتَقِدُونَ أنه كواحد من تلامذة هذا الْمُقَلِّد أَو يقصر عَنْهُ لما يشاهدونه من الْأَوْصَاف الَّتِي قدمنَا ذكرهَا.

So the rational person should imagine where the position of this scholar would be according to the judgement of the people of the world if they saw him in one of the corners of the *masjid* with a man or two men sitting in front of him compared to the position of that *muqallid* whom the *muqallids* gather around. They may assume that he is one of the students of the *muqallid* or think little of him due to their witnessing of the [dazzling gatherings] we described previously.

وَمَعَ هَذَا فَإِنَّهُم لَا يقفون على فَتْوَى من الْفَتَاوَى أَو سجل من الأسجال إِلَّا وَهُوَ بِخَطِّ أهل التَّقْلِيد ومنسوب إِلَيْهِم فيزدادون لَهُم بذلك تَعْظِيمًا ويقدمونهم على عُلَمَاء الِاجْتِهَاد فِي كل إِصْدار وإيراد، فَإذا تكلم عَالِم من عُلَمَاء الِاجْتِهَاد وَالْحَال هَذِه بِشَيْءٍ يُخَالف مَا يَعْتَقِدهُ المقلدة قَامُوا عَلَيْهِ قومه جَاهِلِيَّة وَوَافَقَهُمْ على ذَلِك أهل الدُّنْيَا وأرباب السُّلْطَان فَإذا قدرُوا على الْإِضْرَار بِهِ فِي بدنه وَمَاله فعلوا ذَلِك وهم بفعلهم مشكورون عِنْد أَبْنَاء جنسهم من الْعَامَّة والمقلدة لأنهم قَامُوا بنصرة الدِّين بزعمهم وذبوا عَن الْأَئِمَّة المتبوعين وَعَن مذاهبهم الَّتِي قد اعتقدها أتباعهم فَيَكُون

لَهُم بِهَذِهِ الْأَفْعَال الَّتِي هِيَ عين الْجَهْل والضلال من الجاه والرفعة عِنْد أَبنَاء جنسهم مَا لم يكن فِي حِسَاب.

In addition to this, no *fatwā* or book would they come across except that it is in the handwriting of the people of *taqlīd* and attributed to them, so this would increase them in honour and they will give them preference over the scholars of *ijtihād* in every issuance and dividend. If a scholar of *ijtihād* in this situation were to speak about something contrary to what the *muqallids* believe, the ignorant people would stand up against him and the worldly people and authorities would agree with them in that. If they have the ability to cause harm to the scholar in his body or wealth, they will do so, and their actions would be appreciated by their fellows from the laity and the *muqallids*, as they rendered support to the religion—according to them—and defended the *imāms* they follow, as well as the *madhhabs* which their followers adhere to. Through these actions—which in their essence constitute pure ignorance and misguidance—they would attain high standing and dignity amongst their fellows, and this would be to an absurd level.

وَأما ذَلِك الْعَالم الْمُحِق الْمُتَكَلّم بِالصَّوَابِ فبالحري أَن لَا ينجو من شرهم وَيسلم من ضرهم، وَأما عرضه فَيصير عرضة للشتم والتبديع والتجهيل والتضليل فَمن ذَا تراه ينصب نَفسه للإنكار على هَذِه الْبِدْعَة وَيقوم فِي النَّاس بتبطيل هَذِه الشنعة مَعَ كَون الدُّنْيَا مُؤثرَة وَحب الشّرف وَالْمَال يمِيل بالقلوب على كل حَال.

As for the researching scholar who speaks what is right, he would likely not be saved from their evil nor be free from their harm. His honour will become susceptible to abuse, being declared to be an innovator, ignorant and misguided. So, who will you see exerting himself in repudiating these innovations and standing in the midst of the people to nullify these ills whilst the worldly things influence [the soul,] and the need for prestige and wealth is attached to the hearts in every situation?

فَانْظُر أَيهَا الْمنصف بِعَين الْإِنْصَاف هَل يعد سكُوت عُلَمَاء الِاجْتِهَاد عن إِنْكَار بدعَة التَّقْلِيد مَعَ هَذِه الْأُمُور مُوَافقَة لأَهْلهَا على جوازها؟ كلا وَالله فَإِنَّهُ سكُوت تقية لَا سكُوت مُوَافقَة مرضية وَلَكنهُمْ مَعَ سكوتهم عَن التظاهر بذلك لَا يتركون بَيَان مَا أَخذ الله عَلَيْهِم بَيَانه، فتَارَة يصرحون بذلك فِي مؤلفاتهم وَتارَة يلوحون بِهِ، وَكثير مِنْهُم يكتم مَا يُصَرح بِهِ من تَحْرِيم التَّقْلِيد إِلَى بعد مَوته كَمَا روى الأدفوي عَن شَيْخه الإِمَام ابْن دَقِيق الْعِيد أَنه طلب مِنْهُ ورقا وكتبها فِي مرض مَوته، وَجعلهَا تَحت فرَاشه فَلَمَّا مَاتَ أخرجوها فَإِذا هِيَ فِي تَحْرِيم التَّقْلِيد مُطلقًا. وَمِنْهُم من يُوضح ذَلِك لمن يَثِق بِهِ من أهل الْعلم وَلَا يزالون متوارثين لذَلِك بَينهم طبقَة بعد طبقَة يُوضحهُ السّلف للخلف ويبينه الْكَامِل للمقصر.

So, look O unprejudiced reader with a fair eye: Does the silence of the scholars of *ijtihād* towards repudiating the innovation of *al-taqlīd* in spite of all these issues constitute agreement with the people of *al-taqlīd* on its permissibility? Nay, by Allah it is a silence of fear and not silence of agreement and approval. But despite this silence to avoid problems, they do not abandon explaining what Allah has charged them to explain.[40] At times they explicitly mention

40 Allah states: **{And [mention, O Muhammad], when Allah took a cov-**

this in their books and at times they allude to it. Many of them concealed their recognition of the prohibition of *al-taqlīd* until after their death, just as it was related from al-Adfawī that his *shaykh*, al-Imām Ibn Daqīq al-ʿĪd requested a sheet of paper from him and he wrote something on it during the illness that led to his death and placed it under his bed. When he died, they brought it out and it contained the prohibition of *al-taqlīd* unrestrictedly. Amongst them are those who expressed this to the ones they trusted among the people of knowledge and they would not cease transmitting this amongst themselves generation after generation. The predecessor would express it to the successor and the learned would explain it to the lesser trained.

وَإِن انحجب ذَلِك عَن أهل التَّقْلِيد فَهُوَ غير منحجب عَن غَيرهم وَقد رَأينَا فِي زَمَاننَا مَشَايِخنَا المشتغلين بعلوم الِاجْتِهَاد فَلم نجد عند وَاحِدًا مِنْهُم أَن التَّقْلِيد صَوَاب، وَمِنْهُم من صرح بإنكار التَّقْلِيد من أَصله وَإِنكَار كثير من الْمسَائِل الَّتِي يعتقدها المقلدون فَوَقع بَينه وَبَين أهل عصره قلاقل وزلازل ونالهم من الامتحان مَا فِيهِ توفير أُجُورهم وَهَكَذَا حَال أهل سَائِر الديار فِي جَمِيع الأعصار.

If this is hidden from the people of *taqlīd*, it is not hidden from others. In our era, we have seen our scholars who are preoccupied with the sciences of *ijtihād* and did not find anyone amongst them who held that *taqlīd* is correct. Amongst them was one who publicly refuted *taqlīd* from its foundation and refuted most of the issues

---

enant from those who were given the Scripture, [saying], "You must make it clear to the people and not conceal it." But they threw it away behind their backs and exchanged it for a small price. And wretched is that which they purchased.} [Āli ʿImrān: 187]

the *muqallids* believe in. As a result of this, quarrels and disputes took place between him and his contemporaries. Through these trials they (i.e. the critics of *al-taqlīd*)[41] attained an increase to their reward. And this was the case for the people in all lands and times.

وَبِالْجُمْلَةِ فَهَذَا أَمر يُشَاهِدهُ كل واحد فِي زَمَنه فَإنَّا لم نسْمع بِأَن أهل مَدِينَة من الْمَدَائِن الإسلامية أَجمعُوا أَمرهم على ترك التَّقْلِيد واتباع الْكتاب وَالسّنة لَا فِي هَذَا الْعَصْر وَلَا فِيمَا تقدمه من العصور بعد ظُهُور الْمذَاهب بل أهل الْبِلَاد الإسلامية أجمع أَكْتَع مطبقون على التَّقْلِيد.

In short, everyone will notice this issue in his era. We have not heard of a city amongst the Islamic cities which unanimously agreed upon abandoning *al-taqlīd* and following the Qur'ān and the Sunnah, neither in this generation nor in previous generations after the emergence of the *madhhabs*. Rather, the inhabitants of Islamic lands unanimously agreed upon *al-taqlīd*.

وَمن كَانَ مِنْهُم منتسبا إِلَى الْعلم فَهُوَ إِمَّا أَن يكون مبلغ علمه معرفَة مَا هُوَ مقلد فِيهِ وَهَذَا هو عِنْد التَّحْقِيق لَيْسَ من أهل الْعلم، وَإِمَّا أَن يكون قد اشْتغل بِبَعْض عُلُوم الِاجْتِهَاد وَلم يتأهل للنَّظَر فَوقف تَحت ربقة التَّقْلِيد ضَرُورَة لَا اخْتِيَارا وَإِمَّا أَن يكون عَالما مبرزا جَامعا لعلوم الِاجْتِهَاد فَهَذَا هو الَّذِي يجب عَلَيْهِ أَن يتَكَلَّم بِالْحَقِّ وَلَا يخَاف فِي الله لومة لائم إِلَّا لمسوغ شَرْعِي.

41 [T] This referring to them was interpreted by us based upon context. And Allah knows best.

Those amongst them who are attributed to knowledge may be of those whom the majority of their knowledge is based on *al-taqlīd*, and such a person is not in reality counted amongst the people of knowledge. Or he may be someone who is preoccupied with some of the sciences of *ijtihād* but he is not capable of performing [impartial] scrutiny; so he halted under the noose of *al-taqlīd* out of necessity and not out of choice. Or he may be an outstanding scholar who is versed in all of the sciences of *ijtihād*; such a person is the one that is duty bound to speak the truth and he should not be afraid of the blame of the blamers, except wherein this is justified through the religion.

وَأما من لم يكن منتسبا إِلَى الْعلم فَهُوَ إِمَّا عَامي صرف لَا يعرف التَّقْلِيد وَلَا غَيره، وَإِنَّمَا هو ينتمي إِلَى الْإِسْلَام جملَة وَيفْعل كَمَا يَفْعَله أهل بَلَده فِي صلَاته وَسَائِر عبادته ومعاملاته فَهَذَا قد أراح نَفسه من محنة التعصب الَّتِي يَقع فِيهَا المقلدون وَكفى الله أهل الْعلم شَره، فَهُوَ لَا وازِع لَهُ من نَفسه يحملهُ على التعصب عَلَيْهِم بل رُبمَا نفخ فِيهِ بعض شياطين المقلدة وسعى إِلَيْهِ بعلماء الِاجْتِهَاد فَحَمله على أَن يجهل عَلَيْهِم بِمَا يوبقه فِي حَيَاته وَبعد مماته.

As for one who is not attributed to knowledge, he is sometimes a pure layman who does not understand *al-taqlīd* or other than it. Rather, he only attaches himself to Islam in general. He does as the people of his land do in his prayer and the rest of his acts of worship and dealings; such a person has relieved himself of the trial of partisanship which the *muqallids* have fallen into and which, from his evil (i.e. if he fell into it), Allah saved the people of knowledge. There is no impetus for him which would propel him to show partisanship against them. However, some devilish individuals amongst the *muqallids* may breathe into him and discredit the scholars of *ijtihād* to him, thereby impelling him to behave foolishly towards them, actioning that which will ruin him in his life and after his death.

وَإما أَن يكون مرتفعا عَن هَذِه الطَّبَقَة قَلِيلا فَيكون غير مشتغل بِطَلَب الْعلم لكنه يسْأَل أهل الْعلم عَن أَمر عِبَادَته ومعاملته وَله بعض تَمْيِيز فَهَذَا هُوَ تبع لمن يسْأَله من أهل الْعلم إِن كَانَ يسْأَل المقلدين فَهُوَ لَا يرى الْحق إِلَّا فِي التَّقْلِيد وَإِن كَانَ يسْأَل الْمُجْتَهدين فَهُوَ يعْتَقد أَن الْحق مَا يرشدونه إِلَيْهِ فَهُوَ مَعَ من غلب عَلَيْهِ من الطائفتين.

A person may be above this level a little whereby he is not preoccupied with seeking knowledge but he will ask the people of knowledge about issues pertaining to his acts of worship and transactions. He has some intelligence; thus, he follows whomsoever he asks amongst the people of knowledge. If he asks the *muqallids*, he does not see the truth except in *al-taqlīd*, and if he asks the *mujtahid*, he believes that they are guiding him to the truth. He is with whoever prevails over him amongst the two groups.

وَإما أَن يكون مِمَّن لَهُ اشْتِغَال بِطَلَب علم المقلدين وإكباب على حفظه وفهمه وَلَا يرفع رَأسه إِلَى سواهُ وَلَا يلْتَفت إِلَى غَيره فالغالب على هَؤُلَاءِ التعصب المفرط على عُلَمَاء الِاجْتِهَاد ورميهم بِكُل حجر ومدر وإيهام الْعَامَّة بِأَنَّهُم مخالفون لإِمَام الْمَذْهَب الَّذِي قد ضَاقَتْ أذهانهم عَن تصور عَظِيم قدره، وامتلأت قُلُوبهم من هَيْبَته حَتَّى تقرر عِنْدهم أَنه فِي دَرَجَة

لم يبلغها الصَّحَابَة فضلا عَمَّن بعدهمْ، وَهَذَا وَإِن لم يصرحوا بِهِ فَهُوَ مما تكنه صُدُورهمْ، وَلَا تنطلق بِهِ ألسنتهم.

He may be amongst those who are preoccupied with seeking knowledge of the *muqallids* and diligent in memorising and understanding it. He does not lift his head up nor pay attention to other than it. What is common amongst these people is excessive partisanship against the *mujtahid* scholars, to pelt them with every stone and mud, and enticing the masses to believe that they are opposing the *imām* of the *madhhab*—whilst their intellects have been rendered spent from imagining his esteemed worth and their hearts are filled with awe of him, to the extent that it is established amongst them that he has attained a level which the Companions did not reach, let alone those after them. Even if they do not state this publicly, it is part of what their hearts affirm but their tongues cannot state.

فَمَعَ مَا قد صَار عِنْدهم من هَذَا الِاعْتِقَاد فِي ذَلِك الإِمَام إِذا بَلغهُمْ أَن أحد عُلَمَاء الِاجْتِهَاد الْمَوْجُودين يُخَالِفهُ فِي مَسْأَلَة من الْمسَائِل كَانَ هَذَا الْمُخَالف قد ارْتكب أمرا شنيعا وَخَالف عِنْدهم شَيْئا قَطْعِيا وَأَخْطَأ خطئا لَا يكفره شَيْء وَإِن اسْتدلَّ على مَا ذهب إِلَيْهِ بِالْآيَاتِ القرآنية وَالْأَحَادِيث المتواترة لم يقبل مِنْهُ ذَلِك وَلَا يرفع لما جَاءَ بِهِ رَأْسا كَائِنا من كَانَ وَلَا يزالون منتقصين لَهُ بِهَذِهِ الْمُخَالفَة انتقاصا شَدِيدا على وَجه لَا يستحلونه من الفسقة وَلَا من أهل الْبدع الْمَشْهُورَة كالخوارج وَالرَّوَافِض ويبغضونه بغضا شَدِيدا فَوق مَا يبغضون أهل الذِّمَّة من الْيَهُود وَالنَّصَارَى، وَمن أنكر هَذَا فَهُوَ غير مُحَقّق لأحوال هَؤُلَاءِ.

Since this has become their belief regarding this *imām*, if they are informed that one of the living *mujtahid* scholars disagrees with him on an issue, the one who disagrees with the *imām* has committed a sacrilegious act, contradicted something irrevocable and committed an error that nothing will expiate, even if he cites proof from the Qur'ān and *mutawātir aḥādīth*. Such will not be accepted from him and attention will not be paid to whatever he brings, no matter who it is. They will not cease disparaging him severely for this difference in a manner that they would not deem permissible even for the open sinners or the people of the famous innovations, e.g. the Khawārij and the Rawāfiḍ. They would hate him severely, above the level of hate they would show the Ahl al-Dhimmah amongst the Jews and the Christians. Whoever rejects this has not researched the conditions of these people.

وَبِالْجُمْلَةِ فَهُوَ عِنْدهم ضال مضل وَلَا ذَنْب لَهُ إِلَّا أَنه عمل بِكِتَاب الله وَسنة رَسُول الله صلى الله عَلَيْهِ وَآله وَسلم واقتدى بعلماء الْإِسْلَام فِي أَن الْوَاجِب على كل مُسلم تَقْدِيم كتاب الله وَسنة رَسُوله على قَول كل عَالم كَائِنا من كَانَ.

In brief, according to them such a person is someone astray who will lead others astray, though he committed no sin other than acting upon the Book and the Sunnah of the Messenger of Allah ﷺ, and emulated the scholars of Islam with regard to the fact that it is obligatory upon every Muslim to give preference to the Book of Allah and the Sunnah of His Messenger above the statement of any scholar, no matter who he is.

[أَقْوَال الْأَئِمَّة الْأَرْبَعَة فِي النَّهْي عَن التَّقْلِيد]

[Statements of the Four *Imāms* Regarding the Prohibition of *al-Taqlīd*]

وَمن المصرحين بِهَذِهِ الْأَئِمَّة الْأَرْبَعَة فَإِنَّهُ قد صَحَّ عَن كل وَاحِد مِنْهُم هَذَا الْمَعْنى من طرق مُتعَدِّدَة.

Amongst those who were explicit regarding this were the four *imāms*, and this notion has been authentically narrated from each one of them through numerous chains.

[١- أبو حنيفة]: قَالَ صَاحب الْهِدَايَة: فِي رَوْضَة الْعلمَاء أَنه قيل لأبي حنيفَة إِذا قلت قولا وَكتاب الله يُخَالِفهُ قَالَ اتْرُكُوا قولي بكتاب الله فقيل إذا كان خبر الرسول يخالفه قال اتركوا قولي بِخَبَر رَسُول فَقيل إِذا كَانَ قَول الصَّحَابِيّ يُخَالِفهُ قَالَ اتْرُكُوا قولي بقول الصَّحَابِيّ ... انتهي.

[1. Abu Ḥanīfah:] The author of *al-Ḥidāyah* said: "In *Rawḍatu 'l-'Ulamā*, it states that it was said to Abu Ḥanīfah, 'If you say a word and the Book of Allah contradicts it, [what should we do]?' He said, 'Leave my statement for the Book of Allah.' It was said to him, 'What if the narration of the Messenger contradicts it?' He said, 'Leave my statement for the narration of the Messenger.' It was asked, 'What if a statement of a companion contradicts it? He said: 'Leave my statement for that of the companion...'"[42] End of quote.

42 See *I'lām al-Muwaqqi'īn* (1/282) and *al-Baḥr al-Muḥīṭ* (4/54).

وَقد روى عَنهُ هَذِه الْمَقَالة جمَاعَة من أَصْحَابه وَغَيرهم.

This statement has been reported from him by a group of his disciples and other than them.

[٢- مالك]: وَقد ذكر نور الدّين السنهوري نَحْو ذَلِك، قال: قَالَ ابْن مسدي فِي منسكه: روينَا عَن معن بن عِيسَى قَالَ سَمِعت مَالِكًا يَقُول: إِنَّمَا أَنا بشر أخطئ وَأُصِيب فانظروا فِي رَأْيِي كل مَا وَافق الْكتاب وَالسّنة فَخُذُوا بِهِ وَمَا لم يُوَافق الْكتاب وَالسّنة فاتركوه. انتهى. قال ابن مسدي فقد علم أَن كلما خالف الكتاب والسنة من أَراء مالك فليس بمذهب له بل مذهبه ما وافق الكتاب والسنة. انتهى.

[2. Mālik:] Nūr al-Dīn al-Sanhūrī mentioned something similar to this. He said, "Ibn Musaddī said in his *Mansak*, 'It was narrated to us from Maʿn ibn ʿĪsā that he said, 'I heard Mālik say, 'I am only a human being. I err at times and am correct at others. So, analyse my opinions; whatever is in concordance with the Book and Sunnah, take it and whatever is not, leave it."[43] [End quote.] Ibn Musaddī said, 'It is known that whenever the statements of Mālik contradict the Book and Sunnah, they are not considered his *madhhab*, rather his *madhhab* is whatever agrees with the Book and Sunnah."' [End quote.]

وَنقل الْأَجْهُورِيّ والخرشي هَذَا الْكَلَام وَأَقَرَّاهُ فِي شرحيهما على مُخْتَصر خَلِيل وَقد روى ذَلِك عَن مَالك جمَاعَة من أهل مذْهبه وَغَيرهم.

---

43 See *Jāmiʿ Bayān al-ʿIlm wa Faḍlihi* (1/775, no. 1435), *al-Iḥkām* of Ibn Ḥazm (6/149-150) and *Iʿlām al-Muwaqqiʿīn* (1/75).

Al-Ajhūrī and al-Kharashī both cited this statement and endorsed it in their commentaries upon *Mukhtaṣar Khalīl*.[44] This was narrated from Mālik by a group of his *madhhab's* adherents and others.

[٣- والشافعي]: وَأما الإِمَام الشَّافِعِي: فقد تَوَاتر ذلك عَنهُ تواترا لَا يخفى على مقصر فضلا عَن كَامِل، فَإِنَّهُ نقل ذلك عَنهُ غَالب أَتْبَاعه وَنَقله أَيْضا جَمِيع المترجمين لَهُ إِلَّا من شَذَّ.

[3. Al-Shāfiʿī:] As for al-Imām al-Shāfiʿī, this is mass transmitted from him to the point that the matter is not hidden from the incapable, let alone the capable. This was transmitted from him mostly by his followers and all of those who wrote his biography, except the odd person.

وَمن جملَة من روى عنه ذَلِك الْبَيْهَقِيّ فَإِنَّهُ سَاق إِسْنَادًا إِلَى الرّبيع قَالَ: سَمِعت الشَّافِعِي وَسَأَلَهُ رجل عَن مَسْأَلَة فَقَالَ: يرْوى عَن النَّبِي صلى الله عَلَيْهِ وَآله وَسلم أَنه قَالَ كَذَا وكذا فَقَالَ لَهُ السَّائِل: يَا أَبَا عبد الله أتقول بِهَذَا، فارتعد الشَّافِعِي واصفر وَحَال لَونه وَقَالَ: وَيحك وَأي أَرض تُقِلني وَأي سَمَاء تُظِلنِي إِذا رويت عَن رَسُول الله صلى الله عَلَيْهِ وَآله وَسلم شَيْئا وَلم أقل بِهِ نعم على الرَّأْس وَالْعين نعم على الرَّأْس وَالْعين.

Amongst those who narrated this from him is al-Bayhaqī. He transmitted a chain of narration to al-Rabīʿ who said, "I heard a man asking al-Shāfiʿī about an issue and he said, 'It was reported from the Prophet ﷺ that he said such and such.' Then the questioner asked him, 'O Abā 'Abdillāh, do you hold to this?' To this, al-Shāfiʿī shiv-

44 (1/40-43).

ered, became pale and stated, 'Woe unto you. What earth will carry me and what sky will give me shade if I narrate something from the Messenger of Allah ﷺ whilst not holding it to be my view. Yes, his words are held in high esteem. Yes, his words are held in high esteem.'"[45]

وروى الْبَيْهَقِيّ أَيْضا عَن الشَّافِعِي أَنه قَالَ: إِذا وجدْتُم فِي كتابي خلاف سنة رَسُول الله صلى الله عَلَيْهِ وَآله وَسلم فَقولُوا بِسنة رَسُول الله صلى الله عَلَيْهِ وَآله وَسلم ودعوا مَا قلت: وروى الْبَيْهَقِيّ عَنهُ أَيْضا قَالَ: إِذا حدث الثِّقَة عَن الثِّقَة حَتَّى يَنْتَهِي إِلَى رَسُول الله صلى الله عَلَيْهِ وَآله وَسلم فَهُوَ ثَابت عَن رَسُول الله صلى الله عَلَيْهِ وَآله وَسلم وَلَا يتْرك لرَسُول الله صلى الله عَلَيْهِ وَآله وَسلم حَدِيث أبدا إِلَّا حَدِيث وجد عَن رَسُول الله صلى الله عَلَيْهِ وَآله وَسلم حَدِيث يُخَالِفهُ.

Al-Bayhaqī also reported from al-Shāfiʿī that he said, "If you find in my book something contrary to the Sunnah of the Messenger of Allah ﷺ, then speak on the basis of the Sunnah of the Messenger of Allah ﷺ and ignore what I have said."[46] Al-Bayhaqī also related from him that he said, "If a trustworthy narrator reports from a trustworthy narrator until the transmission ends at the Messenger of Allah ﷺ, then it is confirmed from the Messenger of Allah ﷺ and his ḥadīths should never be left, except when there is a ḥadīth established from the Messenger of Allah ﷺ contrary to it."[47]

---

45 *Al-Manāqib* (1/475). I say: Ibn al-Qayyim mentioned it in *Iʿlām al-Muwaqqiʿīn* (2/286) and Abu Nuʿaym in *al-Ḥilyah* (9/106).

46 *Al-Manāqib* (1/472-473).

47 Ibn al-Qayyim mentioned it in *Iʿlām al-Muwaqqiʿīn* (2/282) and Abu Nuʿaym in *al-Ḥilyah* (9/106).

وروى الْبَيْهَقِيّ أَيْضا عَنهُ أَنه قَالَ لَهُ رجل وَقد روى حَدِيثا أتأخذ بِهذا فَقَال مَتى رويت عَن رَسُول الله صلى الله عَلَيْهِ وَآله وَسلم حَدِيثا صَحِيحا فَلم آخذ بِهِ فأشهدكم أَن عَقْلِي قد ذهب.

Al-Bayhaqī also narrated from al-Shāfi'ī that a man asked him after a ḥadīth was narrated, "Do you hold this view?" He replied, "When I narrate an authentic ḥadīth from the Messenger of Allah ﷺ and I do not take it as my view, I call you to witness that my intellect has departed."[48]

وَحكى ابْن الْقيم فِي إعْلَام الموقعين أَن الرّبيع قَالَ سَمِعت الشَّافِعِي يَقُول: كل مَسْأَلَة يَصح فِيهَا[٤٩] الْخَبَر عَن رَسُول الله صلى الله عَلَيْهِ وَآله وَسلم عِنْد أهل النَّقْل بِخِلَاف مَا قلت فَأَنا رَاجع عَنْهَا فِي حَياتِي وَبعد مماتي. وَقَالَ حَرْمَلَة بن يحيى قَالَ الشَّافِعِي: مَا قلت وَكَانَ النَّبِي صلى الله عَلَيْهِ وَآله وَسلم قد قَالَ بِخِلَاف قولي فَمَا صَحَّ من حَدِيث النَّبِي صلى الله عَلَيْهِ وَآله وَسلم أولى وَلَا تقلدوني.

Ibn al-Qayyim related in *I'lām al-Muwaqqi'īn* that al-Rabī' said, "I heard al-Shāfi'ī say, 'In every issue where the people of narration find a report from the Messenger of Allah ﷺ to be authentic and it is contrary to what I have said, then I retract from it, whether during my lifetime or after my death.'" Ḥarmalah ibn Yaḥyā said, "Al-Shāfi'ī stated, 'For everything I say, if there is something from the Prophet ﷺ contrary to my statement, then the authentic ḥadīth of the

48 *Al-Manāqib* (1/474).

49 [T] In the original text this said (فيه).

Prophet ﷺ takes precedence, and do not blindly follow me.'"[50]

وَقَالَ الْحميدِي سَأَلَ رجل الشَّافِعِي عَن مَسْأَلَة فأفتاه وَقَالَ قَالَ النَّبِي صلى الله عَلَيْهِ وَآله وَسلم كَذَا وَكَذَا فَقَالَ الرجل أَتقول بِهَذَا يَا أَبَا عبد الله فَقَالَ الشَّافِعِي أَرَأَيْت فِي وسطي زنارا؟ أترَانِي خرجت من الْكَنِيسَة؟ أَقُول قَالَ النَّبِي صلى الله عَلَيْهِ وَآله وَسلم وتقول لي أَتَقول بِهَذَا. أأروي عَن النَّبِي صلى الله عَلَيْهِ وَآله وَسلم وَلَا أَقُول بِهِ. انتهى. وَنقل إِمَام الْحَرَمَيْنِ فِي نهايته عَن الشَّافِعِي أَنه قَالَ: إِذا صَحَّ خبر يُخَالف مذهبي فَاتَّبِعُوهُ، وَاعْلَمُوا أَنه مذهبي. انتهى.

Al-Ḥumaydī said, "A man asked al-Shāfiʿī about an issue and he gave him the verdict and said, 'The Prophet ﷺ said such and such.' Then the man said, 'O Abā 'Abdillāh, do you hold this view?' Al-Shāfiʿī said, 'Did you see a strap on my waist? Have you seen me coming out from a church? I say the Prophet ﷺ said such and such and you are asking me if I hold this view. Would I narrate from the Prophet ﷺ without taking it as my view?'"[51] [End quote.] Imāmu 'l-Ḥaramayn transmitted in *al-Nihāyah* from al-Shāfiʿī that he said, "If a narration is authentic, which is contrary to my view, follow it and know that it is my *madhhab*."[52] [End quote.]

وَقد روى نَحْو ذَلِك الْخَطِيب وَكَذَلِكَ الذَّهَبِيّ فِي تَارِيخ الْإِسْلَام والنبلاء وَغير هَؤُلَاءِ مِمَّن لَا يَأْتِي عَلَيْهِ الْحصْر. وَقَالَ الْحَافِظ ابن حجر فِي توالي

---

50 2/285.

51 See *Iʿlām al-Muwaqqiʿīn* (2/285-286).

52 Refer to the previous reference.

التأسيس قد اشْتهر عَن الشَّافِعِي إِذا صَحَّ الحَدِيث فَهُوَ مذهبي وَحكى عَن السُّبْكِيّ أَن لَهُ مصنفا فِي هَذِه الْمَسْأَلَة.

Similar reports have been narrated by al-Khaṭīb and al-Dhahabī in *Tārikhu 'l-Islām* and *al-Nubalā*,[53] and from other sources, the amount of which cannot be enumerated. Al-Ḥāfiẓ Ibn Ḥajar stated in *Tawālī al-Ta'sīs*, "It is well known that al-Shāfi'ī said, 'When a ḥadīth is found to be authentic, it is my *madhhab*.' And it was related by al-Subkī that he has a book on this issue."[54]

[٤- أحمد بن حنبل]: وَأما الإِمَام أَحْمد بن حَنْبَل فَهُوَ أَشد الْأَئِمَّة الْأَرْبَعَة تنفيرا عَن الرَّأْي وأبعدهم عَنهُ وألزمهم للسّنة، وَقد نقل عَنهُ ابْن الْقيم فِي مؤلفاته كإعلام الموقعين مَا فِيهِ التَّصْرِيح بِأَنَّهُ لَا عمل على الرَّأْي أصلا وَهَكَذَا نقل عَنهُ ابْن الْجَوْزِيّ وَغَيره من أَصْحَابه.

[4. Aḥmad ibn Ḥanbal:] As for al-Imām Aḥmad ibn Ḥanbal, he was the strictest of the four *imāms* in fleeing from personal opinion, the furthest of them from it, and the most diligent of them in clinging to the Sunnah. Thus, Ibn al-Qayyim narrated from him in his books like *I'lām al-Muwaqqi'īn* that which explicitly displays him not acting upon personal opinion at all. Likewise, Ibn al-Jawzī and others from his disciples have also reported it from him.

---

53 Al-Dhahabī said in *Siyar A'lām al-Nubalā* (10/35), "Abu Thawr said that he heard al-Shāfi'ī say, "Every ḥadīth from the Prophet ﷺ is my view even if you did not hear it from me."

54 Of Ibn Ḥajar (p. 109). The correct name of the book is *Tawālī al-Ta'nīs bima'ālī Ibn Idrīs*.' See *Tawthīq al-Nuṣūṣ wa Ḍabṭihā 'inda al-Muḥaddithīn* by Dr. Muwaffaq ibn 'Abdullāh ibn Abd al-Qādir (p. 108-113).

وَإِذا كَانَ من الْمانعين للرأي المنفرين عَنهُ فَهُوَ قَائِل بِمَا قَالَه الْأَئِمَّة الثَّلَاثَة المنقولة نصوصهم على أَن الحَدِيث مَذْهَبهم وَيزِيد عَلَيْهِم بِأَنَّهُم سوغوا الرَّأْي فِيمَا لَا يُخَالف النَّص وَهُوَ مَنعه من الأَصْل وسيأتي قريبا النقل عن الإمام أحمد بما فيه التصريح بمنع التقليد.

So, in his forbidding of personal opinion and fleeing from it, he has stated what the three *imāms* stated—whose statements indicate that the ḥadīth is their *madhhab*—and he exceeded them in that they allowed personal opinion in what does not contradict a text but he forbade it absolutely. A narration from al-Imām Aḥmad will follow shortly which contains explicit prohibition of *al-taqlīd*.

وَقد حكى الشعراني فِي الْمِيزَان أَن الْأَئِمَّة الْأَرْبَعَة كلهم قَالُوا إِذا صَحَّ الحَدِيث فَهُوَ مَذْهَبنَا وَلَيْسَ لأحد قِيَاس وَلَا حجَّة. انتهى.

Al-Shaʿrānī mentioned in *al-Mīzān* that all of the four *imāms* said, "When a ḥadīth is *ṣaḥīḥ*, it is our *madhhab* and there is no room for *qiyās* or proof from anyone."[55] [End of quote.]

55 (1/55).

[إجْمَاع الْأئِمَّة الْأَرْبَعَة على تَقْدِيم النَّص]

[The Consensus of the Four *Imāms* on Giving Preference to the Text]

وَإِذا تقرر لَك إِجْمَاع أَئِمَّة الْمذَاهب الْأَرْبَعَة على تَقْدِيم النَّص على آرائهم عرفت أَن الْعَالم الَّذِي عمل بِالنَّصِّ وَترك قَول أهل الْمذَاهب هُوَ الْمُوَافق لما قَالَه أَئِمَّة الْمذَاهب، والمقلد الَّذِي قدم أَقْوَال أهل الْمذَاهب على النَّص هُوَ الْمُخَالف لله وَلِرَسُولِهِ ولإمام مذْهبه وَلغيره من سَائِر عُلَمَاء الْإِسْلَام.

If the consensus of the four *imāms* on giving precedence to a text of the Qur'an or ḥadīth over their personal views is established to you, you should know that the scholar who acts on a text and ignores the statements of the people of the *madhhabs* is in agreement with what the *imāms* of the *madhhabs* have said, and the *muqallid* who gives preference to the statements of the people of the *madhhabs* over a text is opposing Allah, His Messenger, the *imām* of his *madhhab* and others amongst the scholars of Islam.

ولعمري إِن الْقَلَم جرى بِهَذِهِ النقول على وَجل وحياء من رَسُول الله صلى الله عَلَيْهِ وَآله وَسلم فيا لله الْعجب أيحتاج الْمُسلم فِي تَقْدِيم قَول الله أَو قَول رَسُوله على قَول أحد من عُلَمَاء أمته إِلَى أَن يعتضد بِهَذِهِ النقول يَا

لله الْعجب، أَي مُسلم يلتبس عَلَيْهِ مثل هَذَا حَتَّى يحْتَاج إِلَى نقل أَقْوَال
هَؤُلَاءِ الْعلمَاء رَحِمهم الله فِي أَن أَقْوَال الله وأَقْوَال رَسُوله مُقَدّمَة على
أَقْوَالهم فَإِن التَّرْجِيح فرع التَّعَارُض وَمن ذَاك الَّذِي يُعَارِض قَوْله قَول الله أَو
قَول رَسُوله حَتَّى نرْجِع إِلَى التَّرْجِيح والتقديم! سُبْحَانَك هَذَا بهتان عَظِيم.
فَلَا حَيا الله هَؤُلَاءِ المقلدة الَّذين أَلجأُوا الْأَئِمَّة إِلَى التَّصْرِيح بِتَقْدِيم
أَقْوَال الله وَرَسُوله على أَقْوَالهم لما شاهدوهم عَلَيْهِ من الغلو المشابه لغلو
الْيَهُود وَالنَّصَارَى فِي أَحْبَارهم وَرُهْبَانهمْ وَهم الَّذين أَلجأُونا إِلَى نقل هَذِه
الْكَلِمَات وَإِلَّا فَالْأَمْر وَاضِح لَا يلتبس على أَكمه.

Upon my life, that the pen flows out with such words in the presence of apprehension and shyness of the Messenger of Allah ﷺ, by Allah, it is amazing. Why is it that a Muslim needs assistance through these transmissions in giving preference to the statements of Allah and His Messenger over the statements of any scholar? O Allah this is amazing. Meaning, the Muslim is uncertain of such an issue until he has statements from the aforementioned scholars that the statements of Allah and His Messenger take precedence over their words. Indeed, *al-tarjīḥ* (giving preference) is utilised when there is a contradiction, and whose statement would contradict that of Allah or His Messenger to the extent that we would resort to *tarjīḥ* and *taqdīm* (giving preference to one of the statements)!? Glory be to You, this is a great lie. How shameless are those *muqallids* who forced the *imāms* to declare that preference should be given to the statements of Allah and His Messenger over their statements, due to what they saw of extremism which resembled that of the Jews and Christians with regard to their monks and rabbis.[56] And likewise,

___
56 He is referring to the statement of the Most High: {**They have taken their**

they are the ones who forced us to quote these words, as the issue is clear and not ambiguous to anyone.

وَلَو فرضنَا وَالْعِيَاذ بِاللَّه أَن عَالما من عُلَمَاء الْإِسْلَام يَجْعَل قَوْله كَقَوْل الله أَو قَول رَسُوله لَكَانَ كَافِرًا مُرْتَدا فرضا عن أَن يَجْعَل قَوْله أقدم من قول الله وَرَسُوله.

Let us assume—and Allah's refuge is sought—that a scholar amongst the scholars of Islam considers his statement similar to the statement of Allah and His Messenger, he would be deemed a disbeliever and apostate, let alone giving his statement preference over those of Allah and His Messenger.

فَإنَّا لله وَإِنَّا إِلَيْهِ رَاجِعُون مَا صنعت هَذِه الْمذَاهب بِأَهْلِهَا وَإِلَى أَي مَوضِع أخرجتهم، وليت هَؤُلَاءِ المقلدة الجفاة الأجلاف نظرُوا بِعَين الْعقل إِذا حرمُوا النّظر بعين الْعلم ووازنوا بَين رَسُول الله صلى الله عَلَيْهِ وَآله وَسلم وَبَين أَئِمَّة مذاهبهم وتصوروا وقوفهم بَين يَدي رَسُول الله صلى الله عَلَيْهِ وَآله وَسلم فَهَل يخْطر ببال من بقيت فِيهِ بَقِيَّة من عقل من هَؤُلَاءِ المقلدين

---

rabbis and monks as lords besides Allah, and [also] the Messiah, the son of Mary. And they were not commanded except to worship one God; there is no deity [worthy of worship] except Him. Exalted is He above whatever they associate with Him.} [Al-Tawbah: 31] Ibn Jarīr recorded in *Jāmiʿ al-Bayān* (6/10/114-115) and al-Qurtubī in his *Tafsīr* (8/120): Ḥudhayfah was asked about the statement, **{They have taken their rabbis and monks as lords besides Allah...}** Were they worshipping them? He said, "No, if they made something lawful to them, they considered it lawful and when they forbade something to them, they considered it forbidden."

أَن هَؤُلَاءِ الْأَئِمَّة المتبوعين عِنْد وقوفهم المفروض بَين يَدي رَسُول الله صلى الله عَلَيْهِ وَآله وَسلم كَانُوا يردون عَلَيْهِ قَوْله أَو يخالفونه بأقوالهم! كلا وَالله بل هم أتقى لله وأخشى لَهُ، فقد كَانَ أَكَابِر الصَّحَابَة يتركون سُؤَاله صلى الله عَلَيْهِ وَآله وَسلم فِي كثير من الْحَوَادِث هَيْبَة له وتعظيما، وَكَانَ يعجبهم الرجل الْعَاقِل من أهل الْبَادِيَة إِذا وصل يسْأَل رَسُول الله صلى الله عَلَيْهِ وَآله وَسلم ليستفيدوا بسؤاله كَمَا ثَبت فِي الصَّحِيح.

Indeed, *inna 'llāhi wa inna ilayhi rāji'ūn* (indeed to Allah we belong and indeed to Him we will return). This is what these *madhhabs* have become to their people and the place they have taken them to. If only these uncouth and uncivil *muqallids* would examine with a rational eye, since they have been deprived of a knowledgeable eye, and make a comparison between the Messenger of Allah ﷺ and the *imāms* of their *madhhabs*, and imagine their *imāms* before him. Would anyone who possesses a remnant of intellect amongst these *muqallids* think that these great *imāms* that are followed would reject the statement of the Messenger of Allah ﷺ or contradict him with their own views during their imagined standing in front of him? Nay! By Allah they were the most conscious and fearful of Allah. The major companions would leave off asking the Messenger of Allah ﷺ regarding many issues, out of awe and respect for him. They preferred for a rational Bedouin to come and ask the Messenger of Allah ﷺ so that they could take benefit from his questions, as established in *al-Ṣaḥīḥ*.[57]

---

57 He is referring to the ḥadīth recorded by Muslim in his *Ṣaḥīḥ* (10/20) on the authority of Anas that he said, "We were forbidden to ask the Messenger of Allah ﷺ about anything [he did not make clear to us], so we liked that a desert man would come and ask him, and we would listen."

وَكَانُوا يقفون بَين يَدَيْهِ كَأَن على رؤوسهم الطير يرْمونَ بِأَبْصَارِهِمْ إِلَى بَين أَيْديهم وَلَا يرفعونها إِلَى رَسُول الله صلى الله عَلَيْهِ وَآله وَسلم احتشاما وتكريما وَكَانُوا أَحْقَر وَأَقل عِنْد أنفسهم من أَن يعارضوا رَسُول الله صلى الله عَلَيْهِ وَآله وَسلم بآرائهم وَكَانَ التابعون يتأدبون مَعَ الصَّحَابَة بقريب من هَذَا الْأَدَب، وَكَذَلِكَ تابعوا التَّابِعين كَانُوا يتأدبون مع التَّابِعين بقريب من أدب التَّابِعين مَعَ الصَّحَابَة فَمَا ظَنك أَيهَا الْمُقَلّد لَو حضر إمامك بَين يَدي رَسُول الله صلى الله عَلَيْهِ وَآله وَسلم.

They would stand in front of him as if birds were on their heads, aiming at what is in front of them without raising them up[58] towards the Messenger of Allah ﷺ out of bashfulness and respect. The most disgusting thing to them was that they should contradict the Messenger of Allah ﷺ with their personal views. The followers of the companions treated them with similar humility, and the followers of the followers treated them with similar humility, emulating their manner with the companions. So, what do you think, O *muqallid*, if your *imām* were to be standing in front of the Messenger of Allah ﷺ?

فَإِذا فاتك يَا مِسْكين الاهتداء بهدي الْعلم فَلَا يفوتنك الاهتداء بهدي الْعقل، فَإنَّك إِذا استضأت بنوره خرجت من ظلمات جهلك إِلَى نور الْحق. وإِذا عرفت مَا نَقَلْنَاهُ عَن أَئِمَّة الْمذَاهب الْأَرْبَعَة من تَقْدِيم النَّص على آرائهم فقد قدمنَا لَك أَيْضا حِكَايَة الْإِجْمَاع على مَنعهم من التَّقْلِيد

58 Refer to the lengthy ḥadīth in *Ṣaḥīḥ al-Bukhārī* (no. 2731, 2732) from the ḥadīth of al-Miswar ibn Makhramah and Marwān.

وَحَكِينَا لَكَ مَا قَالَهُ الإِمَام أَبُو حَنِيفَة وَمَا قَالَهُ إِمَام دَار الْهِجْرَة مَالِك بن
أَنس مِن ذَلِكَ وَلَاحَ لَكَ مَا نَقَلْنَاهُ قَرِيبًا مَا يَقُول الإِمَام مُحَمَّد بن إِدْرِيس
الشَّافِعِي مِن منع التَّقْلِيد.

O pauper, if following the guidance of knowledge eluded you, you
should not miss out on following the guidance of rationality, because if you are enlightened or guided by its light, you will exit from
the darkness of your ignorance to the light of the truth. [Reflect
upon] what we have transmitted from the *imāms* of the four *madhhabs*, such as giving preference to a legislative text over their personal
opinions, and our presenting to you of reports citing a consensus on
their prohibition of *al-taqlīd*. We also mentioned to you the statements of al-Imām Abu Ḥanīfah and the *imām* of Dār al-Hijrah,
Mālik ibn Anas regarding this, and it is clear to you what we cited
from the statements of al-Imām Muḥammad ibn Idrīs al-Shāfiʿī concerning the prohibition of *al-taqlīd*.

وَقد قَالَ الْمُزَنِيّ فِي أَول مُخْتَصَره مَا نَصه: اخْتصرت هَذَا مِن علم
الشَّافِعِي وَمِن معنى قَوْله لأقراه على مِن أَرَادَهُ مَعَ إِعْلَامه بنهيه عَن تَقْلِيده
وتقليد غَيره لِينْظر فِيهِ لِدِينِهِ ويحتاط فِيهِ لِنَفسِهِ. انتهى. فَانْظُر مَا نَقله هَذَا
الإِمَام الَّذِي هُوَ مِن أَعلم النَّاس بِمذهب الشَّافِعِي رَحمَه الله من تصريحه
بِمَنْع تَقْلِيده وتقليد غَيره.

Al-Muzanī stated at the beginning of his *Mukhtaṣar*, "I have
abridged this from the knowledge of Al-Shāfiʿī and from the purport of his statements, in order to display it to whoever wants it,
whilst declaring his prohibition of himself and others being blindly
followed, so that one place efforts in contemplation for the sake of

his religion and to take the safe side [by avoiding *al-taqlīd*.]"[59] [End quote.] One should ponder at what was cited by this *imām*, who was one of the most learned of people about the *madhhab* of al-Shāfiʿī, regarding his explicit prohibition of *taqlīd* of him or other than him.

وَأما الإِمَام أَحْمد بن حَنْبَل فالنصوص عَنهُ فِي منع التَّقْلِيد كَثِيرَة قَالَ أَبُو دَاوُد قلت لِأَحْمَد الْأَوْزَاعِيّ هو اتبع أم مَالك؟ فَقَالَ: لَا تقلد دينك أحدا من هَؤُلَاءِ مَا جَاءَ عَن النَّبِي صلى الله عَلَيْهِ وَآله وَسلم وَأَصْحَابه فَخذ بِهِ وَقَالَ أَبُو دَاوُد سمعته - يَعْنِي أَحْمد بن حَنْبَل - يَقُول: الِاتِّبَاع أَن يتبع الرجل مَا جَاءَ عَن النَّبِي صلى الله عَلَيْهِ وَآله وَسلم وَأَصْحَابه ثم من هُوَ بعده من التَّابِعين بِخَير. انتهى. فَانْظُر كَيفَ فرق بَين التَّقْلِيد والإتباع.

As for al-Imām Aḥmad ibn Ḥanbal, the narrations from him regarding the prohibition of *al-taqlīd* are many. Abu Dāwūd relayed that he asked Aḥmad, "Should I follow al-Awzāʿī or Mālik?" He replied, "Do not blindly take your religion from any one of these, rather, whatever comes from the Prophet ﷺ and His companions, take it."[60] Abu Dāwūd said that he heard Aḥmad ibn Ḥanbal say, "*Al-ittibāʾ* means that a man follows what comes from the Prophet ﷺ and his companions; then for those after them from the successors, he has a choice."[61] [End quote.] One sees how he differentiated between *al-taqlīd* and *al-ittibāʿ*.

وَقَالَ أبو داود: قال لي أَحْمد لَا تقلدني وَلَا تقلد مَالِكًا وَلَا الشَّافِعِي وَلَا

59 Published with the book, *al-Umm* of al-Shāfiʿī (8/93), Dār al-Fikr edition.
60 *Masāʾil al-Imām Aḥmad* (pp. 276-277).
61 Ibid

الْأَوْزَاعِيّ وَلَا الثَّوْرِيّ وَخذ من حَيْثُ أخذُوا. وَقَالَ من قلَّة فقه الرجل أَن يُقَلّد دينه الرِّجَال.

Abu Dāwūd stated that Aḥmad said to him, "Do not make *taqlīd* of me, nor Mālik, al-Shāfiʿī, al-Awzāʿī or al-Thawrī; rather take from where they took." He said, "From the deficiency of a man's understanding is to make *taqlīd* of men in his religion."[62]

قَالَ ابْن الْقيم: وَلأَجل هَذَا لم يؤلف الإِمَام أَحْمد كتابا فِي الْفِقْه وَإِنَّمَا دون أَصْحَابه مذْهبه من أَقْوَاله وأفعاله وأجوبته وَغير ذَلِك. وَقَالَ ابْن الْجَوْزِيّ فِي تلبيس إِبْلِيس: اعلم أَن الْمُقَلّد على غير ثِقَة فِيمَا قلد، وَفِي التَّقْلِيد إِبْطَال مَنْفَعَة الْعقل ثمَّ أَطَالَ الْكَلَام فِي ذَلِك.

Ibn al-Qayyim said, "Due to this, al-Imām Aḥmad did not author a book in *fiqh*. His disciples recorded his *madhhab* from his statements, actions, responses and so on."[63] Ibn al-Jawzī said in *Talbīs Iblīs*, "Know that a *muqallid* is not upon reliability in what he blindly follows, and *al-taqlīd* contains nullification of the intellect's usefulness." Then he spoke at length with regard to that.[64]

---

62 Ibid; and see *I'lām al-Muwaqqiʿīn* (2/200) and *Īqāẓ al-Hamam* (p.113) by al-Fulānī.

63 See *I'lām al-Muwaqqiʿīn* (2/282).

64 These are the concluding parts of his words (pp. 94-95): "... This is because he was created to contemplate and reflect. Horrible is the one who is given a candle to be guided by but extinguishes it and walks in the dark. Know that the general body of the adherents to *madhhabs* venerate a man and follow his statements without contemplation, and this is the essence of misguidance, for it is necessary that attention be given to the statement and not the one it emanates from."

وَبِالْجُمْلَةِ فنصوص أَئِمَّة الْمذَاهب الْأَرْبَعَة فِي الْمَنْع من التَّقْلِيد وَفِي تَقْدِيم النَّص على آرائهم وآراء غَيرهم لَا تخفى على عَارِف من أتباعهم وَغَيرهم.

In brief, the statements of the four *imāms* of the *madhhabs* with regard to the prohibition of *al-taqlīd* and [the necessity of] giving preference to a text over their personal views and the views of others is not hidden from the learned amongst their followers and others.

[أقوال الأئمة المتبوعين من أهل البيت]

[Statements of the *Imāms* Followed Amongst Ahl al-Bayt]

وَأما نُصُوص سَائِر الْأَئِمَّة المتبوعين على ذَلِك الْأَئِمَّة من أهل الْبَيْت عَلَيْهِم السَّلَام فَهِيَ مَوْجُودَة فِي كتبهمْ مَعْرُوفَة قد نقلهَا العارفون بمذاهبهم عَنْهُم وَمن أحب النّظر فِي ذَلِك فليطالع مؤلفاتهم.

As for the narrations from other *imāms* who are followed concerning this—like the *imāms* from Ahl al-Bayt ﷺ—they are available in their known books. Those who are learned about their *madhhabs* have related it from them. Whoever wishes to look into this should familiarise himself with their books.

وَقد جمع مِنْهَا السَّيِّد الْعَلامَة الإِمَام مُحَمَّد بن إِبْرَاهِيم الْوَزير فِي مؤلفاته مَا يشفي وَيَكْفِي لَا سِيمَا فِي كِتَابه الْمَعْرُوف بالقواعد فَإِنَّهُ نقل الْإِجْمَاع عَنْهُم وَعَن سَائِر عُلَمَاء الْإِسلام على تَحْرِيم تَقْلِيد الْأَمْوَات وَأَطَال فِي ذَلِك وأطاب وناهيك بِالْإِمَامِ الْهَادِي يحيى بن الْحُسَيْن رحمه الله فَإِنَّهُ الإِمَام الَّذِي صَار أهل الديار اليمنية مقلدين لَهُ متبعين لمذهبه من عصره وَهُوَ آخر الْمِائَة الثَّالِثَة إِلَى الْآن مَعَ أَنه قد اشْتهر عِنْد أَتْبَاعه والمطلعين على مذْهبه أَنه صرح تَصْرِيحًا لَا يبْقى عِنْده شكّ وَلَا شُبْهَة بِمَنْع التَّقْلِيد

لَهُ وَهَذِهِ مقَالَة مَشْهُورَة فِي الديار اليمنية يعلمهَا مقلدوه فضلا عَن غيرهم، وَلَكنهُمْ قلدوه شَاءَ أم أبى. وَقَالُوا قد قلدوه وَإِن كَانَ لَا يجوز ذَلِك عملا بِمَا قَالَه بعض الْمُتَأَخِّرين إِنه يجوز تَقْلِيد الإِمَام الْهَادِي وَإِن منع من التَّقْلِيد، وَهَذَا من أغرب مَا يطْرق سَمعك إِن كنت مِمَّن ينصف.

Al-Sayyid al-ʿAllāmah al-Imām Muḥammad ibn Ibrāhīm al-Wazīr has compiled in his books what suffices from their statements, especially in his book known as *al-Qawāʿid*.[65] He cited their consensus and that of the rest of the scholars of Islam upon the prohibition of blindly following the dead. He discussed it at length and spoke good words. Sufficient for you is al-Imām al-Hādī Yaḥyā ibn al-Ḥusayn, for he was the *imām* whom the inhabitants of Yemen made *taqlīd* of, having followers of his *madhhab* from his life time—which was at the tail end of the third century—until today. This is, in spite of the fact that it is well-known amongst his followers and those cognizant of his *madhhab* that he declared explicitly, without any doubt or ambiguity, the prohibition of blindly following him. This dictate is well-known within the lands of Yemen, his blind followers know of it let alone others. However, they adopted his views regardless of whether he desired it or not. They said that they perform *taqlīd* of him even if it is not permissible, acting in accordance to the view of later people, that it is permissible to perform *taqlīd* of al-Imām al-Hādī even if he forbade this. This is amongst the most unusual things that would reach one's ear, if one is of those who are just.

وَبِهَذَا تعرف أَن مؤلفات أَتبَاع الإِمَام الْهَادِي فِي الْأُصُول وَالْفُرُوع وَإِن صرحوا فِي بَعْضهَا بِجَوَاز التَّقْلِيد فَهُوَ على غير مَذْهَب إمَامهمْ وَهَذَا كَمَا

65 *Al-Qawā'id fī al-Ijtihād*, no. 96. See *I'lām al-Mu'allafīn al-Zaydiyyah* (p.829).

وَقع لغَيرهم من أهل الْمذَاهب، وَقد كَانَ أَتبَاع هَذَا الإِمَام فِي العصور السَّابِقَة وَكَذَلِكَ أَتبَاع الإِمَام الْأَعْظَم زيد بن عَليّ رحمه الله فيهم إنْصَاف لَا سِيمَا فِي فتح باب الِاجْتِهَاد وتوسع دَائِرَة التَّقْلِيد وَعدم قصر الْجَوَاز على إِمَام معِين كَمَا يعرف ذَلِك من مؤلفاتهم بِخِلَاف غَيرهم من المقلدة فَإِنَّهُم أوجبوا على أنفسهم تَقْلِيد الْمعِين واستروحوا إِلَى أَن بَاب الِاجْتِهَاد قد انسد وَانْقطع التفضل به من الله على عباده ولقنوا الْعَوام الَّذين هم مشاركون لَهُم فِي الْجَهْل بالمعارف العلمية ودونهُم فِي معرفَة مسَائِل التَّقْلِيد بِأَنَّهُ لَا اجْتِهَاد بعد اسْتِقْرَار الْمذَاهب وانقراض أئمتها.

With this, the reader should know that if some of the books of the followers of al-Imām al-Hādī in fundamental and subsidiary issues declare the permissibility of *al-taqlīd*, this is not upon the *madhhab* of their *imām*. This occurrence amongst them is just like what occurred to others from the adherents of the *madhhabs*. The followers of this *imām* in previous generations as well as the followers of al-Imāmu 'l-Aʿẓam (the great *imām*) Zayd ibn ʿAlī had justness, especially in opening the door of *al-ijtihād*, broadening the scope of *al-taqlīd* and not restricting its permissibility to a specific *imām*. This is known from their books, making them at variance to others amongst the *muqallids* who mandated upon themselves the *taqlīd* of a specific person, going on to say that the door of *al-ijtihād* is closed—thereby cutting off Allah's favour of it upon His slaves. They taught the common people—who are partners with them in ignorance—scientific knowledge and presented them with an understanding of issues related to *al-taqlīd* that dictated the absence of *al-ijtihād* after the establishment of the *madhhabs* and the demise of their *imāms*.

فضموا إِلَى بدعتهم بِدعَة وشنعوا شنعتهم بشنعة وسجلوا على أنفسهم بالجَهْل فَإِن من تجارأ على مثل هَذِه الْمقَالة وَحكم على الله سُبْحَانَهُ بِمثل هَذَا الحكم المتضمن لتعجيزه عَن التفضل على عباده بِمَا أرشدهم إِلَيْهِ من تعلم الْعلم وتعليمه لَا يعجز عَن التجاري على أَن يحكم على عباده بِالْأَحْكَامِ الْبَاطِلَة ويجازف فِي إصداره وإيراده.

Thus, they added innovations to their innovation, made viler their vileness and imposed ignorance upon themselves. Indeed, one who is bold enough to state the like of this statement and pass a judgement upon Allah with the like of this judgement—that comprises of declaring Him of being incapable of bestowing favour upon His slaves with what He guided them to, such as learning and teaching knowledge—is not incapable of venturing into passing judgements upon His slaves with baseless rulings and acting indiscriminately in his judicial duties.

[القول بانسداد باب الاجتهاد بدعة شنيعة]

[Stating That the Door of *al-Ijtihād* Is Closed Is a Repulsive Innovation]

وَيَا لله الْعجب فاقنع هَؤُلَاءِ الجهلة النوكى بِمَا هم فِيهِ من بِدعَة التَّقْلِيد الَّتِي هِيَ أم الْبدع وَرَأس الشنع حَتَّى سدوا على أمة مُحَمَّد صلى الله عَلَيْهِ وَآله وَسلم بَاب معرفَة الشَّرِيعَة من كتاب الله وَسنة رَسُوله وَإنه لَا سَبِيل إِلَى ذَلِك وَلَا طَرِيق حَتَّى كَأَن الأفهام البشرية قد تَغَيَّرت والعقول الإنسانية قد ذهبت وكل هَذَا حرصا مِنْهُم على أَن تعم بِدعَة التَّقْلِيد كل الْأمة وَأَن لَا يرْتَفع عَن طبقتهم السافلة أحد من عباد الله.

O Allah, it is amazing that these imbecilic ignorant people are content with what they are upon of the innovation of *al-taqlīd*—which is the mother of innovations and chief of vileness—so much so that they closed upon the Ummah of Muhammad ﷺ the door of understanding the Sharīʿah from the Book of Allah and the Sunnah of His Messenger; [implying] that there is no means to understanding it, as if the understanding of human beings has changed and the intellects of humans have vanished. All of this is an effort by them for the innovation of *al-taqlīd* to permeate through the entire Ummah, and that none from Allah's slaves rise above their lowly station.

كَأَن هَذِه الشَّرِيعَة الَّتِي بَين أظهرنَا من كتاب الله وَ[سنة][٦٦] رَسُوله قد

66 [T] Added by the translator.

صَارَت مَنْسُوخَة والناسخ لَهَا مَا ابتدعوه من التَّقْلِيد فِي دين الله فَلَا يعْمل النَّاس بِشَيْء مِمَّا فِي كتاب الله وَالسّنة بل لَا شَرِيعَة لَهُم إِلَّا مَا قد تقرر فِي الْمذَاهب أذهبها الله فَإِن يُوَافِقهَا مَا فِي الْكتاب وَالسّنة فبها ونعمت وَالْعَمَل على الْمذَاهب لَا على مَا وافقها مِنْهُمَا وَإِن يُخَالِفهَا أَحدهمَا أَو كلَاهُمَا فَلَا عمل عَلَيْهِ وَلَا يحل التَّمَسُّك بِهِ.

It is as if the Sharīʿah in our midst derived from the Book of Allah and the Sunnah of His Messenger has become abrogated, and the abrogator is their invention of *al-taqlīd* in the religion of Allah. So [according to them], people should not act upon anything as contained in the Book and Sunnah, in fact, there is no Sharīʿah to them except what has been established in the *madhhabs* (may Allah rectify them). If what is in the Book and Sunnah conforms to them, it is good but they act upon the *madhhabs* and not upon what conforms to them from the two scriptural sources. But if one or both of them contradicts the *madhhabs*, they will not act upon it and [they deem it] impermissible to cling to it.

هَذَا حَاصِل قَوْلهم وَمفَاده وَبَيت قصيدهم وَمحل نشيدهم وَلَكنهُمْ رَأَوْا التَّصْرِيح بِمثل هَذَا تستنكره قُلُوب الْعَوام فضلا عَن الْخَواص وتقشعر مِنْهُ جُلُودهمْ وترجف لَهُ أفئدتهم فعدلوا عَن هَذِه الْعبارَة الكفرية والمقالة الْجَاهِلِيَّة إِلَى مَا يلاقيها فِي الْمعنى ويوافقها فِي المفاد وَلكنه ينْفق على الْعَوام بعض نفاق فَقَالُوا قد انسد بَاب الِاجْتِهَاد. وَمعنى هَذَا الانسداد المفترى وَالْكذب البحت أَنه لم يبْق فِي أهل هَذِه الْملَّة الإسلامية من يفهم الْكتاب وَالسّنة وَإِذا لم يبْق من هُوَ كَذَلِك لم يبْق سَبِيل إِلَيْهِمَا.

This is the general overview and purport of their view. However, they noticed that explicitly declaring the like of this would be detested by the hearts of the laity, let alone the distinguished; causing their skin to tremble and their hearts to shiver on account of it, so they avoided these sacrilegious expressions and statements of ignorance for those which would achieve the same purpose and concord in effect. However, they displayed to the common people some hypocrisy, stating that the door of *al-ijtihād* is closed. The meaning of this outright invention and false closing is that no one is left amongst the people of the Islamic religion who understands the Book and the Sunnah; and if there remains none like that, there is no way to understanding them.

وَإِذا انْقَطع السَّبِيل إِلَيْهِمَا فَكل حكم فيهمَا لَا عمل عَلَيْهِ وَلَا الْتِفَات إِلَيْهِ سَوَاء وَافق الْمَذْهَب أَو خَالفه لِأَنَّهُ لم يبْق من يفهمهُ وَيعرف مَعْنَاهُ إِلَى آخر الدَّهْر، فكذبوا على الله وَادعوا عَلَيْهِ سُبْحَانَهُ أَنه لَا يتَمَكَّن من أَن يخلق خلقا يفهمون مَا شَرعه لَهُم وتعبدهم بِهِ حَتَّى كَأَن مَا شَرعه لَهُم فِي كِتَابه وعَلى لِسَان رَسُوله لَيْسَ بشرع مُطلق.

And if the way to understanding them is cut off, then every ruling in them should not be acted upon nor be given any attention to, regardless whether it conforms to the *madhhabs* or contradicts them, as no one is left who understands them and knows their meaning until the end of time. They lied against Allah and claimed against Him that it is not possible for Him to form creations who will understand what He legislated for them and devote themselves to it. It is as if what He ordained for them in His Book and upon the tongue of His Messenger is not an absolute law.

بل شرع مُقيّد مُؤَقّت إِلَى غَايَة هِيَ قيام هَذِه الْمذَاهب، وَبعد ظُهُورهَا لَا كتاب وَلَا سنة بل قد حدث من يشرع لهَذِهِ الْأمة شَرِيعَة جَدِيدَة وَيحدث لَهَا دينا آخر وينسخ بِمَا رَآهُ من رأي وَمَا ظَنّه من الظَّن مَا يقدمهُ من الْكتاب وَالسّنة وَهَذَا وَإِن أنكروه بألسنتهم فَهُوَ لَازم لَهُم لَا محيد لَهُم عَنهُ وَلَا مهرب، وَإِلَّا فَأَي معنى لقَولهم قد انسد بَاب الِاجْتِهَاد وَلم يبْق إِلَّا مجرد التَّقْلِيد فَإِنَّهُم إن أقرُّوا بِأَنَّهُم قَائِلُونَ بِهَذَا لَزِمَهُم الْإِقْرَار بِمَا ذكرْنَاهُ.

Rather, it is restricted and temporal to a target, which is the establishment of the *madhhabs*; and after their emergence, there is no Book or Sunnah. More so, [it is as if] the one who will legislate a new Sharīʿah for this Ummah and invent another religion for it (i.e. for the Ummah, meaning the community), who abrogates with his views and thoughts which are not preceded in the Book and Sunnah has emerged. Even if their tongues reject this, it is inseparable from them and there is no escape or flight from it for them. Otherwise, what alternative meaning would one give to their statement that the door of *al-ijtihād* is closed and nothing is left except absolute *taqlīd*? If they acknowledge that they said this, their acknowledgment makes what we have stated inseparable from them.

وَعند ذَلِك نتلو عَلَيْهِم ﴿اتَّخَذُوا أَحْبَارَهُمْ وَرُهْبَانَهُمْ أَرْبَابًا مِّن دُونِ اللَّهِ﴾ وَإِن أَنْكَرُوا القَوْل بذلك وَقَالُوا بَاب الِاجْتِهَاد مَفْتُوح والتمسك بالتقليد غير حتم فقل لَهُم فَمَا بالكم يَا نوكى ترمون كل من عمل بِالْكتاب وَالسّنة وَأخذ دينه مِنْهُمَا بِكُل حجر وقدر وتستحلون عرضه وعقوبته وتجلبون عَلَيْهِ بخيلكم ورجلكم!

Hence, we recite this to them: **{They took their rabbis and monks to be their lords besides Allah.}**[67] If they reject such a statement and say that the door of *al-ijtihād* is open and clinging to *al-taqlīd* is not obligatory, say to them: What is wrong with you, O imbecile; you throw every possible stone and utensil at those who act upon the Book and Sunnah and extract their religion from them, and you legalise violating his honour and punishing him and you assault him with your horses and foot soldiers?

وَقد علمُوا وَعلم كل من يعرف مَا هم عَلَيْهِ أَنهم مصممون على تغليق بَاب الِاجْتِهَاد وَانْقِطَاع السبيل إِلَى معرفَة الْكتاب وَالسّنة فلزمهم مَا ذكرْنَاهُ بِلَا تردد فَانْظُر أَيهَا الْمنصف مَا حدث بِسَبَب بِدعَة التَّقْلِيد من البلايا الدِّينِيَّة والرزايا الشيطانية، فَإِن هَذِه الْمقَالة بخصوصها - أَعنِي انسداد بَاب الِاجْتِهَاد - لَو لم يحدث من مفاسد التَّقْلِيد إِلَّا هِيَ لَكَانَ فِيهَا كِفَايَة وَنِهَايَة فَإِنَّهَا حَادِثَة رفعت الشَّرِيعَة بأسرها واستلزمت نسخ كَلَام الله وَرَسُوله وَتَقْدِيم غَيرهمَا عليهما واستبدال غَيرهمَا بهما.

Indeed, they and everyone familiar with their nature know that they are determined to close the door of *al-ijtihād* and cut off the means of understanding the Book and Sunnah. So what we have stated is completely applicable to them, without doubt. Thus, O just [reader], look at what has occurred as a result of the innovation of *al-taqlīd* from religious calamities and devilish whisperings. In fact, this statement in particular—i.e. the closure of the door of *al-ijtihād*—if nothing occurred of the evils of *al-taqlīd* except it, it would have sufficed [for its prohibition]; for it is an occurrence that abolishes the Sharīʿah in its entirety and necessitates abrogation of the

67 Sūrah al-Tawbah: 31

word of Allah and His Messenger and gives preference to other than them, replacing both of them with something else.

يَا ناعي الْإِسْلَام قُم وانعه   قد زَالَ عرف وبدا مُنكر

O wailer of Islam, rise and wail over it, convention has dissipated and evil has emerged.

وَمَا ذكرنَا فِيمَا سبق من أَنه كَانَ فِي الزيدية والهادوية بالديار اليمنية إنصاف فِي هَذِه الْمَسْأَلَة بِفَتْح بَاب الِاجْتِهَاد فَذَلِك إِنَّمَا هُوَ فِي الأزمنة السَّابِقَة كَمَا قيدنَاهُ فِيمَا سلف. وَأما فِي هَذِه الْأَزْمِنَة فقد أدركنا مِنْهُم من هُوَ أَشد تعصبا من غَيرهم فَإِنَّهُم إِذا سمعُوا بِرَجُل يَدعِي الِاجْتِهَاد وَيَأْخُذ دينه من كتاب الله وَسنة رَسُوله قَامُوا عَلَيْهِ قيَاما تبْكي له عُيُون الْإِسْلَام وَاسْتَحَلُّوا مِنْهُ مَا لَا يستحلونه من أهل الذِّمَّة بالطعْن واللعن والتفسيق والتكفير والهجم عَلَيْهِ إِلَى دياره ورجمه بالأحجار والاستظهار هتك حرمته.

We stated earlier that the Zaydiyyah and Hādawiyyah in the lands of Yemen are the most just in this issue by their leaving open of the door of *al-ijtihād*. This is in reference to the previous eras specifically, as we established above. As for the current era, we have come across some of them who are worse in partisanship than others. If they were to hear a man calling for *al-ijtihād* and taking his religion from the Book of Allah and the Sunnah of His Messenger, they would rise up against him in a manner that the eyes of Islam would weep for him. They would legalise against him that which they do not legalise against *Ahl al-Dhimmah* such as disparagement, cursing, declaring him a *fāsiq* (open sinner) and a disbeliever, beating him to his house, striking him with stones, and resorting to violating his sanctity.

وَنعلم يَقِينا أنه لَوْلَا خبطهم بسَوط هَيْبَة الْخلَافَة أعز الله أَرْكَانهَا وشيد سلطانها لاستحلوا إِرَاقَة دِمَاء الْعلمَاء المنتمين إِلَى الْكتاب وَالسّنة وفعلوا بهم مَا لَا يَفْعَلُونَهُ بِأَهْل الذِّمَّة وَقد شاهدنا من هَذَا مَا لَا يَتَّسِع الْمقَام لبسطه.

We know for sure that were it not that they were inhibited by the whip of the caliphate—may Allah honour its pillars and strengthen its authority—they would legalise shedding the blood of the scholars who affiliate to the Book and Sunnah, and treat them in a manner that they do not treat *Ahl al-Dhimmah*. We have witnessed this to an extent of which there is no room to discuss here.

وَالسَّبَب فِي بلوغهم إِلَى هَذَا الْمبلغ الَّذِي بلغه مَا غَيرهم أَن جمَاعَة من شياطين المقلدين الطالبين لفوائد الدُّنْيَا بِعلوم الدّين يوهمون الْعَوام الَّذين لَا يفهمون من الأجناد والسوقة وَنَحْوهم بِأَن الْمُخَالف لما قد تقرر بَينهم من الْمسَائِل الَّتِي قلدوا فِيهَا هُوَ من المنحرفين عَن أَمِير الْمُؤمنِينَ عَليّ بن أبي طَالب رضي الله عنه وَأَنه من جملَة المبغضين لَهُ الدافعين لفضله وفضائله المعادين لَهُ وللأئمة من أَوْلَاده.

The reason why they have reached this level which others did not reach, is that a devilish group amongst the *muqallids* seeking after worldly benefits through knowledge of the religion gave the unlearned laity—from the soldiers, general populace and others—a false impression that the one who opposes that which is established amongst them in the matters they blindly follow, is among those who are against the Commander of the Faithful 'Alī ibn Abī Ṭālib and amongst those who hate him, reject his merit and virtues, and that he is amongst those who show enmity to him and the *imāms* amongst his children.

فَإِذا سمع مِنْهُم الْعَاميّ هَذَا مَعَ قد ارتكز فِي ذهنه من كَون هَؤُلَاءِ المقلدة هم الْعلمَاء المبرزون لما يبهره من زيهم والاجتماع عَلَيْهِم وتصدرهم للفتيا وَالْقَضَاء حسبمَا ذكرْنَاهُ سَابِقًا فَلَا يشك أَن هَذِه الْمقَالة صَحِيحَة وَإِن ذَلِك الْعَالم الْعَامِل بِالْكتاب وَالسّنة من أَعدَاء الْقَرَابَة فَيقوم بحمية جَاهِلِيَّة صادرة عَن واهمة دينية قد أَلْقَاهَا إِلَيْهِ من قدمنَا ذكرهم ترويجا لبدعتهم وتنفيقا لجهلهم وقصورهم على من هُوَ أَجْهَل مِنْهُم.

So if the layman hears this from them—in addition to the fact that it is settled in his brain that these *muqallids* are the eminent scholars, due to his awe of their dress, gatherings around them, and the issuance of verdicts and judgement by them, as we mentioned earlier—he will not doubt that these statements are correct and that this scholar who acts upon the Book and Sunnah is an enemy of the Ahl al-Bayt. He thus acts out with the fanaticism of the times of ignorance, which emanates from the religious delusions placed upon him by those whom we have mentioned previously, in order to further their innovation and promote their ignorance and deficiencies to one who is more ignorant than them.

وَإِنَّمَا موهوا على الْعَوام بِهَذِهِ الدقيقة الإبليسية لما يعلمونه من أَن طبائعهم مجبولة على التشيع إِلَى حد يقصر عَنهُ الْوَصْف حَتَّى إن أحدهم سمع

التنقص تصريحا بالجناب الإلهي أو الجناب النَّبَوِيّ لم يغْضب لَهُ عشر معشار مَا يغضبه إِذا سمع التنقيص بالجناب الْعلوِي بِمُجَرَّد الْوَهم وَالْإِيهَام الَّذِي لَا حَقِيقَة لَهُ.

They only gave the laity the false impression with this satanic detail due to them understanding that their natures are disposed to taking sides (i.e. *tashayyuʿ*, lit. supporting, and adhering to Shi'ism) to a limit that description cannot detail, so much so that if any one of them were to hear disparagement of Allah or the Prophet, he would not display anger for it one tenth of what he would display if he heard disparagement of ʿAlī. This is due to their false understanding and baseless delusions.

فبهذه الذريعة الشيطانية والدسيسة الإبليسية صَار عُلَمَاء الِاجْتِهَاد فِي الْقطر اليمني فِي محنة شَدِيدَة بالعامة والذنب كل الذَّنب على شياطين المقلدة فَإِنَّهُم هم الدَّاء العضال والسم الْقِتَال، وَلَو كَانَ للعامة عقول لم يخف عَلَيْهِم بطلَان تلبيس شياطين المقلدة عَلَيْهِم فَإِن من عمل فِي شَيْئا من عباداته أَو معاملاته بِنَصّ الْكتاب أَو السّنة لَا يخْطر ببال من لَهُ عقل أَن ذَلِك يسْتَلْزم الانحراف عن علي رضي الله عنه، وَأَيْنَ هَذَا من ذَاك، وَلَكِن الْعَامَّة قد ضموا إِلَى فقدان الْعلم فقدان الْعقل لَا سِيمَا فِي أَبْوَاب الدّين وَعند تلبيس الشَّيَاطِين.

So through these devilish means and satanic machinations, the scholars of *al-ijtihād* in the region of Yemen suffered grave trials at the hands of the laity, and every sin is upon the devilish *muqallids*, for they are an incurable sickness and the poison [causing] fighting.

If the laity had intellects, the futility of the deception of the devils amongst the *muqallids* would not have been hidden to them. This is because when one performs an act of worship or social transaction based upon a text from the Book or Sunnah, the one with intellect would not imagine that this necessitates deviating from 'Alī. How do these two things correlate? However, the masses often attach to their absence of knowledge the absence of intellect, especially in aspects of the religion and when there is devilish deception.

فَإِنَّا لله وَإِنَّا إِلَيْهِ رَاجِعُون مَا للعامة الَّذين قد أظلمت قُلُوبهم لفقدان نور الْعلم وللاعتراض على الْعلمَاء وَالْتحكم[٦٨] عَلَيْهِم وَمَا بَال هَذِه الْأَزْمِنَة جَاءَت بِمَا لم يكن فِي الْحساب، فَإِن الْمَعْرُوف من خلق الْعَامَّة فِي جَمِيع الْأَزْمِنَة أَنهم يبلغون فِي تَعْظِيم الْعلمَاء إِلَى حد يقصر عَنهُ الْوَصْف وَرُبمَا يزدحموا عَلَيْهِم للتبرك بتقبيل أَطْرَافهم ويستجلبون مِنْهُم الدُّعَاء ويقرون بِأَنَّهُم حجج الله على عباده فِي بِلَاده ويطيعونهم فِي كل مَا يأمرونهم بِهِ ويبذلون أنفسهم وَأَمْوَالهمْ بَين أَيْديهم لَا جرم حملهمْ على هَذِه الأفاعيل الشيطانية والأخلاق الْجَاهِلِيَّة أباليس المقلدة بالذريعة الَّتِي أسلفنا بَيَانهَا.

Indeed, to Allah we belong, and indeed to Him we will return. What is wrong with these lay people whose hearts have become dark due to the deprivation of the light of knowledge, turning away from the scholars and deriding them? What is wrong with these times wherein it arose that which cannot be accounted? Indeed, it is common

68 [T] This may be a typo, and Allah knows best.

We have translated it as (تَهَكّم), i.e. with a (ه) instead of a (ح).

knowledge that the character of the laity during all eras was that they used to excel in respecting the scholars to a level bereft of description. They would crowd around them to seek blessing from them by kissing their limbs, requesting supplication from them and asserting that they are Allah's proofs over His slaves in His lands and they would comply with everything they ordered them to. In addition, they would expend themselves and their wealth for them. Surely, the devilish *muqallids* are the ones who forced them to these satanic actions and ignorant characteristics through the means we have explained earlier.

فَانْظُر هَل هَذِه الْأَفْعَال الصادرة من مقلدة الْيمن هِيَ أَفعَال من يعْتَرف بِأَن بَاب الِاجْتِهَاد مَفْتُوح إِلَى قيام السَّاعَة وَأَن تَقْلِيد الْمُجْتَهدين لَا يجوز لمن بلغ رتبة الِاجْتِهَاد وَأَن رُجُوع الْعَالم إِلَى اجْتِهَاد نَفسه بعد إحرازه للاجْتِهَاد وَلَو فِي فن وَاحِد وَمَسْأَلَة وَاحِدَة كَمَا صرح لَهُم بذلك المؤلفون لفقه الْأَئِمَّة وحرروه فِي الْكتب الْأُصُولِيَّة والفروعية.

So look at these actions that emanated from the *muqallids* in Yemen; they are the actions of those who acknowledge that the door of *al-ijtihād* is open until the Hour's establishment; and that *taqlīd* of the *mujtahid* is not permissible for whoever has reached the level of performing *al-ijtihād*; and that a scholar should refer to his personal *ijtihād* after his attainment of [the level to exercise] *al-ijtihād*, even if it is in one field and one issue. This is in concurrence to that which was explained to them by the authors of books regarding the *fiqh* of the *imāms*, and documented in the books of *al-uṣūl* (fundamental issues) and *al-furū'* (subsidiary issues).

كلا وَالله بل صنع من يعادي كتاب الله وَسنة رَسُوله الطَّالِب لَهما

والراغب فيهمَا وَيمْنَع الِاجْتِهَاد وَيُوجب التَّقْلِيد ويحول بَين المتشرعين والشريعة ويحيلها عَلَيْهِم فهما وإدراكا كَمَا صنعه غَيرهم من مقلدة سَائِر الْمذَاهب بل زادوا عَلَيْهِم فِي الغلو والتعصب بِمَا تقدم ذكره.

Nay! By Allah, this is the work of one who opposes the Book of Allah and the Sunnah of His Messenger, and opposes those who seek them and have interest in them. He forbids *al-ijtihād* and mandates *al-taqlīd*, thereby placing a barrier between those who [seek to] adhere to the religious law and the Sharīʿah, deceiving them in understanding and cognition as it was done by others amongst the *muqallids* of the other *madhhabs*. Rather, they exceeded them in extremism and partisanship, as mentioned previously.

وَمَعَ هَذَا فالأئمة قد صَرَّحُوا فِي كتبهمْ الفروعية والأصولية بتعداد علم الِاجْتِهَاد وَأَنَّهَا خَمْسَة وَأَنه يَكْفِي الْمُجْتَهد فِي كل فن مُخْتَصر من المختصرات، وَهَؤُلَاء المقلدة يعلمُونَ أَن كثيرا من الْعلمَاء الْعَالمين بِالْكتاب وَالسّنة المعاصرين لَهُم يعْرفُونَ من كل فن من الْفُنُون الْخَمْسَة أَضْعَاف أضعاف الْقدر الْمُعْتَبر ويعرفون علوما غير هَذِه الْعُلُوم. وهم وَإِن كَانُوا جُهَّالًا لَا يعْرفُونَ شَيْئا من المعارف لكِنهمْ يسْأَلُون أهل الْعلم عَن مقادير الْعلمَاء فيفيدونهم ذَلِك.

Despite this, the scholars have declared in their books of *uṣūl* and *furūʿ* the listing of the knowledge of *al-ijtihād* and that it consists of five[69]; and that a summarised text is sufficient for a *mujtahid* in every

69 One. He should possess knowledge of the texts of the Qur'ān and Sunnah. If he falls short in either of them, he is not a *mujtahid*; and it is not permis-

sible for him to perform *al-ijtihād*. It is not a condition that he must know all of the Qur'ān and Sunnah. Rather, he should know that which is related to rulings from them. Al-Ghazālī and Ibn al-'Arabī said, "That which is in the Mighty Book of this (i.e. *āyāt* of rulings) is about five hundred *āyāt* and the claim of exclusivity in this amount is only with regard to the apparent. Otherwise, in the Mighty Book, there are some *āyāt* from which multiples of legislative rulings can be derived from.' See *al-Baḥr al-Muḥīṭ* (6/199) and *al-Mustaṣfā* (4/6).

Two. He should be learned about the issues of consensus in order to not issue verdicts contrary to it, if he is one of those who uses the proof of consensus and considers it to be a legislative proof.

Three. He should be knowledgeable about the Arabic language to a level that would allow him to explain strange words that have been mentioned in the Qur'ān and Sunnah. It is not a condition that he should preserve them in his heart. Rather, what is given consideration is that he should be able to extract them from books of the scholars who are concerned with that.

Four. He should possess knowledge of the principles of jurisprudence due to its inclusion in what is required, and he should be versed in it and study both concise and lengthy works of this field as much as he can. This is because, this knowledge is the pillar and canopy of *al-ijtihād* and the foundation upon which the pillars of its building would rest. He should also look into every issue in a manner that would lead him to the truth in it, for if he does this, he will be able to refer the subsidiary issues to the fundamental ones with less work. But if he is deficient in this science, refutation will be difficult for him and he would wonder about in it and be confused. Al-Ghazālī said in *al-Mustaṣfā* (4/10), "The greatest sciences for *al-ijtihād* comprises of three fields: ḥadīth, language and the principles of *al-fiqh*."

Five. He should possess knowledge of what abrogates and what is abrogated in a manner that nothing is hidden from him of that, lest he becomes guilty of using what has been abrogated for a judgement.

The scholars differ on stipulating the condition of knowledge of subsidiary subject. These *muqallids* know that most of the scholars who know the Book and Sunnah—who are their contemporaries—understand each of the five aspects extremely well, and they have knowledge of sciences other than them. Even though they are ignorant and bereft of knowledge, they should ask the people of knowledge about the worth of the scholars and they will inform them of that.

وَبِهَذَا تعرف أنه لَا حَامِل لَهُم على ذَلِك إِلَّا مُجَرّد التعصب لمن قلدوه وَتجَاوزوا الْحَد فِي تَعْظِيمة وامتثال رَأْيه على حد لَا يُوجد عِنْدهم للصحابة بل لَا يُوجد عِنْدهم لكَلَام الله وَرَسُوله.

With this, the reader should know that nothing propels them towards this except mere partisanship to the one whom they are making *taqlīd* of; and they exceeded the limit in revering him and complying with his personal view to a level that they did not accord to the companions. In fact, they did not accord it to the words of Allah and His Messenger.

---

issues. A group among them, which include al-Ustādh Abu Isḥāq and al-Ustādh Abu Manṣūr held the view that it is a condition whilst others are of the view that it is not a condition.

Others consider the totality of the knowledge of *al-ijtihād* to be the knowledge of *al-jarḥ* (criticism) and *al-ta'dīl* (praise) and that it is like it but it falls under the knowledge of the Sunnah.

Others consider the totality of the knowledge of *al-ijtihād* to be the knowledge of *al-qiyās* with its conditions and pillars. They said: This is because it is the pivot of *al-ijtihād* and foundation of personal view. And from it emanated *fiqh* and it falls under the knowledge of principles of jurisprudence, for it is a door amongst its doors.

See *al-Iḥkām* of al-Āmidī (4/171), *al-Baḥr al-Muḥīṭ* (6/205) and *al-Mustaṣfā* (4/10-15).

[إِبْطَال التَّقْلِيد]

[Nullification of *al-Taqlīd*]

أخرج الْبَيْهَقِيّ وَابْن عبد الْبر عَن حُذَيْفَة بن الْيَمَان أَنه قيل لَهُ فِي قَوْله تَعَالَى: ﴿اتَّخَذُوا أَحْبَارَهُمْ وَرُهْبَانَهُمْ أَرْبَابًا مِّن دُونِ اللَّهِ﴾ أكانوا يَعْبُدُونَهُمْ فَقَالَ: لَا وَلَكِن يحلونَ لَهُم الْحَرَام فيحلونه ويحرمون عَلَيْهِم الْحَلَال فيحرمونه فصاروا بذلك أَرْبَابًا.

Al-Bayhaqī[70] and Ibn ʿAbd al-Barr[71] related from Ḥudhayfah ibn al-Yamān that it was said to him concerning the statement of Allah: **{They took their rabbis and their monks to be their lords besides Allah.}**[72] "Were they worshipping them?" He replied, "No, but they would make lawful to them the prohibited and they would consider it as lawful; and they would prohibit them the lawful and they would consider it as unlawful; thus, they became lords."

وَقد روى نَحْو ذَلِك مَرْفُوعا من حَدِيث عدي بن حَاتِم كَمَا قَالَ الْبَيْهَقِيّ وَأخرج نَحْو هَذَا التَّفْسِير ابْن عبد الْبر عَن بعض الصَّحَابَة بِإِسْنَاد مُتَّصِل بِهِ قَالَ: أما إنهم لَو أمروهم أَن يعبدوهم مَا أطاعوهم وَلَكنهُمْ أمروهم فَجعلُوا حَلَال الله حَرَامًا وَحَرَامه حَلَالا فأطاعوهم فَكَانَت تِلْكَ الربوبية.

70 *Al-Sunan al-Kubrā* (10/116).

71 *Jāmiʿ Bayān al-ʿIlm wa Faḍlihi* (2/975). It is a *ḥasan ḥadīth*.

72 Al-Tawbah: 31

A similar narration in *marfū'* form has been related from the ḥadīth of 'Adī ibn Ḥātim, as reported by al-Bayhaqī.[73] Ibn Abd al-Barr has recorded the like of this explanation from a companion with a connected chain.[74] He said, "If they had ordered them to worship them, they would not have obeyed them. But they commanded by making the lawful things of Allah unlawful and His unlawful to be lawful. So they obeyed them, and this falls under *al-rubūbiyyah* (Allah's lordship)."

وَمن ذلك قَوْله تَعَالَى: ﴿وَكَذَٰلِكَ مَآ أَرْسَلْنَا مِن قَبْلِكَ فِي قَرْيَةٍ مِّن نَّذِيرٍ إِلَّا قَالَ مُتْرَفُوهَا إِنَّا وَجَدْنَآ آبَاءَنَا عَلَىٰٓ أُمَّةٍ وَإِنَّا عَلَىٰٓ آثَارِهِم مُّقْتَدُونَ ۝٢٣ قَالَ أَوَلَوْ جِئْتُكُم بِأَهْدَىٰ مِمَّا وَجَدتُّمْ عَلَيْهِ آبَآءَكُمْ﴾ فآثروا الاقتداء بآبائهم قَالُوا ﴿إِنَّا بِمَآ أُرْسِلْتُم بِهِ كَافِرُونَ﴾.

Another example is the statement of Allah the Most High: **{"And similarly, We did not send before you any warner into a city except that its affluent said, "Indeed, we found our fathers upon a religion, and we are, in their footsteps, following." [Each warner] said, "Even if I brought you better guidance than that [religion] upon which you found your fathers?"}** They preferred following their fathers so much so that they said: **{"Indeed we, in that with which you were sent, are disbelievers."}**[75]

وَقَالَ عز وَجل: ﴿إِذْ تَبَرَّأَ الَّذِينَ اتُّبِعُوا مِنَ الَّذِينَ اتَّبَعُوا وَرَأَوُا الْعَذَابَ وَتَقَطَّعَتْ بِهِمُ الْأَسْبَابُ ۝١٦٦ وَقَالَ الَّذِينَ اتَّبَعُوا لَوْ أَنَّ لَنَا كَرَّةً فَنَتَبَرَّأَ مِنْهُمْ كَمَا تَبَرَّءُوا مِنَّا كَذَٰلِكَ

---

73 *Al-Sunan al-Kubrā* (10/116).

74 *Jāmi' Bayān al-'Ilm wa Faḍlihi* (2/976-977).

75 Al-Zukhruf: 23-24

﴿يُرِيهِمُ اللَّهُ أَعْمَالَهُمْ حَسَرَاتٍ عَلَيْهِمْ وَمَا هُم بِخَارِجِينَ مِنَ النَّارِ﴾

Allah also states: **{[And they should consider that] when those who have been followed disassociate themselves from those who followed [them], and they [all] see the punishment, and cut off from them are the ties [of relationship], those who followed will say, "If only we had another turn [at the worldly life] so we could disassociate ourselves from them as they have disassociated themselves from us." Thus will Allah show them their deeds as regrets upon them. And they are never to emerge from the Fire.}**[76]

وَقَالَ الله عز وَجل: ﴿مَا هَٰذِهِ التَّمَاثِيلُ الَّتِي أَنتُمْ لَهَا عَاكِفُونَ ۝٥٢ قَالُوا وَجَدْنَا آبَاءَنَا لَهَا عَابِدِينَ﴾.

Allah said: **{What are these images, to which you are devoted? They said, "We found our fathers worshipping them."}**[77]

وَقَالَ تعالى: ﴿إِنَّا أَطَعْنَا سَادَتَنَا وَكُبَرَاءَنَا فَأَضَلُّونَا السَّبِيلَا﴾.

The Most High said: **{And they will say: "Our Lord! Verily, we obeyed our chiefs and our great ones, and they misled us from the [Right] Way."}**[78]

فَهَذِهِ الْآيَات وَغَيرهَا مِمَّا ورد فِي مَعْنَاهُ ناعية على المقلدين مَا هم فِيهِ وَهِي وَإِن كَانَ تنزيلها فِي الْكفَّار لكنها قد صَحَّ تَأْوِيلهَا فِي المقلدين لِاتِّحَاد الْعلَّة، وَقد تقرر فِي الْأُصُول أَن الِاعْتِبَار بِعُمُوم اللَّفْظ لَا بِخُصُوص السَّبَب،

76 Al-Baqarah: 166-167
77 Al-Anbiyā: 52-53
78 Al-Ahzāb: 67

وَأن الحكم يَدُور مَعَ الْعلَّة وجودا وعدما. وَقد احْتج أهل الْعلم بِهَذِهِ الْآيَات على إبْطَال التَّقْلِيد وَلم يمنعهُم من ذَلِك كَونهَا نازلة فِي الْكفَّار.

These *āyāt* and others are amongst the *āyāt* which should serve as an omen to the *muqallids* for what they are upon. Though they were revealed concerning the disbelievers, interpreting them to apply to the *muqallids* is valid due to the concordance of the effective cause (*'illa*). It is established in *al-uṣūl* that consideration should be given to the general wording and not the particular cause; and that the ruling depends on its reason (*'illa*); if the reason is present, the ruling applies.[79] The people of knowledge have used these *āyāt* as proof for the nullity of *al-taqlīd*, and the fact that it was revealed concerning the disbelievers did not inhibit them from this.

وَأخرج ابْن عبد الْبر بِإِسْنَاد مُتَّصِل بمعَاذ رَضِي الله عَنهُ أَنه قَالَ: إن وراءكم فتْنا يكثر فِيهَا المَال وَيفتح فِيهَا الْقُرْآن حَتَّى يقرأه الْمُؤمن وَالْمُنَافِق وَالْمَرْأَة وَالصَّبِيّ وَالْأسود والأحمر فيوشك أحدهم أَن يَقُول قد قَرَأت الْقُرْآن فَمَا أَظن يتبعوني حَتَّى أبتدع لَهُم غَيره فإياكم وَمَا ابتدع فَإِن كل بِدعَة ضَلَالَة ...

Ibn 'Abd al-Barr reported with a chain connected to Mu'ādh that he said, "Behind you are trials. Wealth will be in abundance and the Qur'ān will be opened so much so that a believer, a hypocrite, woman, a child, the black and white will recite it. A time will come when one of them will say, 'I have read the Qur'ān and I do not think they will follow me until I introduce other than it to them.' So, beware

79 See *Irshād al-Fuḥūl* (p. 699).

of what has been invented for every innovation is misguidance..."[80]

وَأَخرج أَيْضا عَن ابْن عَبَّاس أَنه قَالَ: وِيل لِلأَتباع من عثرات الْعَالم قيل
كَيفَ ذَلِك؟ قَالَ يَقُول الْعَالم شَيْئا بِرَأْيِه ثمَّ يجد من هُوَ أَعلم بِرَسُول الله
صلى الله عَلَيْهِ وَآله وَسلم مِنْهُ فَيَترك قَوْله، ثمَّ يمْضِي الأَتباع.

Ibn 'Abd al-Barr also reported from Ibn 'Abbās that he said, "Woe to those who follow after the slips of the scholar." They asked, "How is that?" He replied, "The scholar says something based upon his personal opinion, then he finds someone who is more knowledgeable [in the Sunnah] of the Messenger of Allah ﷺ than him and he abandons his view. However, those who imitate him keep [following his prior view.]"[81]

وَأَخرج أَيْضا عَن عَلِيّ بن أَبِي طَالب رَضِي الله عَنهُ أَنه قَالَ: يَا كميل إِن
هَذِه الْقُلُوب أَوعية فَخَيرهَا أَوعاها للخير، وَالنَّاس ثَلَاثَة: فعالم رباني ومتعلم
على سَبِيل نجاة وهمج رعاع أَتبَاع كل ناعق لم يستضيئوا بِنور الْعلم وَلم
يلجأوا إِلَى ركن وثيق.

Ibn 'Abd al-Barr also reported that 'Alī ibn Abī Ṭālib said, "O Kumayl, these hearts are containers, and the best of them are those which retain the most good. People are of three categories: The nurturing scholar, the student on the path of salvation and the riffraff of society, who follow every crowing of crows, have never sought enlightenment through the light of knowledge nor turned to a strong

80 *Jāmiʿ Bayān al-ʿIlm wa Faḍlihi* (2/981, no. 1871).
81 *Jāmiʿ Bayān al-ʿIlm wa Faḍlihi* (2/984, no. 1877).

refuge."[82]

وَأخرج عَنهُ أَيْضا أَنه قَالَ: إِيَّاكُمْ والاستنان بِالرِّجَالِ فَإِن الرجل يعْمل بِعَمَل أهل الْجنَّة ثمَّ يَنْقَلِب لعلم الله فِيهِ بِعَمَل أهل النَّار فَيَمُوت وَهُوَ من أهل النَّار.

Ibn 'Abd al-Barr also related that he said, "Beware of copying men, for a man may perform the deeds of the people of Paradise, then change based upon Allah's knowledge and perform the actions of the people of Hell. Then he will die and be amongst the people of Hell."[83]

وَأخرج عَن ابْن مَسْعُود أَنه قَالَ: أَلا لَا يقلدن أحدكُم دينه رجلا إِن آمن آمن وَإِن كفر كفر فإنه لا أسوة فِي الشَّرّ.

Ibn 'Abd al-Barr related that Ibn Mas'ūd said, "Nay! None of you should blindly follow his religion from any man; if he is saved, he is saved, and if he disbelieves, he disbelieves. There is no example to be followed in evil."[84]

وروى ابْن عبد الْبر بِإِسْنَادِهِ إِلَى عَوْف بن مَالك الاشجعي قَالَ: قَالَ رَسُول الله صلى الله عَلَيْهِ وَآله وَسلم: ((تفترق أمتِي على بضع وَسبعين فرقة

---

82 *Jāmi' Bayān al-'Ilm wa Faḍlihi* (2/984, no. 1878) with a *ḍa'īf jiddan* chain. Its chain contains Abu Ḥamzah al-Thumālī whose name is Thābit ibn Abu Ṣafiyyah. He is *ḍa'īf* and a Rāfiḍī. His *shaykh,* Abd al-Raḥmān ibn Jundub al-Fazārī is *majhūl* (unknown), as stated by al-Ḥāfiẓ in *al-Lisān* (3/408).
83 *Jāmi' Bayān al-'Ilm wa Faḍlihi* (2/987, no. 1881) with a *ḍa'īf* chain.
84 *Jāmi' Bayān al-'Ilm wa Faḍlihi* (2/988, no. 1882).

أعظمها فتْنَة قوم يقيسون الدّين برأيهم يحرمُونَ مَا أحل الله وَيحلون بِهِ مَا حرم الله)). وَأخرجه الْبَيْهَقِيّ أَيْضا.

Ibn ʿAbd al-Barr related with a chain traced to ʿAwf ibn Mālik al-Ashjaʿī that he said, "The Messenger of Allah ﷺ said, 'My Ummah will be divided into seventy odd sects and the greatest of them in trials are those who interpret the religion with their personal opinion, prohibiting what Allah has legalised and permitting what Allah has prohibited."[85] Al-Bayhaqī also reported it.[86]

قَالَ ابْن الْقيم بعد إِخْرَاجه من طرق: هَؤُلَاءِ - يعني رجال إِسْنَاده - كلهم ثِقَات حفاظ إِلَّا حريز بن عُثْمَان فَإِنَّهُ كَانَ منحرفا عَن عَليّ، وَمَعَ هَذَا احْتج بِهِ البُخَارِيّ فِي صَحِيحه. وَقد روى عَنهُ أيضا أَنه تَبرأ مِمَّا نسب إِلَيْهِ من الانحراف.

After mentioning it through different chains, Ibn al-Qayyim said, "The men in its chain are all trustworthy and *ḥuffāẓ* except Harīz ibn ʿUthmān, for he was against ʿAlī. Despite this, al-Bukhārī depended upon him in his *Ṣaḥīḥ.*[87] And it has been related from him that he disassociated himself from the deviation of *inḥirāf* that has been attributed to him."

وروى ابْن عبد الْبر بِإِسْنَادِهِ إِلَى أبي هُرَيْرَة قَالَ: قَالَ رَسُول الله صلى الله

85 *Jāmiʿ Bayān al-ʿIlm wa Faḍlihi* (2/1039 no 1997).

86 *Al-Madkhal* (p. 188, no. 207). I say: It was recorded by al-Ḥākim in *al-Mustadrak* (4/430) who graded it as *ṣaḥīḥ* upon the conditions of the two *shaykhs*, and al-Khaṭīb in *al-Faqīh wa 'l-Muttafaqih* (no. 473) and *Tārīkh Baghdād* (3/307-311), it is a *ḍaʿīf* hadith.

87 In *Hadī al-Sārī* (p. 396).

عَلَيْهِ وَآله وَسلم: ((تعْمل هَذِه الْأمة بُرْهَة بِسنة رَسُول الله ثمَّ يعْملُونَ بِالرَّأْيِ فَإِذا فعلوا ذَلِك فقد ضلوا)). وَأخرجه أَيْضا بِإِسْنَاد آخر فِيهِ جبارَة ابْن الْمُغلس وَفِيه مقَال.

Ibn 'Abd al-Barr related with a chain to Abu Hurayrah that he said, "The Messenger of Allah ﷺ said, "This Ummah will act upon the Sunnah of Allah's Messenger for a short while and then they will act upon their personal opinion. When they do that, they will have gone astray."[88] He also recorded it with another chain which contains Jubārah ibn Mughallis and some have expressed reservations about his reliability.[89]

وروى أَيْضا بِإِسْنَاد إِلَى عمر بن الْخطاب أَنه قَالَ وَهُوَ على الْمِنْبَر: يَا أَيهَا النَّاس إِن الرَّأْي إِنَّمَا كَانَ من رَسُول الله صلى الله عَلَيْهِ وَآله وَسلم مصيبا لِأَن الله كَانَ يرِيه، وَإِنَّمَا هُوَ منا الظَّنّ والتكلف. وَأخرجه أيضا الْبَيْهَقِيّ فِي الْمدْخل. وروى ابْن عبد الْبر بِإِسْنَادِهِ إِلَى عمر أَيْضا أَنه قَالَ أهل الرَّأْي أَعدَاء السّنَن أعيتهم الْأَحَادِيث أَن يعوها وتفلتت مِنْهُم أَن يرووها فَاشتقُوا الرَّأْي.

He also recorded with a chain to 'Umar ibn al-Khaṭṭāb that he said whilst upon the pulpit, "O people, the personal opinion emanating from the Messenger of Allah ﷺ is always correct, due to Allah's inspiration. But personal opinion from us is mere assumption and

88 *Jāmi' Bayān al-'Ilm wa Faḍlihi* (2/1039, no. 1998).
89 *Jāmi' Bayān al-'Ilm wa Faḍlihi* (2/1040, no. 1999); it is a *ḍa'īf* ḥadīth.

guesswork."[90] Al-Bayhaqī also reported it in *al-Madkhal*.[91] Ibn 'Abd al-Barr related with a chain to 'Umar that he also said, "The people of opinion are the enemies of the Sunnah; the *aḥādīth* thwarted their effort to *memorise* them and escaped from being narrated by them. So fear personal opinion."[92]

وروى ابْن عبد الْبر بِإِسْنَادِهِ إِلَيْهِ أَيْضا قَالَ: اتَّقوا الرَّأْي فِي دينكُمْ.

Ibn 'Abd al-Barr also reported that he said, "Fear personal opinion in your religion."[93]

وَرُوِيَ عَنهُ أَيْضا قَالَ إِن أَصْحَاب الرَّأْي أَعدَاء السّنَن أعيتهم أَن يحفظوها وتفلتت مِنْهُم أَن يعوها واستحيوا حِين يسْأَلُوا أَن يَقُولُوا لَا نعلم فعارضوا السّنَن برأيهم فإياكم وإياهم.

He also reported that he said, "The adherents of personal opinion are the enemies of the Sunnah, it thwarted their effort of memorising it and it escaped from them lest they retain it. They are shy to say we do not know when they are asked, thus, they contradicted the Sunnah with their opinion. So, beware of them."[94]

وَأخرج ابْن عبد الْبر بِإِسْنَادِهِ إِلَى ابْن مَسْعُود قَالَ: لَيْسَ عَام إِلَّا الَّذِي بعده شَرّ مِنْهُ، لَا أَقُول عَام أمطر من عَام وَلَا عَام أخصب من عَام ولا أمير خير من أَمِير وَلَكِن ذهَاب خياركم وعلمائكم ثمَّ يحدث قوم يقيسون الْأُمُور

---

90 *Jāmi' Bayān al-'Ilm wa Faḍlihi* (2/1041, no. 2000); it is a *ṣaḥīḥ* narration.
91 P. 189, no. 210, and he reported it in *al-Sunan al-Kubrā* (10/117).
92 *Jāmi' Bayān al-'Ilm wa Faḍlihi* (2/1041, no. 2001); it is a *ṣaḥīḥ* narration.
93 *Jāmi' Bayān al-'Ilm wa Faḍlihi* (2/1041, no. 2002).
94 *Jāmi' Bayān al-'Ilm wa Faḍlihi* (2/1042, no. 2003).

برأيهم فيهدم الْإِسْلَام ويثلم. وَأخرجه الْبَيْهَقِيّ بِإِسْنَاده رِجَاله ثِقَات.

Ibn 'Abd al-Barr recorded with a chain to Ibn Mas'ūd that he said, "There will be no year except that which is after it is worse than it; I am not saying a year will be more rainy than a year, nor that a year will be more fertile than a year, nor that a leader will be better than a leader; rather, [I am speaking in regards to] the departure of your best people and your scholars. Then some people will emerge interpreting the religion with their personal opinion, thereby destroying Islam and damaging it."[95] Al-Bayhaqī reported it with its chain and its men are *thiqāt* (reliable narrators).[96]

وَأخرج أَيْضا ابْن عبد الْبر عَن ابْن عَبَّاس قَالَ: إِنَّمَا هُوَ كتاب الله وَسنة رَسُوله فَمن قَالَ بعد ذَلِك بِرَأْيِهِ فَمَا أدري أَفِي حَسَنَاته أم فِي سيئاته.

Ibn 'Abd al-Barr reported that Ibn 'Abbās said, "It is only the Book of Allah and the Sunnah of his Messenger. Whoever says anything thereafter based upon his personal opinion, I do not know whether it is from his good deeds or evil deeds."[97]

وَأخرج أَيْضا عَن ابْن عَبَّاس أَنه قَالَ: تمتّع رَسُول الله صلى الله عَلَيْهِ وَآله وَسلم فَقَالَ عُرْوَة: نهى أَبُو بكر وَعمر عَن الْمُتْعَة فَقَالَ ابْن عَبَّاس: أَرَاهُم سيهلكون أَقُول قَالَ رَسُول الله صلى الله عَلَيْهِ وَآله وَسلم وَيَقُول قَالَ أَبُو بكر وَعمر.

He also related that Ibn 'Abbās said, "The Messenger of Allah ﷺ

95 *Jāmi' Bayān al-'Ilm wa Faḍlihi* (2/1043, no. 2008).

96 *Al-Madkhal* (p. 186, no. 205).

97 *Jāmi' Bayān al-'Ilm wa Faḍlihi* (2/1046, no. 2013) with a *ḍa'īf isnād*.

performed temporary marriage." 'Urwah then said, "Abu Bakr and 'Umar forbade temporary marriage." Ibn 'Abbās replied, "I am sure they will perish, I say that the Messenger of Allah ﷺ said, but they counter with Abu Bakr and 'Umar said."[98]

وَأخرج أَيْضا عَن أبي الدَّرْدَاء أَنه قَالَ: من يعذرني من مُعَاوِيَة أحدثه عَن رَسُول الله صلى الله عَلَيْهِ وَآله وَسلم ويخبرني بِرَأْيِه وَمثله عَن عبَادَة.

Ibn 'Abd al-Barr related from Abu Dardā that he said, "Who will apologise to me for Mu'āwiyah. I narrate from the Messenger of Allah ﷺ to him and I am being informed of his personal opinion."[99] 'Ubādah has a similar narration.

وَأخرج أَيْضا عَن عمر رَضِي الله عَنهُ قَالَ: السّنة مَا سنه رَسُول الله صلى الله عَلَيْهِ وَآله وَسلم لَا تجْعَلُوا خطأ الرَّأْي سنة للْأمة.

He also related from 'Umar that he said, "The Sunnah is that which emanates from the Messenger of Allah's ﷺ way. Do not consider a mistaken opinion to be a *sunnah* for the Ummah."[100]

وَأخرج أَيْضا عَن عُرْوَة بن الزبير أَنه قَالَ: لم يزل أَمر بني إِسْرَائِيل مُسْتَقِيمًا حَتَّى أدْركْت فيهم المولدون أَبنَاء سَبَايَا الْأُمَم فَأَخذُوا فيهم بِالرَّأْيِ فأضلوا بني إِسْرَائِيل.

He also reported from 'Urwah ibn al-Zubayr that he said, "The affair of Banī Isrā'īl did not cease to be upright until those who were given

98 *Jāmi' Bayān al-'Ilm wa Faḍlihi* (2/210, no. 2381).
99 *Jāmi' Bayān al-'Ilm wa Faḍlihi* (2/1210, no. 2379).
100 *Jāmi' Bayān al-'Ilm wa Faḍlihi* (2/1047, no. 2014).

birth by the female slaves of other nations emerged amongst them. So, they took to personal opinion, and so Banī Isrāʿīl went astray."[101]

وَأخرج أَيْضا عَن الشّعبِيّ أنه قَالَ: إيَّاكُمْ والمقايسة فوالَّذِي نَفسِي بِيَدِهِ لَئِن أَخَذْتُم بالمقايسة لتحلن الْحَرَام ولتحرمن الْحَلَال، وَلَكِن مَا بَلغَكُمْ مِمَّن حفظ عَن أَصْحَاب رَسُول الله صلى الله عَلَيْهِ وَآله وَسلم فاحفظوه. وروى ابْن عبد الْبر أَيْضا ذمّ الرَّأْي والتبرؤ مِنْهُ والتنفير عَنهُ بِكَلِمَات تقَارب هَذِه الْكَلِمَات عَن مَسْرُوق وَابْن سِيرِين، وَعبد الله بن الْمُبَارك، وسُفْيَان، وَشُرَيْح، وَالْحسن الْبَصْرِيّ، وَابْن شهَاب.

He also related that Al-Shaʿbī said, "Beware of *qiyās* (deductive analogy). By the One in whose hand lies my soul, if you hold on to analogy you will surely permit the unlawful and prohibit the lawful. However whatever reaches you from the companions of the Messenger of Allah ﷺ, preserve it."[102] Ibn ʿAbd al-Barr has also reported the condemnation of personal opinion and disassociation from it with statements similar to these from: Masrūq,[103] Ibn Sīrīn,[104] ʿAbdullāh

---

101 *Jāmiʿ Bayān al-ʿIlm wa Faḍlihi* (2/1047, no. 2015) with a *ṣaḥīḥ isnād*.

102 *Jāmiʿ Bayān al-ʿIlm wa Faḍlihi* (2/1047, no. 2016) with an *isnād* which is *ḍaʿīf jiddan*.

103 No. (2018) with a *ḍaʿīf isnād*. On the authority of al-Shaʿbī from Masrūq who said, "I do not make analogy of anything with something.' He was asked why and he said, 'Out of fear that my feet should slip."

104 No. (2019, 2020), both *isnāds* are *ṣaḥīḥ*. Ibn Sīrīn said, "They used to hold that it is on the path so long as it is upon the narrations."

ibn al-Mubārak,[105] Sufyān,[106] Shurayḥ,[107] al-Ḥasan al-Baṣrī[108] and Ibn Shihāb.[109]

وَذكر الطَّبَرِيّ فِي كتاب تَهْذِيب الْآثَار لَهُ بِإِسْنَادِهِ إِلَى مَالك قَالَ: قَالَ
مَالك: قبض رَسُول الله صلى الله عَلَيْهِ وَآله وَسلم وَقد تمّ هَذَا الْأَمر
واستكمل فَإِنَّمَا يَنْبَغِي أَن تتبع آثَار رَسُول الله صلى الله عَلَيْهِ وَآله وَسلم
وَلَا تتبع الرَّأْي فَإِنَّهُ مَتى اتبع الرَّأْي جَاءَ رجل آخر أقوى فِي الرَّأْي مِنْك
فاتبعته فَأَنت كلما جَاءَ رجل غَلَبَك اتبعته. أرى هَذَا لَا يتم.

Al-Ṭabarī mentioned in his book, *Tahdhīb al-Āthā*r with a chain to Mālik that he said, "The Messenger of Allah ﷺ passed away with this religion completed and perfected. So it is necessary for you to follow the narrations of the Messenger of Allah ﷺ and not follow personal opinion, because whenever personal opinions are followed,

105 No. (2021) with a *ṣaḥīḥ isnād* from 'Abdullāh ibn al-Mubārak who said to a man, 'If you are tested with judgeship, stick to the narrations."

106 No. (2022) with a *ṣaḥīḥ isnād*. Sufyān said, "The religion is only with the narrations. The religion is only with the narrations."

107 No. (2024) on the authority of Shurayḥ who said, "The Sunnah has preceded your analogy. So follow and do not innovate, for you will never go astray so long as you cling to the narrations."

108 No. (2026). Ḥasan said, "Those who came before you were destroyed when the paths became numerous to them and they deviated from the path. They abandoned the narrations and talked about the religion with their personal opinion. So they went astray and led others astray."

109 No. (2028) with a *ḍa'īf isnād*. Ibn Shihāb said—whilst he was mentioning what happened to the people as a result of personal opinion (*al-rảy*, or rational discretion) and their abandonment of the Sunnah, "The Jews and Christians were only stripped of the knowledge that was in their possession when they gave preference to *al-rảy* and held onto it."

another man will come who is stronger in opinion than you and you will follow him. Whenever a person comes and overpowers you, you will follow him. And I view that this cycle will not come to an end."[110]

وروى ابْن عبد الْبر عَن مَالك بن دِينَار أَنه قَالَ لِقَتَادَة: أَتَدْرِي أَي علم رفعت، قُمْت بَين الله وبين وعباده، فَقلت هَذَا لَا يصلح وَهَذَا يصلح.

Ibn 'Abd al-Barr related from Mālik ibn Dīnār that he said to Qatādah, "Do you know which is the knowledge that will elevate you? Stand up between Allah and His slaves and say 'this is not good' and 'this is good'."[111]

وروى ابْن عبد الْبر أَيْضا عَن الأوزاعي أَنه قَالَ: عَلَيْك بآثار من سلف وَإِن رفضك النَّاس وَإِيَّاك وآراء الرِّجَال وَإِن زخرفوا لَك القَوْل.

Ibn 'Abd al-Barr also related from al-Awzā'ī that he said, "Stick to the narrations of those who have preceded, even if the people reject you; and beware of the personal opinions of men, even if they beautify the speech to you."[112]

وَرُوِيَ أَيْضا عَن مَالك أَنه قَالَ: مَا عَلمته فَقل بِهِ وَدلّ عَلَيْهِ وَمَا لم تعلم فاسكت وَإِيَّاك أَن تقلد النَّاس قلادة سوء.

He also recorded that Mālik said, "Whatever you know, speak about it and guide to it; and whatever you do not know be silent regarding

110 Ibn 'Abd al-Barr attributed it to him in *Jāmi' Bayān al-'Ilm* (no. 2072). Ibn 'Abd al-Barr recorded it in *Jāmi' Bayān al-'Ilm* (2/1080, no. 2117) with a *ḍa'īf isnād*.

111 *Jāmi' Bayān al-'Ilm wa Faḍlihi* (no. 2074).

112 *Jāmi' Bayān al-'Ilm wa Faḍlihi* (no. 2077) with a *ḥasan isnād*.

it. Beware of blind following the people in an evil manner."[113]

وَرُوِيَ أَيْضا عن القعْنبِي أَنه دخل على مَالك فَوَجَدَهُ يبكي فَقَالَ: مَا الَّذِي يبكيك؟ فَقَالَ: يَا ابْن قعنب إنا لله على مَا فرط مني، لَيْتَني جلدت بِكُل كلمة تَكَلَّمت بهَا فِي هَذَا الْأَمر سَوْطًا وَلم يكن فرط مني مَا فرط من هَذَا الرَّأْي وَهَذِه الْمسَائِل وَقد كَانَت لي سَعَة فِيمَا سبقت إِلَيْهِ.

He also related from al-Qaʿnabī that he entered upon Mālik and met him weeping. He asked, "Why do you weep?" He replied, "O son of Qaʿnab! Allah shall judge me for what occurred from me without careful attention. Would that I be flogged for every word I uttered concerning this religion instead of all that I have uttered inadvertently using my own deduction and in discussing these issues whilst I could have refrained as others had preceded me in speaking."[114]

وَرُوِيَ أَيْضا عَن سَحْنُون أَنه قَالَ: مَا أَدْرِي مَا هَذَا الرَّأْي سفكت بِهِ الدِّمَاء واستحلت بِهِ الْفروج واستحقت بِهِ الْحُقُوق.

He also related from Saḥnūn that he said, "I do not know what this *rāy* (personal opinion) is, which has caused bloodshed, legalised the private parts and made rights to be entitled."[115]

وَرُوِيَ أَيْضا عَن أَيُّوب أَنه قيل لَهُ مَا لك لَا تنظر فِي الرَّأْي؟ فَقَالَ أَيُّوب قيل للحمار مَا لَك لَا تجتر؟ قَالَ أكره مضغ الْبَاطِل.

113 *Jāmiʿ Bayān al-ʿIlm wa Faḍlihi* (no. 2080) with a *ṣaḥīḥ isnād*.
114 *Jāmiʿ Bayān al-ʿIlm wa Faḍlihi* (no. 2081) and it is a *ṣaḥīḥ* narration.
115 *Jāmiʿ Bayān al-ʿIlm wa Faḍlihi* (no. 2082) and it is a *ṣaḥīḥ* narration.

He also related from Ayyūb that it was said to him, "Why do you not look into *al-rảy* (personal opinion)?" Ayyūb said, "It was said to the donkey, 'Why do you not ruminate?' And he replied, 'I hate to chew falsehood.'"[116]

وَرُوِيَ عَن الشّعبِيّ أَيْضا أَنه قَالَ: وَالله لقد بغض إِلَيّ هَؤُلَاءِ الْقَوْم الْمَسْجِد حَتَّى لَهو أبْغض إِلَيّ من كناسَة دَارِي، قيل لَهُ من هم. قَالَ هَؤُلَاءِ الآرائيون وَكَانَ فِي ذَلِك الْمَسْجِد الحكم وَحَمَّاد وأصحابهم.

He also related from al-Sha'bī that he said, "By Allah, indeed these people made me dislike [attending] the *masjid* to the extent it has become more detested to me than the refuse of my house." He was asked, "Who are they?" He replied, "The people of opinion." And in that *masjid* were al-Ḥakam, Ḥammād and their companions."[117]

وَذكر ابْن وهب أَنه سمع مَالِكًا يَقُول: لم يكن من أَمر النَّاس وَلَا من مضى من سلفنا وَلَا أدْركْت أحدا اقْتدي بِهِ يَقُول فِي شَيْء هَذَا حَلَال وَهَذَا حرَام مَا كَانُوا يجترئون على ذَلِك وَإِنَّمَا كَانُوا يَقُولُونَ نكره هَذَا ونرى هَذَا حسنا وَيتقى هَذَا وَلَا نرى هَذَا. وَزَاد بعض أَصْحَاب مَالك عَنهُ فِي هَذَا الْكَلَام أَنه قَالَ: وَلَا يَقُولُونَ حَلَال وَلَا حرَام. أما سَمِعت قَول الله عز وَجل ﴿قُلْ أَرَأَيْتُم مَّا أَنزَلَ اللهُ لَكُم مِّن رِّزْقٍ فَجَعَلْتُم مِّنْهُ حَرَامًا وَحَلَالًا قُلْ آللهُ أَذِنَ لَكُمْ أَمْ عَلَى اللهِ تَفْتَرُونَ﴾ الْحَلَال مَا أحله الله وَرَسُوله وَالْحرَام مَا حرمه الله وَرَسُوله.

116 *Jāmi' Bayān al-'Ilm wa Faḍlihi* (no. 2085) with a *ṣaḥīḥ isnād*.
117 *Jāmi' Bayān al-'Ilm wa Faḍlihi* (no. 2089) with a *ḍa'īf isnād*.

Ibn Wahb mentioned that he heard Mālik say, "It is not from the affairs of the people, nor those who have preceded amongst our pious predecessors and I have not met anyone whom I follow saying concerning anything: this is lawful and this is unlawful. They did not engage in that, rather they used to say, 'We dislike this,' 'We hold that this is good,' 'This is proper,' and 'We do not hold that this is good.'"[118] Some of the companions of Mālik added to this statement that he said regarding this, "They do not say this is lawful nor unlawful. Did you not hear the statement of Allah: **{Say, "Have you seen what Allah has sent down to you of provision of which you have made [some] lawful and [some] unlawful?" Say, "Has Allah permitted you [to do so], or do you invent [something] about Allah?"}**[119] The lawful is what Allah and His Messenger have permitted, whilst the unlawful is that which Allah and His Messenger have prohibited."

وروى ابْن عبد الْبر أَيْضا عَن أَحْمد بن حَنْبَل أَنه قَالَ: رَأْي الأوزاعي ورأي مَالك ورأي أبي حنيفَة كُله رَأْي وَهُوَ عِنْدِي سَوَاء وَإِنَّمَا الْحجَّة فِي الْآثَار.

Ibn 'Abd al-Barr reported from Aḥmad ibn Ḥanbal that he said, "The opinion of al-Awzā'ī, the opinion of Mālik and the opinion of Abu Ḥanīfah are all opinions. They are all equal to me; the proof is only in the narrations."[120]

وَرُوِيَ أَيْضا عَن سهل بن عبد الله التستري أَنه قَالَ: مَا أحدث أحد فِي الْعلم شيئا إِلَّا سُئِلَ عَنهُ يَوْم الْقِيَامَة فَإِن وَافق السّنة سلم وَإِلَّا فَهُوَ العطب.

He also related that Sahl ibn 'Abdullāh al-Tastarī said, "No one in-

118 *Jāmi' Bayān al-'Ilm wa Faḍlihi* (no. 2091) with a *ḍa'īf isnād*.
119 Yūnus: 59
120 *Jāmi' Bayān al-'Ilm wa Faḍlihi* (no. 2107) with a *ṣaḥīḥ isnād*.

troduces anything in knowledge except that he will be asked about it on the Day of Resurrection; if it conforms to the Sunnah, he is saved, otherwise he is ruined."[121]

وَقَالَ الشَّافِعِي فِي تَفْسِيرِ الْبِدْعَة الْمَذْكُورَة فِي الْحَدِيث الثَّابِت فِي الصَّحِيح مِن قَوْلِه صلى الله عَلَيْهِ وَآلَه وَسلم: ((خير الْحَدِيث كتاب الله وَخير الْهدي هدي مُحَمَّد، وَشر الْأُمُور محدثاتها وكل بِدعَة ضَلَالَة)): إن المحدثات مِن الْأُمُور ضَرْبَان:

Al-Shāfiʿī stated in explanation of the term *al-bidʿah* (innovation) that is mentioned in a ḥadīth established in *al-Ṣaḥīḥ*, wherein the Prophet ﷺ stated, "The best of speech is the Book of Allah and the best guidance is the guidance of Muḥammad; and the worst of affairs are the newly invented matters. And every innovation is misguidance"[122]: Newly invented matters are of two types:

أَحدهمَا: مَا أَحدث يُخَالف كتابا أَو سنة أَو أثرا أَو إِجْمَاعًا فَهَذِهِ الْبِدْعَة الضَّلَالَة.

First: Whatever is introduced into the religion which contradicts the Qurʾān, Sunnah, *āthār* (narrations) or consensus; this is a misguided innovation.

وَالثَّانِيَة: مَا أَحدث مِن الْخَيْر لَا خلاف فِيهِ لوَاحِد مِن هَذِهِ الْأمة وَهَذِه محدثة غير مذمومة. وَقد قَالَ عمر فِي قيام شهر رَمَضَان نعمت الْبِدْعَة

121 *Jāmiʿ Bayān al-ʿIlm wa Faḍlihi* (no. 2117).
122 Reported by Muslim in his *Ṣaḥīḥ*, (no. 592/867)

هَذِه.

Second: Whatever is introduced of good in which there is no disagreement regarding it from anyone amongst the Ummah; this newly invented matter is not blameworthy. [This is because] 'Umar stated regarding the night prayer in Ramaḍān, "What an excellent innovation this is."[123]

وَأخرج الْبَيْهَقِيّ فِي الْمدْخل عَن ابْن مَسْعُود أَنه قَالَ: اتبعُوا وَلَا تبتدعوا فقد كفيتم.

Al-Bayhaqī reported in *al-Madkhal* from Ibn Mas'ūd that he said, "Follow and do not innovate, for indeed you have been sufficed."[124]

وَأخرج عَن عبَادَة بن الصَّامِت قَالَ: سَمِعت رَسُول الله صلى الله عَلَيْهِ وَآله وَسلم يَقُول: ((يكون بعدِي رجال يعرفونكم مَا تنكرون وَيُنْكِرُونَ عَلَيْكُم مَا تعرفُون فَلَا طَاعَة لمن عصى الله، وَلَا تعملوا برأيكم)).

He also reported that 'Ubādah ibn al-Ṣāmit said, "I heard the Messenger of Allah ﷺ state, 'There will be some men after me who will approve for you what you do not accept and condemn for you what you approve. There is no obedience to whoever disobeys Allah and do not act upon your personal opinion.'"[125]

---

123 Mālik reported this narration in *al-Muwatta* (1/114) and al-Bukhārī in his *Ṣaḥīḥ* (no. 2010).

124 P. 186, no. 204 with a *ṣaḥīḥ isnād*. I say: al-Ṭabarānī recorded it in *al-Kabīr* (9/198, no. 8770) and al-Haythamī cited it in *al-Majma'* (1/181) and stated that its men are *ṣaḥīḥ*.

125 Reported by al-Bayhaqī in *al-Madkhal* (p. 187, no. 206). I say: Aḥmad (5/325) recorded a similar version from the path of al-Ḥakam ibn Nāfi'—Abu

وَأَخْرَجَ عَنْ عمر أَنه قَالَ: اتَّقوا الرَّأْي فِي دينكُمْ.

He related from ʿUmar that he said, "Fear personal opinion in your religion."[126]

وَأَخْرَجَ عَنْهُ أَيْضا بِسَنَد رِجَاله ثِقَات أَنه قَالَ يَا أَيهَا النَّاس اتهموا الرَّأْي على الدّين.

He also related from ʿUmar with a chain whose narrators are *thiqāt* that he said, "O people, avoid personal opinion in the religion."[127]

---

al-Yamān—Ismāʿīl ibn Iyāsh—ʿAbdullāh ibn Khuthaym and its *isnād* is *ḍaʿīf* due to the weakness of Ismāʿīl ibn Iyāsh in his narrations from other than the people of his land; and this is one of them.

ʿAbdullāh ibn al-Imām Ahmad reported it in *Zawāʾid al-Musnad* (5/329) from the path of Suwayd ibn Saʿīd—Yaḥyā ibn Sulaym—Ibn Khuthaym—Ismāʿīl ibn ʿUbayd ibn Rifāʿah—his father ʿUbayd—ʿUbādah ibn al-Ṣāmit. Al-Ḥākim recorded it in *al-Mustadrak* (3/356) from the path of ʿAbdullāh ibn Wāqid—ʿAbdullāh ibn ʿUthmān ibn Khuthaym—Abu 'l-Zubayr—Jābir—ʿUbādah. Al-Ḥākim said, "The *isnād* of this ḥadīth is *ṣaḥīḥ* but they [al-Bukhārī and Muslim] did not record it. Al-Dhahabī said, "'Abdullāh ibn Wāqid is alone in reporting it and he is weak."

It has a *shāhid* (witnessing report) through the ḥadīth of Ibn Masʿūd, as recorded by Aḥmad (1/399-400) and Ibn Mājah (2/956, no. 2865) with the wording, "Your affairs after me will be with men who will extinguish the Sunnah and act upon innovation. They will delay the prayer from its time." I said, "O Messenger of Allah, what should I do if I meet them?" He said, "O ʿAbdullāh, are you asking me what you should do? There is no obedience to the one who disobeys Allah." I say: The ḥadīth of ʿUbādah ibn al-Ṣāmit is *ṣaḥīḥ* and the ḥadīth of Ibn Masʿūd is also *ṣaḥīḥ*. See *al-Ṣaḥīḥah* (no. 590).

126 Al-Bayhaqī in *al-Madkhal* (p. 190, no. 210).
127 Al-Bayhaqī in *al-Madkhal* (p. 192-193, no. 217, 218).

وَأخرج أَيْضا عَن عَليّ بن أبي طَالب أَنه قَالَ: لَو كَانَ الدّين بِالرَّأْيِ لَكَانَ بَاطِن الْخُفّ أَحَق بِالْمَسْحِ من ظاهرهما وَلَكِن رَأَيْت رَسُول الله صلى الله عَلَيْهِ وَآله وَسلم يمسح على ظاهرهما. وَهُوَ أثر مَشْهُور أخرجه غير الْبَيْهَقِيّ أَيْضا.

Al-Bayhaqī related from ʿAlī ibn Abī Ṭālib that he said, "If the religion was based upon personal opinion, it would be more important to wipe the under part of the *khuffs* than the upper, but I saw the Messenger of Allah ﷺ wiping over the upper part."[128] This is a famous narration which has also been recorded by other than al-Bayhaqī.[129]

وَأخرج الْبَيْهَقِيّ أَيْضا مَا يُفِيد الْإِرْشَاد إِلَى إتباع الْأَثر والتنفير عَن إتباع الرَّأْي عَن ابْن عمر وَابْن سِيرِين وَالْحسن وَالشعْبِيّ وَابْن عَوْف والأوزاعي وسُفْيَان وَالثَّوْري وَالشَّافِعِيّ وَابْن الْمُبَارك وَعبد الْعَزِيز بن أبي سَلمَة وَأبي حنيفَة وَيحي بن آدم وَمُجاهد.

Al-Bayhaqī also related other reports indicating a directive to follow the narrations and avoid following personal opinion from: Ibn ʿU-

128 Al-Bayhaqī in *al-Madkhal* (p. 193, no. 219) and *al-Sunan al-Kubrā* (1/292).

129 Such as Abu Dāwūd (no. 162), al-Dāraquṭnī (1/199, no. 23), al-Bayhaqī (1/292), al-Dārimī (1/181), Ibn Abī Shaybah (1/181) from the narration of ʿAbd Khayr on the authority of ʿAlī. It is a *ḥasan* ḥadīth.

mar,[130] Ibn Sīrīn,[131] al-Ḥasan,[132] al-Shaʿbī,[133] Ibn ʿAwn,[134] al-Awzāʿī,[135] Sufyān al-Thawrī,[136] al-Shāfiʿī,[137] Ibn al-Mubārak,[138] ʿAbd al-Azīz ibn

130 Ibn ʿUmar said, "People will continue to be upon the right path so long as they follow the narrations." Reported by al-Bayhaqī in *al-Madkhal* (no. 220).

131 Al-Bayhaqī reported in *al-Madkhal* (no. 223) from Ibn Sīrīn that he said, "The first person to perform analogy (*qiyās*) was Iblīs, and the sun and the moon were worshipped through making analogical deductions."

132 Al-Bayhaqī recorded in *al-Madkhal* (no. 224) from al-Ḥasan that he used to say, "Keep your desires and personal views away from Allah's religion and be sincere to Allah's Book for yourselves and your religion."

133 Al-Bayhaqī recorded in *al-Madkhal* (no. 225) that al-Shaʿbī said, "By Allah, if you take to analogical deduction, you will prohibit the lawful and legalise the unlawful."

134 Al-Bayhaqī recorded in *al-Madkhal* (no. 231) from Ibn ʿAwn—Muḥammad—Shurayḥ that he said, "I am sufficed by the narration[s] (*al-athar*)." Meaning the narrations of the Prophet ﷺ.

135 Recorded by al-Bayhaqī in *al-Madkhal* (no. 233) from al-Awzāʿī who said, "Stick to the narrations of those who preceded even if the people reject you; and beware of the opinion of men even if they beautify it with speech. So indeed, the affair will become clear [to others] whilst you are upon the straight path regarding it."

136 Recorded by al-Bayhaqī in *al-Madkhal* (no. 235) from Sufyān al-Thawrī who said, "All of knowledge is the knowledge of the narrations."

137 Recorded by al-Bayhaqī in *al-Madkhal* (no. 249) that al-Shāfiʿī said, "If you find something contrary to the Sunnah of the Messenger of Allah ﷺ in my book, hold onto the Sunnah and leave what I said."

138 Recorded by al-Bayhaqī in *al-Madkhal* (no. 240) from Ibn al-Mubārak that he said, "Let that which you rely upon be the narration[s] and take from opinion (*al-raʾy*) that which explains the ḥadīth to you."

Abī Salamah,[139] Abu Ḥanīfah,[140] Yaḥyā ibn Ādam[141] and Mujāhid.[142]

وَأخرج أَبُو دَاوُد وأبن ماجة وَالْحَاكِم من حَدِيث عبد الله بن عَمْرو بن الْعَاصِ أَن رَسُول الله صلى الله عَلَيْهِ وَآله وَسلم قَالَ: ((الْعلم ثَلَاثَة فَمَا سوى ذَلِك فضل: آيَة محكمَة وَسنة قَائِمَة وفريضة عادلة)). وَفِي إِسْنَاده عبد الرَّحْمَن بن زِيَاد الافريقي وَعبد الرَّحْمَن بن رَافع وَفِيهِمَا مقَال.

139 Recorded by al-Bayhaqī in *al-Madkhal* (no. 242): 'Abd al-'Azīz ibn Abī Salamah said, "When I came to Iraq, the people of Iraq came to me and said, 'Narrate *al-rày* (personal opinion/reasoning) from Rabī'ah to us.' I said, 'O people of Iraq, you are saying Rabī'ah uses personal opinion ([t] i.e. he is from the people of *al-rày*). No, by Allah I have not seen anyone who is more mindful of the Sunnah than him."

140 Recorded by al-Bayhaqī in *al-Madkhal* (no. 245) from Yaḥyā ibn Ḍurays who said, "I witnessed Sufyān when a man came to him and said, 'Why do you place blame upon Abu Ḥanīfah?' He said, 'What does he do?' He said: 'I heard him state, 'I take from the Book of Allah, whatever I do not find in it then I take from the Sunnah. If I do not find it in the Book of Allah nor in the Sunnah, I take to the statements of the companions. I take the statement of whoever amongst them I wish and I leave the view of whomever amongst them I wish. I do not leave their statements for the statements of others.'"

141 Recorded by al-Bayhaqī in *al-Madkhal* (no. 29) from Yaḥyā ibn Ādam who said, "The statement of the Prophet ﷺ does not need accompaniment with that of anyone else."

142 Recorded by al-Bayhaqī in *al-Madkhal* (no. 30) from Mujāhid who said, "Everyone's statement can be accepted or rejected besides the Prophet ﷺ." Al-Ḥāfiẓ in *al-Fatḥ* (13/289) attributed these narrations to al-Bayhaqī in al-Madkhal and to Ibn 'Abd al-Barr, grading the chains to be good (*jayyid*).' See *I'lām al-Muwaqqi'īn* (1/73-79).

Abu Dāwūd,[143] Ibn Mājah[144] and al-Ḥākim[145] reported a ḥadīth of 'Abdullāh ibn 'Amr ibn al-'Āṣ wherein the Messenger of Allah ﷺ said, "Knowledge has three categories, anything else is extra: a precise *āyah*, an established Sunnah and a just obligatory act." The chain of narration contains 'Abd al-Raḥmān ibn Ziyād al-Afrīqī and 'Abd al-Raḥmān ibn Rāfi' and there are reservations concerning their reliability.

قَالَ ابْن عبد الْبر: السّنة الْقَائِمَة الثَّابِتَة الدائمة المحافظ عَلَيْهَا مَعْمُولا بهَا لقِيَام إسنادها.

Ibn 'Abd al-Barr said, "The established, confirmed and lasting Sunnah is constantly adhered to and acted upon because it is proven through its known source."[146]

وَالْفَرِيضَة العادلة المساوية لِلْقُرْآنِ فِي وجوب الْعَمَل بهَا وَفِي كَونهَا صدقا وصوابا.

The just obligatory act is equal to the Qur'ān in regard to the obligation of acting upon it and based upon the fact that it is the truth and correct.

وَأخرج الديلمي فِي مُسْند الفردوس وَأَبُو نعيم وَالطَّبَرَانِيّ فِي الْأَوْسَط والخطيب وَالدَّارَقُطْنِيّ وَابْن عبد الْبر عَن عبد الله بن عمر بن الْخطاب مَوْقُوفا: الْعلم ثَلَاثَة أَشْيَاء كتاب نَاطِق، وَسنة مَاضِيَة، وَلَا أَدْرِي. وَإِسْنَاده

143 *Al-Sunan* (no. 2885).
144 *Al-Sunan* (no. 54).
145 *Al-Mustadrak* (4/332) and it is a *ḍa'īf* ḥadīth.
146 *Jāmi' Bayān al-'Ilm wa Faḍlihi* (1/752).

حسن.

It was reported by al-Daylamī in *Musnad al-Firdaws*,[147] Abu Nu'ay-m,[148] al-Ṭabarānī in *al-Awsaṭ*,[149] al-Khaṭīb,[150] al-Dāraquṭnī[151] and Ibn 'Abd al-Barr[152] from Ibn 'Umar ibn al-Khaṭṭāb in *mawqūf* form, "Knowledge is based upon three things: the [ever-]uttered book (i.e. the Qur'ān), an established Sunnah and [saying] I do not know." Its chain is *ḥaṣan*.

وَأخرج ابْن عبد الْبر عَن ابْن عَبَّاس أَن النَّبِي صلى الله عَلَيْهِ وَآله وَسلم قَالَ: ((إِنَّمَا الْأُمُور ثَلَاثَة: أَمر تبين لَك رشده فَاتبعهُ، وَأمر تبين لَك زيغه فاجتنبه وَأمر اخْتلف فِيهِ فكله إِلَى عالمه)).

Ibn 'Abd al-Barr related from Ibn 'Abbās that the Prophet ﷺ said, "There are only three affairs: An affair that its rightness is clear to you, so follow it; an affair whose deviation is clear to you, so avoid it, and an affair in which there is a divergence of opinion, refer it to one who knows it."[153]

147 No. 4197.

148 Al-'Irāqī attributed it to him in *Takhrīj al-Iḥyā* (1/204).

149 (1/299, no. 1001). Al-Haythamī mentioned it in *al-Majma'* (1/172) and said, "Its chain contains 'Ḥusayn' without any ascription reporting it from Mālik ibn Anas. Also, Ibrāhīm ibn al-Mundhir reported it from him and I could not locate his biography."

150 Amongst the names of those who reported from Mālik from the narration of 'Umar ibn 'Iṣām—Mālik—Nāfi'—Ibn 'Umar in *mawqūf* form. *Takhrīj al-Iḥyā* (1/203, no. 184).

151 *Al-Sunan* (4/68).

152 *Jāmi' Bayān al-'Ilm wa Faḍlihi* (no. 1387).

153 *Jāmi' Bayān al-'Ilm wa Faḍlihi* (no. 1388) with a *ḍa'īf jiddan* (very weak) *isnād*.

وَالْحَاصِل أَن كَون الرَّأْي لَيْسَ من الْعلم لَا خلاف فِيهِ بَين الصَّحَابَة وَالتَّابِعِينَ وتابعيهم.

In short, there is no disagreement amongst the companions, their successors and the followers of their successors concerning the fact that personal opinion (*al-rảy*) is not a part of knowledge.

قَالَ ابْن عبد الْبر: وَلَا أعلم بَين مُتَقَدِّمي عُلَمَاء هَذِه الْأمة وسلفها خلافًا أَن الرَّأْي لَيْسَ بِعلم حَقِيقَة، وَأما أُصُول الْعلم فالكتاب وَالسّنة ... انتهى.

Ibn ʿAbd al-Barr said, "I do not know of any divergence of opinion between the foremost scholars of this Ummah and its pious predecessors that personal opinion is not knowledge in reality. As for the foundation of knowledge, it is the Qur'ān and the Sunnah."[154]

وَقَالَ ابْن عبد الْبر: حد الْعلم عِنْد الْعلمَاء والمتكلمين فِي هَذَا الْمَعْنى هُوَ مَا استيقنته وتبينته، وكل من استيقن شَيْئا وتبينه فقد علمه وعَلى هَذَا من لم يستيقن الشَّيْء وَقَالَ بِهِ تقليدا فَلم يعلم.

Ibn ʿAbd al-Barr also said, "The definition of knowledge according to the scholars and those who have spoken on this matter is ascertainment and identification; and so, anyone who is sure of something and it is clear to him, indeed knows it. On the basis of this, whoever is not certain of something and speaks about it out of *taqlīd* does not know.[155]

والتقليد عِنْد جمَاعَة الْعلمَاء غير الإتباع لِأَن الاتباع هُوَ أَن تتبع الْقَائِل

154 (2/765).
155 (2/765).

على مَا بان لَك من فضل قَوْله وَصِحَّة مذْهبه. والتقليد أَن تَقول بقوله وَأَنت لَا تعرفه وَلَا وَجه القَوْل وَلَا مَعْنَاهُ، وتأبى من سواهُ. أو أن يتبين لَك خطؤه فتتبعه مهابة خِلَافه، وَأَنت قد بَان لَك فَسَاد قَوْله وَهَذَا يحرم القَوْل بِهِ فِي دين الله سُبْحَانَهُ ... انتهى.

Al-taqlīd according to a group of scholars contrasts with *al-ittibā*. This is because *al-ittibā* is to follow someone's view based upon something clarifying the merit of his view and correctness of his *madhhab*, whilst *al-taqlīd* is to hold to his view without knowing him, the basis of the view or its meaning; and dismissing other than him. Or when his error is made manifest to you, you still follow him out of fear of contradicting him whilst the invalidity of his view has become clear to you. It is forbidden to hold such a view in the religion of Allah." [End quote.]

وَمِمَّا يدل على مَا أجمع عَلَيْهِ السّلف من أَن الرَّأْي لَيْسَ بِعلم قَول الله عز وَجل: ﴿فَإِن تَنَازَعْتُمْ فِي شَيْءٍ فَرُدُّوهُ إِلَى اللهِ وَالرَّسُولِ﴾ قَالَ عَطاء بن أبي رَبَاح وَمَيْمُون بن مهْرَان وَغَيرهمَا: الرَّد إِلَى الله هُوَ الرَّد إِلَى كِتَابه، وَالرَّدّ إِلَى رَسُول الله هُوَ الرَّد إِلَى سنته بعد مَوته.

Amongst that which indicates that the pious predecessors unanimously agreed that personal opinion is not knowledge, is the statement of Allah: **{And if you disagree over anything, refer it to Allah and the Messenger.}**[156] 'Aṭā ibn Abī Rabāḥ,[157] Maymūn ibn Mahrān[158] and others said: Referring to Allah means referring to His

156 An-Nisā: 59

157 *Jāmi' Bayān al-'Ilm wa Faḍlihi* (no. 1413).

158 *Jāmi' Bayān al-'Ilm wa Faḍlihi* (no. 1414) with a *ḥasan isnād*.

Book and referring to the Messenger of Allah is to refer to his Sunnah after his death.

وَعَن عَطاء فِي قَوْله تَعَالَى: ﴿أَطِيعُوا اللَّهَ وَأَطِيعُوا الرَّسُولَ﴾ قَالَ طَاعَة الله وَرَسُوله إتباع الْكتاب وَالسّنة ﴿وَأُولِي الْأَمْرِ مِنكُمْ﴾ قَالَ أولُوا الْعلم وَالْفِقْه وَكَذَا قَالَ مُجَاهِد.

'Aṭā stated regarding the statement of Allah: **{Obey Allah and obey the Messenger}**[159] "Obedience to Allah and His Messenger is to follow the Qur'ān and Sunnah. **{Those in authority amongst you}** refers to the people of knowledge and understanding."[160] Mujāhid stated the same.[161]

وَيدل على ذَلِك من السّنة حَدِيث الْعِرْبَاض بن سَارِيَة وَهُوَ ثَابت وَرِجَاله رجال الصَّحِيح قَالَ وعظنا رَسُول الله صلى الله عَلَيْهِ وَآله وَسلم موعظة ذرفت مِنْهَا الْعُيُون ووجلت مِنْهَا الْقُلُوب فَقُلْنَا يَا رَسُول الله إِن هَذِه لموعظة مُودع فَمَاذَا تعهد إِلَيْنَا؟ فَقَالَ: ((تركتكم على الْبَيْضَاء لَيْلهَا كنهارها لَا يزِيغ عَنْهَا بعدِي إِلَّا هَالك، وَمن يَعش مِنْكُم فسيرى اخْتِلَافا كثيرا فَعَلَيْكُم بِمَا عرفتم من سنتي وَسنة الْخُلَفَاء المهديين الرَّاشِدين. وَعَلَيْكُم بِالطَّاعَةِ وَإِن كَانَ عبدا حَبَشِيًّا عضوا عَلَيْهَا بالنواجذ فَإِنَّمَا الْمُؤمن كَالْجملِ الْآنف كلما قيد انْقَادَ)).

159 Al-Nisā: 59
160 *Jāmi' Bayān al-'Ilm wa Faḍlihi* (no. 1417) with a *ḥasan isnād*.
161 *Jāmi' Bayān al-'Ilm wa Faḍlihi* (no. 1418) with a *ḍa'īf isnād*.

What indicates to this from the Sunnah is the ḥadīth of al-ʿIrbāḍ ibn Sāriyah which is established and its men are the men of *al-Ṣaḥīḥ*. He said, "The Messenger of Allah ﷺ gave us an admonition which caused the eyes to shed tears and the hearts to tremble. We said, 'O Messenger of Allah, it is as if this is a farewell admonition, so with what do you enjoin us?' He said, 'I am leaving you upon a [path of] brightness of which its night is like its day. No one will deviate from it after I am gone except one who is doomed. Whomever amongst you lives will see great conflict. I urge you to adhere to what you know of my Sunnah and the way of the Rightly Guided Caliphs. And you must obey, even if he is an Abyssinian slave. Cling stubbornly to this (lit. with your molars), for the true believer is like a camel with a ring on its nose; wherever it is driven, it complies."[162]

وَأخرجه أَيْضا ابْن عبد الْبر بِإِسْنَاد صَحِيح وَزَاد: ((وَإِيَّاكُم ومحدثات الْأُمُور فَإِن كل بدعة ضَلَالَة)). وفي رواية: ((إِيَّاكُم ومحدثات الْأُمُور فَإِن كل محدثة بِدعَة وكل بِدعَة ضَلَالَة)).

Ibn ʿAbd al-Barr also recorded this with a *ṣaḥīḥ* chain and added, "Beware of newly invented matters in the religion; for every innovation is misguidance."[163] And in another version, "Beware of newly invented matters, for every newly invented matter is an innovation, and every innovation is misguidance."[164]

وَالْأَحَادِيث فِي هَذَا الْبَاب كَثِيرَة جدا وَيَكْفِي في دفع الرَّأْي وَأَنه لَيْسَ من الدّين قَوله الله عز وَجل: ﴿الْيَوْمَ أَكْمَلْتُ لَكُمْ دِينَكُمْ وَأَتْمَمْتُ عَلَيْكُمْ

162 It is a *ṣaḥīḥ* ḥadīth.
163 *Jāmiʿ Bayān al-ʿIlm wa Faḍlihi* (2/1164, no. 2305) with a *ṣaḥīḥ isnād*.
164 *Jāmiʿ Bayān al-ʿIlm wa Faḍlihi* (2/1164).

نِعْمَتِي وَرَضِيتُ لَكُمُ الْإِسْلَامَ دِينًا﴾.

The *aḥādīth* on this issue are plentiful, and it suffices to refute personal opinion (*al-rảy*) and to display that it is not from the religion with the statement of Allah: **{This day I have perfected for you your religion and completed My favor upon you and have approved for you Islam as religion.}**[165]

فَإِذا كَانَ الله قد أكمل دينه قبل أَن يقبض إِليه نبيه صلى الله عَلَيْهِ وَآله وَسلم فَمَا هَذَا الرَّأْي الَّذِي أحدثه أَهله بعد أَن أكمل الله دينه؟ إِن كَانَ من الدّين فِي اعْتِقَادهم فَهُوَ لم يكمل عِنْدهم إِلَّا برأيهم وَهَذَا فِيهِ رد لِلْقُرْآنِ، وَإِن لم يكن من الدّين فَأَي فَائِدَة في الِاشْتِغَال بِمَا لَيْسَ من الدّين.

Thus, if Allah has perfected His religion before taking the life of His Prophet ﷺ, what is the need of this personal opinion that its practitioners have invented after Allah perfected His religion? If they believe that it is part of the religion, this dictates that the religion is not complete according to them except with their opinion. This entails rejection of the Qur'ān. So, if it is not a part of it, what is the benefit of preoccupying oneself with what is not part of the religion?

وَهَذِه حجَّة قاهرة وَدَلِيل عَظِيم لَا يُمكن صَاحب الرَّأْي أَن يَدْفَعهُ بدافع أبدا فَاجْعَلْ هَذِه الْآيَة الشَّرِيفَة أول مَا تصك بِهِ وُجُوه أهل الرَّأْي وترغم بِهِ آنافهم، وتدحض بِهِ حججهم فقد أخبرنَا الله فِي مُحكم كِتَابه أَنه أكمل

165 Al-Mā'idah: 4

دينه وَلم يمت رَسُول الله صلى الله عَلَيْهِ وَآله وَسلم إِلَّا بعد أَن أخبرنَا بِهَذَا الْخَبَر عَن الله عز وَجل. فَمن جَاءَنَا بالشَّيْء من عِنْد نَفسه وَزعم أَنه من ديننا قُلْنَا لَهُ الله أصدق مِنْك فَاذْهَبْ فَلَا حَاجَة لنا فِي رَأيك.

This is a strong proof and powerful evidence, which the adherents of personal opinion will never have the ability to refute. So, make this noble *āyah* the first utensil with which you strike the faces of the people of *al-rày*, humble them and dismantle their proofs. Allah has informed us clearly in His Book that He has perfected the religion and that the Messenger of Allah ﷺ did not die except after he informed us about this from Allah. Thus, whoever emerges amongst us with something from himself and claims that it is part of our religion, we should say to him, "Allah is more truthful than you. Leave, as we have no need for your personal opinion."

وليت المقلدة فهموا هَذِه الْآيَة حق الْفَهم حَتَّى يستريحوا ويريحوا.

I wish the *muqallids* comprehended this *āyah* the way it should be comprehended, so that they would find rest and comfort.

وَمَعَ هَذَا فقد أخبرنَا فِي كِتَابه أَنه أحَاط بِكُل شَيْء فَقَالَ: ﴿مَّا فَرَّطْنَا فِي الْكِتَابِ مِن شَيْءٍ﴾ وَقَالَ تَعَالَى: ﴿وَنَزَّلْنَا عَلَيْكَ الْكِتَابَ تِبْيَانًا لِّكُلِّ شَيْءٍ وَهُدًى وَرَحْمَةً﴾.

In addition to this, He has informed us in His Book that He encompasses everything. He states: **{We have neglected nothing in the Book...}**[166] And He states: **{And We have sent down to you the**

166 Al-An'ām: 38

Book as an exposition of everything, a guidance, a mercy...}[167]

ثمَّ أَمر عباده بالحكم بكتابه فقَالَ: ﴿وَأَنِ احْكُم بَيْنَهُم بِمَا أَنزَلَ اللَّهُ وَلَا تَتَّبِعْ أَهْوَاءَهُمْ﴾.

Then He commanded His slaves to judge with his Book. He states: **{And so judge between them by what Allah has revealed and follow not their vain desires...}**[168]

وَقَالَ: ﴿إِنَّا أَنزَلْنَا إِلَيْكَ الْكِتَابَ بِالْحَقِّ لِتَحْكُمَ بَيْنَ النَّاسِ بِمَا أَرَاكَ اللَّهُ ۚ وَلَا تَكُن لِّلْخَائِنِينَ خَصِيمًا﴾.

He states: **{Indeed, We have revealed to you, [O Muhammad], the Book in truth so you may judge between the people by that which Allah has shown you. And do not be for the deceitful an advocate.}**[169]

وَقَالَ: ﴿إِنِ الْحُكْمُ إِلَّا لِلَّهِ ۖ يَقُصُّ الْحَقَّ ۖ وَهُوَ خَيْرُ الْفَاصِلِينَ﴾.

He states: **{The decision is only for Allah, He declares the truth, and He is the best of judges.}**[170]

وَقَالَ: ﴿وَمَن لَّمْ يَحْكُم بِمَا أَنزَلَ اللَّهُ فَأُولَٰئِكَ هُمُ الْكَافِرُونَ﴾.

He states: **{And whosoever does not judge by what Allah has revealed, such are the disbelievers.}**[171]

---

167 Al-Naḥl: 89
168 Al-Mā'idah: 49
169 Al-Nisā: 105
170 Al-An'ām: 57
171 Al-Mā'idah: 44

وقال: ﴿وَمَن لَّمْ يَحْكُم بِمَا أَنزَلَ اللَّهُ فَأُولَٰئِكَ هُمُ الظَّالِمُونَ﴾.

He states: **{And whosoever does not judge by that which Allah has revealed, such are the wrongdoers.}**[172]

وَقَالَ: ﴿وَمَن لَّمْ يَحْكُم بِمَا أَنزَلَ اللَّهُ فَأُولَٰئِكَ هُمُ الْفَاسِقُونَ﴾.

He states: **{And whosoever does not judge by what Allah has revealed [then] such are the defiantly disobedient.}**[173]

وَأمر عباده أَيْضا فِي مُحكم كِتَابه بِاتِّبَاع مَا جَاءَ بِهِ رَسُوله صلى الله عَلَيْهِ وَآله وَسلم قَالَ سُبْحَانَهُ: ﴿وَمَا آتَاكُمُ الرَّسُولُ فَخُذُوهُ وَمَا نَهَاكُمْ عَنْهُ فَانتَهُوا ۚ وَاتَّقُوا اللَّهَ ۖ إِنَّ اللَّهَ شَدِيدُ الْعِقَابِ﴾.

And He clearly commanded His slaves in His Book to follow what His Messenger brought forth. Allah states: **{And whatsoever the Messenger gives you, take it, and whatsoever he forbids you, abstain [from it,] and fear Allah. Verily, Allah is severe in punishment.}**[174]

وقال: ﴿قُلْ إِن كُنتُمْ تُحِبُّونَ اللَّهَ فَاتَّبِعُونِي يُحْبِبْكُمُ اللَّهُ﴾.

He states: **{Say: If you love Allah then follow me, Allah will love you...}**[175]

وَقَالَ: ﴿وَأَطِيعُوا اللَّهَ وَالرَّسُولَ لَعَلَّكُمْ تُرْحَمُونَ﴾.

---

172 Al-Mā'idah: 45
173 Al-Mā'idah: 47
174 Al-Ḥashr: 7
175 Āli 'Imrān: 31

He states: **{And obey Allah and the Messenger, that you may obtain mercy.}**[176]

وَقَالَ: ﴿أَطِيعُوا اللَّهَ وَالرَّسُولَ فَإِن تَوَلَّوْا فَإِنَّ اللَّهَ لَا يُحِبُّ الْكَافِرِينَ﴾.

He states: **{Say, "Obey Allah and the Messenger." But if they turn away, then indeed, Allah does not like the disbelievers.}**[177]

وَقَالَ: ﴿وَمَن يُطِعِ اللَّهَ وَالرَّسُولَ فَأُولَٰئِكَ مَعَ الَّذِينَ أَنْعَمَ اللَّهُ عَلَيْهِم مِّنَ النَّبِيِّينَ وَالصِّدِّيقِينَ وَالشُّهَدَاءِ وَالصَّالِحِينَ وَحَسُنَ أُولَٰئِكَ رَفِيقًا﴾.

He states: **{And whoever obeys Allah and the Messenger, those will be with the ones upon whom Allah has bestowed favor of the prophets, the steadfast affirmers of truth, the martyrs and the righteous. And excellent are those as companions.}**[178]

وَقَالَ: ﴿مَّن يُطِعِ الرَّسُولَ فَقَدْ أَطَاعَ اللَّهَ وَمَن تَوَلَّىٰ فَمَا أَرْسَلْنَاكَ عَلَيْهِمْ حَفِيظًا﴾.

He states: **{He who obeys the Messenger, has indeed obeyed Allah, but he who turns away, then we have not sent you as a watcher over them.}**[179]

وَقَالَ: ﴿يَا أَيُّهَا الَّذِينَ آمَنُوا أَطِيعُوا اللَّهَ وَأَطِيعُوا الرَّسُولَ وَأُولِي الْأَمْرِ مِنكُمْ فَإِن تَنَازَعْتُمْ فِي شَيْءٍ فَرُدُّوهُ إِلَى اللَّهِ وَالرَّسُولِ إِن كُنتُمْ تُؤْمِنُونَ بِاللَّهِ وَالْيَوْمِ الْآخِرِ ذَٰلِكَ خَيْرٌ وَأَحْسَنُ تَأْوِيلًا﴾.

---

176 Āli 'Imrān: 132
177 Āli 'Imrān: 32
178 Al-Nisā: 69
179 Al-Nisā: 80

He states: **{O you who have believed, obey Allah and obey the Messenger and those in authority among you. And if you disagree over anything, refer it to Allah and the Messenger, if you should believe in Allah and the Last Day. That is the best [way] and best in result.}**[180]

وَقَالَ: ﴿وَمَن يُطِعِ اللَّهَ وَرَسُولَهُ يُدْخِلْهُ جَنَّاتٍ تَجْرِي مِن تَحْتِهَا الْأَنْهَارُ خَالِدِينَ فِيهَا وَذَٰلِكَ الْفَوْزُ الْعَظِيمُ ۝١٣ وَمَن يَعْصِ اللَّهَ وَرَسُولَهُ وَيَتَعَدَّ حُدُودَهُ يُدْخِلْهُ نَارًا خَالِدًا فِيهَا وَلَهُ عَذَابٌ مُّهِينٌ﴾.

He states: **{...And whosoever obeys Allah and His Messenger will be admitted to Gardens under which rivers flow, to abide therein, and that will be the great success. And whosoever disobeys Allah and His Messenger, and transgresses His limits, He will cast him into the Fire, to abide therein; and he shall have a disgraceful torment.}**[181]

وَقَالَ: ﴿وَأَطِيعُوا اللَّهَ وَأَطِيعُوا الرَّسُولَ وَاحْذَرُوا فَإِن تَوَلَّيْتُمْ فَاعْلَمُوا أَنَّمَا عَلَىٰ رَسُولِنَا الْبَلَاغُ الْمُبِينُ﴾.

He states: **{And obey Allah and the Messenger, and beware. Then if you turn away, you should know that it is Our Messenger's duty to convey [the Message] in the clearest way.}**[182]

وقال: ﴿وَأَطِيعُوا اللَّهَ وَرَسُولَهُ إِن كُنتُم مُّؤْمِنِينَ﴾.

He states: **{... And obey Allah and His Messenger, if you are**

180 Al-Nisā: 59
181 Al-Nisā: 13-14
182 Al-Mā'idah: 92

faithful believers.}[183]

وَقَالَ: ﴿وَأَطِيعُوا اللَّهَ وَرَسُولَهُ وَلَا تَنَازَعُوا فَتَفْشَلُوا وَتَذْهَبَ رِيحُكُمْ ۖ وَاصْبِرُوا إِنَّ اللَّهَ مَعَ الصَّابِرِينَ﴾.

He states: **{And obey Allah and His Messenger, and do not dispute [with one another] lest you lose courage and your strength depart, and be patient. Surely, Allah is with the patient.}**[184]

وَقَالَ: ﴿قُلْ أَطِيعُوا اللَّهَ وَأَطِيعُوا الرَّسُولَ ۖ فَإِن تَوَلَّوْا فَإِنَّمَا عَلَيْهِ مَا حُمِّلَ وَعَلَيْكُم مَّا حُمِّلْتُمْ ۖ وَإِن تُطِيعُوهُ تَهْتَدُوا ۚ وَمَا عَلَى الرَّسُولِ إِلَّا الْبَلَاغُ الْمُبِينُ﴾.

He states: **{Say: Obey Allah and obey the Messenger, but if you turn away, he is only responsible for the duty placed upon him and you for that placed upon you. If you obey him, you shall be on the right guidance. The Messenger's duty is only to convey [the message] in a clear manner.}**[185]

وَقَالَ: ﴿وَأَقِيمُوا الصَّلَاةَ وَآتُوا الزَّكَاةَ وَأَطِيعُوا الرَّسُولَ لَعَلَّكُمْ تُرْحَمُونَ﴾.

He states: **{And establish the prayer, give *zakāt* and obey the Messenger, that you may receive mercy.}**[186]

وَقَالَ: ﴿وَمَن يُطِعِ اللَّهَ وَرَسُولَهُ فَقَدْ فَازَ فَوْزًا عَظِيمًا﴾.

He states: **{And whosoever obeys Allah and His Messenger he**

183 Al-Anfāl: 1
184 Al-Anfāl: 46
185 Al-Nūr: 54
186 Al-Nūr: 56

has indeed achieved a great achievement.}[187]

وَقَالَ: ﴿يَا أَيُّهَا الَّذِينَ آمَنُوا أَطِيعُوا اللَّهَ وَأَطِيعُوا الرَّسُولَ وَلَا تُبْطِلُوا أَعْمَالَكُمْ﴾.

He states: **{O you who believe, obey Allah and the Messenger and do not render your deeds vain.}**[188]

وَقَالَ: ﴿إِنَّمَا كَانَ قَوْلَ الْمُؤْمِنِينَ إِذَا دُعُوا إِلَى اللَّهِ وَرَسُولِهِ لِيَحْكُمَ بَيْنَهُمْ أَن يَقُولُوا سَمِعْنَا وَأَطَعْنَا ۚ وَأُولَٰئِكَ هُمُ الْمُفْلِحُونَ﴾.

He states: **{The only words of the faithful believers, when they are called to Allah and His Messenger, to judge between them, is that they say, "We hear and we obey." And such are the prosperous ones.}**[189]

وَقَالَ: ﴿لَّقَدْ كَانَ لَكُمْ فِي رَسُولِ اللَّهِ أُسْوَةٌ حَسَنَةٌ﴾.

He states: **{Indeed in the Messenger of Allah you have a good example to follow...}**[190]

والاستكثار من الِاسْتِدْلَال على وجوب طَاعَة الله وَرَسُوله لَا يَأْتِي بفائدة زائدة فَلَيْسَ أحد من الْمُسلمين يُخَالف في ذَلِك، وَمن أنكرهُ فَهُوَ كَافِر خَارج عَن حزب الْمُسلمين. إِنَّمَا أوردنا هَذِه الْآيَات الشَّرِيفَة لقصد تليين قلب الْمُقَلّد الَّذِي قد جمد وَصَارَ كالجلمد فَإِنَّهُ إِذا سمع مثل هَذِه

187 Al-Aḥzāb: 71
188 Muḥammad: 33
189 Al-Nūr: 51
190 Al-Aḥzāb: 21

الْأَوَامِر القرآنية رُبمَا امتثلها وَأخذ دينه عَن كتاب الله وَسنة رَسُوله طَاعَة لأوامر الله تَعَالَى.

Citing an excess of such proofs displaying the obligation of obeying Allah and His Messenger will not bring additional benefit, as there is no one among the Muslims who differs with this, and whoever rejects it is a disbeliever, who is removed from the party of the Muslims. We have only cited these noble *āyāt* with the intent of softening the heart of the *muqallid*, which has hardened and become like a stone. If he hears the like of these commandments from the Qur'ān, he may comply with them and take his religion from the Book of Allah and the Sunnah of His Messenger out of obedience to the decree of Allah.

فَإِن هَذِه الطَّاعَة وَإِن كَانَت مَعْلُومَة لكل مُسلم كَمَا تقدم لَكِن الْإِنْسَان قد يذهل عَن القوارع القرآنية والزواجر النَّبَوِيَّة فَإِذا ذكر بهَا ذكر وَلَا سِيمَا من نَشأ على التَّقْلِيد وَأدْركَ سلفه ثابتين عَلَى غير متزحزحين عَنهُ، فَإِنَّهُ يَقع فِي قلبه أَن دين الْإِسْلَام هُوَ هَذَا الَّذِي هُوَ عَلَيْهِ وَمَا كَانَ مُخَالفا لَهُ فَلَيْسَ من الْإِسْلَام فِي شَيْء فَإِذا رَاجع نَفسه رَجَعَ. وَلِهَذَا تَجِد الرجل إِذا نَشأ على مَذْهَب من هَذِه الْمذَاهب ثمَّ سمع قبل أَن يتمرن بِالْعلمِ وَيعرف مَا قَالَه النَّاس خلافًا يُخَالف ذَلِك المألوف استنكره وأباه قلبه وَنفر عَنهُ طبعه، وَقد رَأينَا وَسَمعنَا من هَذَا الْجِنْس من لَا يَأْتِي عَلَيْهِ الْحصْر.

Though this obedience is known to every Muslim—as has preceded, a person may be distracted from the strong injunctions of the Qur'ān and the admonishments from the Prophetic Sunnah. However, if he is reminded of them then he will be affected, especially one who grew up upon *taqlīd* and witnessed his predecessors established upon it without budging from it, for it will be settled in his mind that the religion of Islam is that which he is upon and whatever opposes it is not part of Islam at all. Then, if he reconsiders the issue, he may retract. Consequently, you may see a man nurtured upon a *madhhab* amongst the *madhhabs* then he hears something which opposes that convention before being trained in knowledge, he would reject it; his heart would deny it and his nature would flee from it. We have seen and heard from many of this type, an amount which cannot be accounted.

وَلَكِن إِذا وازن الْعَاقِل بعقله بَين من اتبع أحد أَئِمَّة الْمذَاهب فِي مَسْأَلَة من مسَائِله الَّتِي رَوَاهَا عَنهُ الْمُقَلّد وَلَا مُسْتَند لذَلِك الْعَالم فِيهَا بل قَالَهَا بمحض الرَّأْي لعدم وُقُوفه على الدَّلِيل، وَبَين من تمسك فِي تِلْكَ الْمَسْأَلَة بخصوصها بِالدَّلِيلِ الثَّابِت فِي الْقُرْآن أَو السّنة أَفَادَهُ الْعقل أَن بَينهمَا مسافات تنقطع فِيهَا أَعْنَاق الْإِبِل بل لَا جَامع بَينهمَا لِأَن من تمسك بِالدَّلِيلِ أَخذ بِمَا أوجب الله عَلَيْهِ الْأَخْذ بِهِ وَاتبع مَا شَرعه الشَّارِع لجَمِيع الْأمة أَولهَا وَآخِرهَا وحيها وميتها، وَأحدهم هَذَا الْعَالم الَّذِي تمسك الْمُقَلّد لَهُ بمحض رَأْيه وهذا العالم هُوَ مَحْكُوم عَلَيْهِ بالشريعة لَا أَنه حَاكم فِيهَا وَهُوَ تَابع لَهَا لَا متبوع فِيهَا.

However, if a rational person weighs with his intellect between (a) one who follows an *imām* of a *madhhab* in an issue amongst the issues that have been reported from him by the *muqallid* without the scholar supporting it with a proof; rather he held it based upon mere personal opinion due to it not being grounded in evidence, and (b) one who adheres to proof established in the Qur'ān and Sunnah on that particular issue; the intellect will show him that between them are distances that would cut the necks of camels. In fact, there is no commonality between them, as the one who adheres to a proof adheres to what Allah has enjoined upon him, adhering to it and following what the Legislator has ordained for the entire Ummah—its first and last, its living and its dead. One of them (i.e. from the Ummah) is the scholar whom the *muqallid* sticks to due to his mere opinion. This scholar is charged with the Sharīʿah and not to be a judge in it. He is subservient to it and not followed regarding it.

فَهُوَ كمن تبعهُ فِي أَن كل وَاحِد مِنْهُمَا فَرْضه الْأَخْذ بِمَا جَاءَ عَن الشَّارِع لَا فرق بَينهمَا إِلَّا في كَون الْمَتْبُوع عَالما وَالتَّابِع جَاهِلا. فالعالم يُمكنهُ الْوُقُوف على الدَّلِيل من دون أَن يرجع إِلَى غَيره لِأَنَّهُ قد استعد لذَلِك بِمَا اشْتغل بِهِ من الطّلب وَالْوُقُوف بَين يَدي أهل الْعلم والتخرج بهُم فِي معارف الِاجْتِهَاد، وَالْجَاهِل يُمكنهُ الْوُقُوف على الدَّلِيل بسؤال عُلَمَاء الشَّرِيعَة على طَرِيقَة طلب الدَّلِيل واسترواء النَّص وَكَيف حكم الله فِي محكم كتابه أَو على لِسَان رَسُوله فِي تِلْكَ الْمَسْأَلَة.

He is just like the one who is following him in the sense that each of them is duty bound to adhere to what has come from the Legislator. There is no difference between them except in the fact that the one who is followed is a scholar whilst the follower is ignorant. It is possible for a scholar to arrive at a proof without referring to others, as he has prepared for this by preoccupying himself with seeking knowledge, standing before the people of knowledge and benefiting from them in the skills of *al-ijtihād*. It is also possible for an ignorant person to arrive at a proof by asking the scholars of the Ṣharīʿah by way of seeking proof, seeking narration of the text and enquiring about how Allah judged regarding the issue in the *muḥkam* (clear) [*āyāt*] of His Book or upon the tongue of His Messenger.

فيفيدونه النَّص إن كَانَ مِمَّن يعقل الْحجَّة إِذا دلّ عَلَيْهَا أَو يفيدونه مَضْمُون النَّص بالتعبير عَنهُ بِعِبَارَة يفهمها فهم رُوَاة وَهُوَ مسترو وَهَذَا عَامل بالرواية لَا بِالرَّأْيِ، والمقلد عَامل بِالرَّأْيِ لَا بالرواية لِأَنَّهُ يقبل قَول الْغَيْر من دون أَن يُطَالِبهُ بِحجَّة. وَذَلِكَ هُوَ فِي سُؤَاله مطَالب بِالْحجَّةِ لَا بِالرَّأْيِ فَهُوَ قبل رِوَايَة الْغَيْر لَا رَأْيه وهما من هَذِه الْحَيْثِيَّة متقابلان. فَانْظُر كم الْفرق بَين المنزلتين.

Then they will show him the text—if he is amongst those who understands proofs when they are shown to him—or they will explain to him the purport of the text with a statement that he understands. Thus, they are the reporters whilst he is the one being reported to, and this procedure is based upon acting upon narration, not upon personal opinion. Contrarily, the *muqallid* acts upon personal opinion and not upon narration, as he accepts the view of others without seeking proof. The former individual, in asking, is seeking proof and not personal opinion. So, he accepts the narration of others and not their personal opinion. Therefore, from this perspective they are opposites. So, look at the difference between the two states.

فَإِن الْعَالم الَّذِي قَلّدهُ غَيره إِذا كَانَ قد أجهد نَفسه فِي طلب الدَّلِيل وَلم يجده ثمَّ اجتهد رَأْيه فَهُوَ مَعْذُور. وَهَكَذَا إِذا أخطأ فِي اجْتِهَاده فَإِنه مَعْذُور بل مأجور للْحَدِيث الْمُتَّفق عَلَيْهِ: ((إِذا اجْتهد الْحَاكِم فَأصَاب فَلهُ أجران

وَإِنِ اجْتَهد فَأَخْطَأَ فَلَهُ اجرٌ)).

A scholar whom others blindly follow, if he resorted to personal opinion after having exerted himself in seeking proof but could not find anything, he is excused. Similarly, if he errs in his *ijtihād*, he is excused. In fact, he will be rewarded due to the *muttafaqun 'alayhi* (agreed upon) ḥadīth, "When a judge passes a judgement, having exerted his efforts to judge correctly and is right, he will have two rewards. When he exerts his efforts [likewise] but errs, he will have one reward."[191]

فَإِذَا وقف بَيْن يَدي الله وَتبين خطأه كَانَ بِيَدِهِ هَذِه الْحجَّة الصَّحِيحَة بِخلَاف الْمقلد له فَإِنَّهُ لَا يجد حجَّة يُدْلِي بهَا عِنْد السُّؤَال فِي موقف الْحساب لِأَنَّهُ قلد فِي دين الله من هُوَ مُخطِئٌ، وَعدم مُؤَاخذَة الْمُجْتَهد على خطأه لَا يسْتَلْزم عدم مُؤَاخذَة من قَلَّدهُ فِي ذَلِك الْخَطَأَ لَا عقلا وَلَا شرعا وَلَا عَادَة، فَإِن استروح الْمُقَلّد إِلَى مَسْأَلَة تصويب الْمُجْتَهد فالقائل بهَا إِنَّمَا قَالَ إِن الْمُجْتَهد مُصِيب بِمَعنى أَنه لَا يَأْثم بِالْخَطَأَ بل يُؤجر على الْخَطَأَ بعد تَوْفِيَة الِاجْتِهَاد حَقه وَلم يقل أَنه مُصِيب للحق الَّذِي هُوَ حكم الله فِي الْمَسْأَلَة، فَإِن هَذَا خلاف مَا نطق بِهِ رَسُول الله صلى الله عَلَيْهِ وَآله وَسلم فِي هَذَا الْحَدِيث حَيْثُ قَالَ: ((إِن اجْتهد الْحَاكِم فَأَصَاب فَلَهُ أَجْرَانِ وَإِن اجتهد فَأَخطَأَ فَلَهُ أَجرٌ)).

When this scholar stands in front of Allah and his error becomes clear, he has this authentic proof unlike the *muqallid*, for he will not

---

191 Reported by al-Bukhārī (7352) and Muslim (1716).

find a proof to use as evidence during his questioning at the station of accountability. This is because he blindly followed one who erred in Allah's religion; and the fact that a *mujtahid* is not answerable for his error does not necessitate that the one who adopted his view will not be answerable for that error; not rationally, technically or conventionally. If the *muqallid* resorts to the issue of *taṣwību 'l-mujtahid* (correctness of the *mujtahid*), those who hold this view only say that the *mujtahid* is right in the sense that he is not sinful on account of the error, and that he will be rewarded for the error after fulfilling the rights of *al-ijtihād*. They do not say that he has attained the truth, which is the judgement of Allah in the issue. This is contrary to what the Messenger of Allah ﷺ stated in the ḥadīth, "When a judge passes a judgement, having exerted his efforts to judge correctly and is right, he will have two rewards. When he exerts his efforts [likewise] but errs, he will have one reward."

فَانْظُر هَذِه الْعبارَة النَّبَوِيَّة فِي هَذَا الحَدِيث الصَّحِيح الْمُتَّفق عَلَيْهِ عِنْد أهل الصَّحِيح والمتلقى بِالْقبُولِ بَين جَمِيع الْفرق فَإِنَّهُ قَالَ ((وَإِن اجْتهد فَأَخْطَأَ ..)) فقسم مَا يصدر عَن الْمُجْتَهد فِي مسَائِل الدّين إِلَى قسمَيْنِ: أَحدهمَا هُوَ فيه مُصِيب وَالْآخر هُوَ فيه مُخطئ فَكيف يَقُول قَائِل إنه مُصِيب للحق سَوَاء أصَاب أَو أَخطَأ وَقد سَمَّاهُ رَسُول الله صلى الله عَلَيْهِ وَآله وَسلم مخطئا فَمن زعم أَن مُرَاد الْقَائِل بتصويب الْمُجْتَهد الْإِصَابَة للحق مُطبقًا فقد غلط عَلَيْهِم غَلطا بَينا، وَنسب إِلَيْهِم مَا هم عَنهُ بَرَاء.

Look at this prophetic expression in this authentic ḥadīth which is agreed upon according to the people of authentication and considered acceptable amongst all sects. He said, "When he exerts his efforts [likewise] but errs." He divided that which emanates from a *mujtahid* in religious issues into two: (i) wherein he is correct and (ii) wherein he is incorrect. In light of this, why would someone state that he is right irrespective of whether he is correct or incorrect whilst the Messenger of Allah ﷺ said that he is mistaken? Whoever claims that the meaning of those who mentioned "the correctness of the *mujtahid*" is that he is in the right absolutely has indeed erred clearly in regards to them and attributed to them what they are free of.

وَلِهَذَا أوضح جمَاعَة من الْمُحَقِّقين مُرَاد الْقَائِلين بتصويب الْمُجْتَهدين بِأَن مقصودهم أَنهم مصيبون من الصَّوَاب الَّذِي لَا يُنَافِي الْخَطَأ لَا من الْإِصَابَة الَّتِي هِيَ مُقَابلَة للخطأ فَإِن تسمية المخطئ مصيبا هي باعتبار قيام النص على أنه مأجور في الخطئه لا باعتبار أنه لم يُخطئ فَهَذَا لَا يقول بِهِ عَالم، وَمن لم يفهم هَذَا الْمَعْنى فَعَلَيهِ أَن يتهم نَفسه ويحيل الذَّنب على قصوره وَيقبل مَا أوضحه لَهُ من هُوَ أعرف مِنْهُ بفهم كَلَام الْعلمَاء.

As such, a group of researching scholars explained that what is meant by those who mention "the correctness of the *mujtahid*" is that the *mujtahids* are correct in a manner that does not negate error, but it is not the correctness which is the opposite of error. This is because calling the one who errs as one who is correct is with regard to establishing the text that he will be rewarded in his error and not with regard to the fact that he did not err. Thus, this is not something which would be stated by any scholar. And whoever does not understand this meaning, it is incumbent upon him to blame himself, admit the sin for his shortcomings and accept what has been explained to him by one more capable than him in understanding the words of the scholars.

وَإِن استروح الْمُقَلّد إِلَى الِاسْتِدْلَال بقوله تَعَالَى ﴿فَاسْأَلُوا أَهْلَ الذِّكْرِ إِن كُنتُمْ لَا تَعْلَمُونَ﴾.

If the *muqallid* resorts to using as proof the statement of the Most High: **{So ask the people of the Scripture if you do not know.}**[192]

فَهُوَ يقْتَصر على سُؤال أهل الْعلم عَن الحكم الثَّابِت فِي كتاب الله وَسنة رَسُوله حَتَّى يبينوه لَهُ كَمَا أَخذ الله عَلَيْهِم من بَيَان أَحْكَامه لِعِبَادِهِ فَإِن معنى هَذَا السُّؤَال الَّذِي شرعه الله هُوَ السُّؤَال عَن الْحجَّة الشَّرْعِيَّة وطلبها من الْعَالم فَيكون رَاوِيا وَهَذَا السَّائِل مسترويا، والمقلد يقر على نَفسه بِأَنَّهُ يقبل قَول الْعَالم وَلَا يُطَالِبهُ بِالْحجَّةِ، فالآية هِيَ دَلِيل الإتباع لَا دَلِيل التَّقْلِيد وَقد أوضحنا الْفرق بَينهمَا فِيمَا سلف هَذَا على فرض أَن المُرَاد بهَا السُّؤَال الْعَام، وَقد قدمنَا أَن السِّيَاق يُفِيد أَن المُرَاد بهَا السُّؤَال الْخَاص لِأَن الله يَقُول: ﴿وَمَآ أَرْسَلْنَا قَبْلَكَ إِلَّا رِجَالًا نُّوحِيٓ إِلَيْهِمْ ۖ فَاسْأَلُوا أَهْلَ الذِّكْرِ إِن كُنتُمْ لَا تَعْلَمُونَ﴾.

This is restricted to asking the people of knowledge about the established ruling in the Book of Allah and the Sunnah of His Messenger so that they explain it to him, just as Allah has enjoined them to explain His rulings to His slaves. The meaning of this enquiring which Allah has ordained is to ask regarding proofs of the Sharīʿah and to seek it from the scholar, and by doing so the scholar serves as

192 Al-Anbiyā: 7

a narrator whilst the questioner is the one being narrated to. [This is contrary to] the *muqallid*, who admits that he accepts the statement of a scholar and does not seek the proof. The aforementioned *āyah* is a proof for *al-ittibā'* (following the texts) and not a proof for *al-taqlīd*, and we have already covered the difference between them.[193] This is based upon supposing that the intended meaning is a general question, but we have stated earlier that the context indicates that what is intended is a specific question, as Allah states: **{And We sent not before you, [O Muhammad], except men to whom We revealed [the message], so ask the people of the Scripture if you do not know.}**[194]

وَقد قدمنَا طرفا من تَفْسِير أهل الْعلم لهَذِهِ الْآيَة وَبِهَذَا يظْهر لَك أَن هَذِه الْحجَّة الَّتِي احْتج بهَا الْمُقَلّد هِيَ حجَّة داحضة على فرض أَن المُرَاد الْمَعْنى الْخَاص وَهِي عَلَيْهِ لَا لَهُ على فرض أَن المُرَاد الْمَعْنى الْعَام.

193 The difference between *al-ittibā* and *al-taqlīd*: *Al-ittibā* refers to following the proof and acting upon the revelation. Allah has called acting upon revelation *al-ittibā* in many places. Among them are: **{Follow, [O mankind], what has been revealed to you from your Lord.}** [Al-A'rāf: 3] And His statement: **{Follow, [O Muhammad], what has been revealed to you from your Lord...}** [Al-An'ām: 106]

Therefore, *al-ittibā* has to do with every ruling whose proof emanates from the Qur'ān, Sunnah and *al-ijmā'*. As for the issue of *al-taqlīd*, it is in the area of *al-ijtihād*. There is no *ijtihād* nor *taqlīd* when there are authentic clear texts of revelation free from objection.

There is no condition for *al-ittibā* and acting upon the revelation other than knowledge of what will be acted on; and this is not conditional on attaining the pre-requisites of *al-ijtihād*. See *I'lām al-Muwaqqi'īn* (2/190-210) and *Irshād al-Fuḥūl* (p. 881).

194 Al-Anbiyā: 7

We have presented some of the explanations of the people of knowledge regarding this *āyah*. With this, it would be clear to you that this proof which the *muqallid* depends upon is baseless [for their argument]—assuming that what is meant [in the *āyah*] is a specific meaning—and serves against him and not for him, supposing that the meaning [in the *āyah*] is general.

[أسئلة للمقلدين]

[Questions for the *Muqallids*]

ثمَّ نقُول للمقلد أَيْضا أَنْت فِي تقليدك الْعَالم فِي مسَائِل الْعِبَادَات والمعاملات إِمَّا أَن تكون فِي أصل مَسْأَلَة جَوَاز التَّقْلِيد مقلدا أَو مُجْتَهدا: إِن كنت مقلد فقد قلدت فِي مَسْأَلَة لَا يُجِيز إمامك التَّقْلِيد فِيهَا لِأَنَّهَا مَسْأَلَة أصولية والتقليد إِنَّمَا هُوَ فِي مسَائِل الْفُرُوع فَمَاذَا صنعت فِي نَفسك يَا مِسْكين؟

Further, we say to the *muqallid*: In your blind following of a scholar in issues of worship and dealings, it is either that you believe the permissibility of *al-taqlīd* as a *muqallid* (i.e. through blind following) or as a *mujtahid* (i.e. through exercising *ijtihād*). If you were a *muqallid*, you have performed *taqlīd* in an issue in which your *imām* did not permit *taqlīd* in due to it being a fundamental issue, whilst *taqlīd* should be in subsidiary issues. So, what is this that you have done to yourself, O pauper?

وَكَيف وَقعت فِي هَذِه الهوة الْمظْلمَة وَأَنت تَجِد عَنْهَا فرجا ومخرجا.

How did you fall into this dark pit when you could find a relief and way out of it?

وَإِن كنت فِي أصل هَذِه الْمَسْأَلَة مُجْتَهدا فَلَا يجوز لَك التَّقْلِيد لِأَنَّك لَا

تقدر على الِاجْتِهَاد فِي مثل هَذِه الْمسَائِل الْأُصُولِيَّة المتشعبة المشكلة إِلَّا وَأَنت مِمَّن علمه الله علما نَافِعًا تخرج بِهِ من الظُّلُمَات إِلَى النُّور.

And if you were a *mujtahid* regarding this subject matter, it is not permissible for you to perform *taqlīd*, because you would not be able to exert *ijtihād* in the like of such complex, fundamental, difficult issues except that you are from amongst those whom Allah has blessed with beneficial knowledge that exits one from darkness into light.

فَمَا بالك توقع نَفسك فِيمَا لَا يجوز لَهَا وتقلد الرِّجَال فِي دين الله بعد أَن أراحك الله مِنْهُ وأقدرك على الْخُرُوج مِنْهُ.

Why would you put yourself into what is not permissible for you and adopt the view of men in Allah's religion after Allah has relieved you of it and given you the ability to come out of it?

هَذَا على مَا هُوَ الْحق من أَن الِاجْتِهَاد لَا يَتَبَعَّض، وَأَنه لَا يقدر على الِاجْتِهَاد فِي بعض الْمسَائِل إِلَّا من قدر على الِاجْتِهَاد فِي جَمِيعهَا لِأَن الِاجْتِهَاد هُوَ ملكة تحصل للنَّفس عِنْد الْإِحَاطَة بمعارفه الْمُعْتَبرَة وَلَا ملكة لمن لم يعرف إِلَّا الْبَعْض من ذَلِك.

This is based upon the truth that *al-ijtihād* cannot be divided[195] and

195 Further detail regarding this can be found in *al-Kawkab al-Munīr* (4/473-475) and *Taysīr al-Taḥrīr* (4/183). The view that *al-ijtihād* can be divided is the view of most theologians (al-Mutakallimūn), al-Mu'tazilah and most of the jurists. It is the view of the Ḥanafī, Mālikī, Shāfi'ī and Hanbalī schools of *fiqh*. It was endorsed by al-Āmidī, Ibn Ḥājib, Ibn Daqīq al-'Īd and

that none will be able to exercise *al-ijtihād* in some issues except one who is able to exercise it in all of them. This is because *al-ijtihād* is a rank that a person obtains through the vastness of his relevant knowledge and not an endowment given to someone who does not know except some of its issues.

فَإِن استروحت إِلَى أَن الِاجْتِهَاد يَتَبَعَّض أعدنا عَلَيْكَ السُّؤَال فَنَقُول: هَل عرفت أَن الِاجْتِهَاد يَتَبَعَّض بِالِاجْتِهَادِ أَم بالتقليد؟ فَإِن كنت عرفت ذَلِكَ بالتقليد فَالْمَسْأَلَة أصولية لَا يجوز التَّقْلِيد فِيهَا باعترافك واعتراف إِمَامك. وَإِن كنت عرفت ذَلِكَ بِالِاجْتِهَادِ فَهَذِهِ أَيْضا مَسْأَلَة أُخْرَى من مَسَائِل الْأُصُول أقدرك الله على الِاجْتِهَاد فِيهَا فَهَلَّا صنعت هَذَا الصنع فِي مَسَائِل الْفُرُوع فَإِنَّكَ على الِاجْتِهَاد فِيهَا أَقدر مِنْكَ على الِاجْتِهَاد فِي مَسَائِل الْأُصُول.

If you resort to the fact that *al-ijtihād* can be divided, we will pose to you a question: Did you come to know that *al-ijtihād* can be divided through *al-ijtihād* or *al-taqlīd*? If you came to know this through *al-taqlīd*, then it is not permissible to perform *taqlīd* in fundamental issues based upon your acknowledgement and the admission of your *imām*. But if you came to know of this through *al-ijtihād*, this is another issue amongst the fundamental issues, which Allah has given you the ability to perform *ijtihād* in. Why did you not do this act (i.e. *al-ijtihād*) in subsidiary issues (i.e. in *fiqh*), for exercising *ijtihād* in them is more probable for you than performing *ijtihād* in

---

Ibn al-Subkī. See *I'lām al-Muwaqqi'īn* (4/275) and *al-Iḥkām* of al-Āmidī (2/386). It was also said that it cannot be divided, others said that it can be divided in a subject (*bāb*) not in an issue (*mas'alah*), and others said in inheritance excluding other subjects.

fundamental issues?

فَاصْنَعْ من مسَائِل الْفُرُوع هَكَذَا واستكثر من عُلُوم الِاجْتِهَاد حَتَّى تصير من أَهله ويفرج الله عَنْك هَذِه الْغُمَّة ويكشف عَنْك بِمَا علمك هَذِه الظلمَة فَإنَّك إِذا رفعت نَفسك إِلَى الِاجْتِهَاد الْأَكْبَر فالمسافة قريبَة، وَمن قدر على الْبَعْض قدر على الْكل.

If you exercise yourself in the subsidiary issues in this manner and increase your grasp over the sciences of *al-ijtihād*, you will be amongst its people and Allah will relieve you of this distress, and remove this darkness from you through what He has taught you. And if you elevate yourself to the level of the greater *ijtihād*, the distance [to attaining this relief from Allah] will draw closer. Whoever is able [to perform *al-ijtihād*] in some issues will be able to perform [it] in all issues.

وَمن عرف الْحق فِي المعارك الْأُصُولِيَّة عرفه فِي الْمسَائِل الفروعية وستعرف بعد أَن تعرف عُلُوم الِاجْتِهَاد كَمَا يَنْبَغِي بطلَان مَا تظنه الْآن من جَوَاز التَّقْلِيد وَمن تبعض الِاجْتِهَاد، بل لَو طرحت عَنْك العصبية وجردت نَفسك لفهم مَا حررته لَك فِي هَذِه الورقات من أَوله إِلَى آخِره لقادك عقلك وفهمك إِلَى أَنه الصَّوَاب قبل أَن تجمع معارف الِاجْتِهَاد فالفهم قد تفضل الله بِهِ على غَالب عباده وَالْحق لَا يحتجب عَن أهل التَّوْفِيق والإنصاف شَاهد صدق على وجدان الْحق، وَلِهَذَا قَالَ صلى الله عَلَيْهِ وَآله وَسلم: ((أعلم النَّاس أبصرهم بِالْحَقِّ إِذا اخْتلف النَّاس)) وَهُوَ حَدِيث

أخرجه الْحَاكِم فِي مُسْتَدْركه وَصَححهُ وَأخرجه أَيْضا غَيره.

Whoever knows the truth in contentious fundamental issues will know it in the subsidiary issues, and you will know [it] after coming to understand the sciences of *al-ijtihād*, just as it is necessary now to nullify what you are thinking of the permissibility of *al-taqlīd* and the division of *al-ijtihād*. Rather, if you were to be freed of partisanship and exerted yourself in comprehending what I have written to you in these pages from the beginning until the end, your intellect and understanding would lead you to say that it is correct, [even] before you acquire the knowledge of *al-ijtihād*. Allah has indeed blessed most of His slaves with understanding and the truth is not concealed from the people of success, whilst the fair-minded is always a truthful witness to its presence. Consequently, the Messenger of Allah ﷺ said: "The most knowledgeable of the people are those who are most discerning of the truth when the people differ." This is a ḥadīth recorded by al-Ḥākim in his *Mustadrak*[196] and which he graded as *ṣaḥīḥ*, and others have also reported it.[197]

فَإِن طَال بك اللجاج وسلكت من جهالتك فِي فجاج، وتوقحت غير محتشم، وأقدمت غير محجم، فَقلت إِن مَسْأَلَة جَوَاز التَّقْلِيد هِيَ وَإِن كَانَت مَسْأَلَة أصولية وَقد أطبق النَّاس على أَنه لَا يجوز التَّقْلِيد فِي مسَائِل الْأُصُول وَصَارَ هَذَا مَعْرُوفا عِنْد أَبنَاء جنس من المقلدين لكني أَقُول بِأَن

---

196 (2/480) from the ḥadīth of Ibn Masʿūd, and al-Ḥākim said, "The *isnād* of this ḥadīth is *ṣaḥīḥ* but they did not record it." Al-Dhahabī commented on it saying, "It is not *ṣaḥīḥ*, because even though al-Ṣaʿaq is strong, his *shaykh* is *munkar al-ḥadīth* (i.e. his ḥadīth are rejected). Al-Bukhārī said this."

197 Like al-ʿAqīlī in *al-Ḍuʿafā* (3/408) under the biography of ʿAqīl al-Jaʿdī from the path of al-Ṣaʿaq.

التَّقْلِيد فِيهَا وَفِي سَائِر مسَائِل الْأُصُول جَائِز.

However, if you continue to be obstinate and embark upon the long road because of your ignorance, behave in an insolent manner without modesty and advance without restraint, and [continue] saying [the like of,] "In regards to the issue of the permissibility of *al-taqlīd*, although it is a fundamental issue—and the people have agreed that *al-taqlīd* is not permissible in fundamental issues and this has become well known amongst some of the *muqallids*—I say that *al-taqlīd* is permissible in it and all other fundamental issues."

فَنَقُول وَمن أَيْن عرفت جَوَاز التَّقْلِيد فِي مسَائِل الْأُصُول هَل كَانَ هَذَا مِنْك تقليدا أَم اجْتِهَادًا؟ فَإِن قلت تقليدا فَنَقُول وَمن ذَاك الَّذِي قلدته فَإِن قد حكينا لَك فِيمَا سبق أَن أَئِمَّة الْمذَاهب يمْنَعُونَ التَّقْلِيد كَمَا يمنعهُ غَيرهم فِي مسَائِل الْفُرُوع فرضا عَن مسَائِل الْأُصُول، فَإِن قلت قلدتهم أَو قلدت وَاحِدًا مِنْهُم وَهُوَ الَّذِي التزمت مذْهبه فِي جَمِيع مَا قَالَه من دون أَن تطالبه بِحجَّة فقد كذبت عَلَيْهِ وعللت نَفسك بالأباطيل، فَإِن غَيْرك مِمَّن هُوَ أعلم مِنْك بمذهبه واعرف بنصوصه قد نقل عَنهُ أَنه يمْنَع التَّقْلِيد وَإِن قلت قلدت غَيره فَمن هُوَ؟ ثمَّ كَيفَ سمحت نفسك فِي هَذِه الْمَسْأَلَة بخصوصها بِالْخرُوجِ عَن مذْهبه وتقليد غَيره.

We say, from where did you come to know the permissibility of *al-taqlīd* in fundamental issues? Is this out of *taqlīd* or out of *ijtihād* from you? If you say out of *taqlīd*, we say, who is the person that you have blind followed, for we have narrated to you as preceded that the *imāms* of the *madhhabs*—as well as others—forbid *al-taqlīd* in subsidiary issues, let alone in fundamental issues. If you say: I blindly followed them or one of them, and he is the one who's *madhhab* I am clinging to in everything he says without seeking proof from him. Then you have lied against him and furnished a justification via the baseless. This is because others who are more learned than you about his *madhhab* or more knowledgeable of its texts have reported from him that he forbade *al-taqlīd*. And if you say: I blindly followed other than him, then who is it? And how could you permit yourself in this particular issue to omit yourself from his *madhhab* and perform *taqlīd* of others?

وَبِالْجُمْلَةِ فَمن تلاعب بنفسه وبِدِينِهِ إِلَى هَذَا الْحَد فَهُوَ بالبهيمة أشبه، وليت أَن هَؤُلَاءِ المقلدة قلدوا أئمتهم فِي جَمِيع مَا يقولونه، فَإِنَّهُم لَو فعلوا كَذَلِك لَزِمَهُم أَن يقلدوهم فِي مَسْأَلَة التَّقْلِيد، وهم يَقُولُونَ بِعَدَمِ جَوَازه كَمَا عرفت سَابِقًا، وَحِينَئِذٍ يقتدون بهم فِي هَذِه الْمَسْأَلَة وَلَا يتم لَهُم ذَلِك إِلَّا بترك التَّقْلِيد فِي جَمِيع الْمسَائِل فيريحون أنفسهم ويخلصون من هَذِه الشبكة بالوقوع فِي حَبل من حبالها.

In brief, whomsoever plays with his religion and himself to this limit is akin to a beast. Would that these *muqallids* blindly imitate their *imāms* in everything they said, for if they had done that, it would have been binding upon them to imitate them in the issue of *al-taqlīd*, for they were of the view that it is not permissible, as the reader has seen. Therefore, they should follow them in this issue and this cannot be completed except through the abandonment of blind following in all religious issues, so as to give themselves rest and free themselves from this dragnet by loosening one of its ropes.

ثمَّ نقُول لهَذَا الْمُقَلّد أَيْضا من أَيْن عرفت أَن إمامك الذي قلدته مجتهد فإن قال عرفت أنه جَامع لعلوم الِاجْتِهَاد، فَنَقُول لَهُ وَمن أَيْن لَك هَذِه الْمعرفَة يَا مِسْكين فَأَنت تقر على نَفسك بِالْجَهْلِ وتكذبها فِي هَذِه الدَّعْوَى وَلَوْلَا جهلك لم تقلد غَيْرك، وَإِن قَالَ عرفتها بإخبار أهل الْعلم أن إمامي قد جمع عُلُوم الِاجْتِهَاد فَنَقُول هَذَا الَّذِي أخْبرك هَل هُوَ مقلد أم مُجْتَهد؟ إن قلت هُوَ مقلد فَمن أَيْن للمقلد هَذِه الْمعرفَة وَهُوَ مقرّ على نَفسه بِمَا أَقرَرت بِهِ على نَفسك من الْجَهْل وَإِن قلت أخْبرك بذلك رجل مُجْتَهد فَنَقُول من أَيْن عرفت أَنه مُجْتَهد وَأَنت مقرّ على نَفسك بِالْجَهْلِ ثمَّ نعود عَلَيْك بالسؤال الأول إِلَى مَا لَا نِهَايَة لَهُ.

Moreover, we say to this *muqallid* again, from where did you come to know that your *imām* whom you make *taqlīd* of is a *mujtahid*? If he says, "I knew that he possessed a grasp of the entirety of the sciences of *al-ijtihād*." We will say to him: Where did you obtain this knowledge from, O pauper? You acknowledged that you are ignorant yet you are denying it through this claim, and if not for your ignorance, you would not have blindly followed others. If he says, "I knew it through information from the people of knowledge that my *imām* has acquired a grasp of the entirety of the sciences of *al-ijtihād*." We will say: The one who informed you, is he a *muqallid* or a *mujtahid*? If you say that he is a *muqallid*, then where did a *muqallid* attain this knowledge, whilst he has acknowledged what you have acknowledged in that you are ignorant? If you say that you were informed by a *mujtahid*, we will say, where did you obtain the knowledge that he is a *mujtahid* whilst you have acknowledged that you are ignorant? Then we will repeat the first question to you in an endless cycle.

ثمَّ نقُول للمقلد من أَيْن عرفت أَن الْحق بيد الإِمَام الَّذِي قلدته وَأَنت تعلم أَن غَيره من الْعلمَاء قد خَالفه فِي كل مَسْأَلَة من مسَائِل الْخلاف إِن قلت عرفت ذَلِك تقليدا فَمن أَيْن للمقلد معرفَة الْحق والمحقين وَهُوَ مقرّ على نَفسه بِأَنَّهُ لَا يُطَالب بِالْحجَّةِ وَلَا يَعْقِلهَا إِذا جَاءَتْهُ فما لك يَا مِسْكين وَلِلْكذب على نَفسك بِمَا يشْهد عَلَيْك بِبُطْلَانِهِ لسَانك، بل يشْهد عَلَيْك كل مجتهد ومقلد بِخِلَاف دعواك.

In addition, we will say to the *muqallid*: From where did you ascertain that the truth is with the *imām*[198] whom you make *taqlīd* of whilst you know that other scholars have contradicted him in every issue amongst the issues wherein there is variance. If you say, "I came to know this through *taqlīd*." From where will the *muqallid* come to know the truth and the truthful ones when he has admitted that he does not seek after proof nor understand it when it comes to him? O pauper, why do you lie against yourself with what your tongue testifies against you of its futility. In fact, every *muqallid* and *mujtahid* bears witness against you with what is contrary to your claim.

وَإِن قلت عرفت ذَلِك بِالِاجْتِهَادِ فلست حِينَئِذٍ مُقَلدًا وَلَا من أهل التَّقْلِيد بل التَّقْلِيد عَلَيْك حرَام فما لك تغمط نعْمَة الله عَلَيْك وتنكرها وَالله يَقُول: ﴿وَأَمَّا بِنِعْمَةِ رَبِّكَ فَحَدِّثْ﴾ وَرَسُول الله صلى الله عَلَيْهِ وَآله وَسلم يَقُول: ((إِن الله يحب أَن يرى أثر نعْمَته على عَبده)) وَأثر نعْمَة الْعلم أَن يعْمل

198 See *I'lām al-Muwaqqi'īn* (208-211).

الْعَالم بِعِلْمِهِ وَيَأْخُذ مَا تعبده الله بِهِ من الْجِهَة الَّتِي أمره الله بِالْأَخْذِ مِنْهَا فِي مُحكم كِتَابه وعَلى لِسَان رَسُوله تلك الْجِهَة هِيَ الْكتاب وَالسّنة وكَمَا تقدم سرد أَدِلَّة ذَلِك، وَهُوَ أَمر مُتَّفق عَلَيْهِ لَا خلاف فِيهِ.

And if you say, "I came to know of this through *ijtihād*." Then, in this case you are not a *muqallid* nor amongst the people of *al-taqlīd*. Rather, *al-taqlīd* is unlawful for you. So why do you belittle the blessings of Allah upon you and deny them? Allah states: **{And proclaim the Grace of your Lord.}**[199] And the Messenger of Allah ﷺ said, "Verily Allah loves to see the traces of His bounty upon His slave."[200] The traces of the blessing of knowledge is for the scholar to act upon his knowledge and acquire what he will use to worship Allah from the place Allah has ordered him to take from in the clear *āyāt* of His Book and upon the tongue of his Messenger. That place is the Book of Allah and the Sunnah, just as proofs for this have preceded, and it is an issue that is agreed upon without any divergence of opinion.

وعَلى كل حَال فَأَنت بتقليدك مَعَ كونك قاصرا ممَّن عمل فِي دين الله

199 Al-Ḍuḥā:11

200 Recorded by al-Tirmidhī (no. 2819) with this wording from the ḥadīth of 'Amr ibn Shu'ayb—his father—his grandfather; and he said that it is a *ḥasan* ḥadīth, and it is as he stated. Also reported by al-Nasā'ī (8/196, no. 5294), Abu Dāwūd (no. 4063), al-Ḥākim (4/181), Aḥmad (3/473), Ibn Sa'd (6/28), al-Bayhaqī (10/10) from the path of Abu Isḥāq—Abu al-Aḥwas—his father who said, "I came to the Prophet ﷺ wearing a cheap dress. He asked, 'Do you have property?' I said, 'Yes.' He said, 'From which kinds of property do you have?' I said, 'Allah has bestowed upon me from camels, sheep, horses and slaves.' He said, 'Then, when Allah bestows wealth upon you, let the traces of Allah's blessings and bounty be shown on you." It is a *ṣaḥīḥ* ḥadīth.

بِغَيْر بَصِيرَة وَترك مَا لا شك فِيهِ إِلَى مَا فِيهِ الشَّك واستبدل بالْحق شَيْئا لَا يَدْرِي مَا هُوَ، وَإِن كنت مُجْتَهدا فَأَنت مِمَّن أضلّهُ الله على علم وَختم على سَمعه وَبصره فَلم يَنْفَعهُ علمه وَصَارَ مَا علمه حجَّة عَلَيْهِ وَرجع من النُّور إِلَى الظُّلُمَات وَمن الْيَقِين إِلَى الشَّك وَمن الثريا إِلَى الثرى فلا لعا لك بل لِلْيَدَيْنِ وَلِلْفَمِ.

Nevertheless, with your blind following—despite being incapable—you are amongst those who act in the religion of Allah without insight and abandon what contains no doubt for that which contains doubt; and you replace the truth with something of which you do not know its source. If you are a *mujtahid*, then you are amongst those whom Allah has sent astray due to knowledge and has set a seal upon his hearing and sight; so that his knowledge does not avail him. What he knows will serve as a proof against him and he has omitted himself from the light into the darkness; from certainty into doubt and from grace to grass. Indeed, you have no aid; how pitiful you are.

هَذَا إِن كَانَ ذَلِك الْمُقَلّد يَدعِي أن إمَامه على حق فِي جَمِيع مَا قَالَه وَإِن كَانَ يقر بِأَن فِي قَوْله الْحق وَالْبَاطِل وَأَنَّهُ بشر يُخطئ ويصيب لَا سِيمَا فِي مَحْض الرَّأْي الَّذِي هُوَ على شفا جرف هار فَنَقُول لَهُ إِن كنت قَائِلا بِهَذَا فقد أصبت وَهُوَ الَّذِي يَقُوله إمامك لَو سَأَلَهُ سَائل عَن مذْهبه وَجَمِيع مَا دونه من مسَائِله، وَلَكِن أخبرنَا مَا حملك أَن تجْعَل مَا هُوَ مُشْتَمل على الْحق وَالْبَاطِل قلادة فِي عُنُقك تلتزمه وَتَدين بِهِ غير تَارِك لشَيْء مِنْهُ فَإِن الْخَطَأ من إمامك قد عذره الله فِيهِ بل جعل لَهُ أجرا فِي مُقَابلَته كَمَا تقدم

تَقْرِيره لِأَنَّهُ مُجْتَهد وللمجتهد إن أَخطَأ أجر كَمَا صرح بذلك رَسُول الله صلى الله عَلَيْهِ وَآله وَسلم.

This is if such a *muqallid* claims that his *imām* is upon the truth in everything he says. But if he acknowledges that his statements contain truth and falsehood, and that he is a human who errs [sometimes] and is correct [sometimes,] especially in pure personal opinion—which is [akin in danger to one being] upon the edge of a bank about to collapse. We will say to him: If you state this then you are right, as this is what your *imām* would say if a questioner were to ask him about his *madhhab* and the entirety of what he has recorded of its issues. But inform us of what causes you to place something comprising of truth and falsehood as a collar around your neck, clinging to it and taking it as your religion without leaving anything from it. Indeed, an error from your *imām* may be excused by Allah. In fact, He has set a reward for him in exchange for it—as it was explained earlier—due to him being a *mujtahid*; and a *mujtahid* will have a reward if he errs, as stated by the Messenger of Allah ﷺ.

فَأَنت من أخْبرك بأنك مَعْذُور في اتباع الْخَطَأ؟ وَأي حجَّة قَامَت لَك على ذَلِك، فَإِن قلت إِنَّك لَو تركت التَّقْلِيد وَسَأَلت أهل الْعلم عَن النُّصُوص لَكُنْت غير قَاطع بِالصَّوَابِ بل يحْتَمل أَن الَّذِي أخذت بِهِ وَسَأَلت عَنهُ هُوَ حق وَيحْتَمل أَنه بَاطِل فنقول ليس الأمر كذلك فإن التمسك بالدليل الصحيح كله حق وليس شيء منه بباطل، والمفروض أَنَّك ستسأل عَن دينك فِي عباداتك ومعاملاتك عُلَمَاء الْكتاب وَالسّنة وهم أتقى لله من أَن يفتوك بِغَيْر مَا سَأَلت عَنهُ فَإِنَّك إِنَّمَا سَأَلتهمْ عن كتاب الله أو سنة رَسُوله

فِي ذَلِك الحكم الَّذِي أردْت الْعَمَل بِهِ، وهم بل جَمِيع الْمُسلمين يعلمُونَ أَن كتاب الله وَسنة رَسُوله حق لَا بَاطِل وهدى لا ضلالة.

As for you, who informed you that you are excused for following an error? Which proof affirmed this to you in respect of that? If you state: If you leave *al-taqlīd* and ask the people of knowledge about the text, you will not be sure of the truth; rather it is possible that what you acquired and asked about is the truth and it is also possible that it is falsehood. We reply: The issue is not like that. When adhering to a sound evidence, all of it is the truth and there is nothing of it that is falsehood. What is obligatory is that you ask about your religion as regards to your acts of worship and dealings from the scholars of the Book and Sunnah, and they are too conscious of Allah for them to issue a verdict to you contrary to what you have asked them. This is because you only asked them about the Book of Allah and the Sunnah of His Messenger in this judgement which you intended to act upon. They, rather, the entire Muslim body know that the Book of Allah and the Sunnah of His Messenger is the truth and not falsehood, and guidance not misguidance.

وَلَو فَرضنَا أَن المسؤول قصر فِي الْبَحْث فأفتاك مثلا بِحَدِيث ضَعِيف وَترك الصَّحِيح أَو بِآيَة الْمَنْسُوخَة وَترك المحكمة لم يكن عَلَيْك فِي ذَلِك بَأْس فَإِنَّك قد فعلت مَا هُوَ فرضك واسترويت أهل الْعلم عَن الشَّرِيعَة المطهرة لَا عَن آراء الرِّجَال، وَلَيْسَ للمقلد أَن يَقُول كمقالك هَذَا فيزعم أَن إِمَامه أتقى لله من أَن يَقُول بقول بَاطِل لأَنا نقُول هُوَ معترف أَن بعض رَأْيه خطأ وَلم يَأْمُرك بِأَن تتبعه فِي خطئه بل نهاك عَن تَقْلِيده ومنعك من ذَلِك كَمَا تقدم تحريره عَن أَئِمَّة الْمذَاهب وَعَن سَائِر الْمُسلمين، بِخِلَاف من سَأَلته عَن

الْكتاب وَالسّنة فأفتاك بذلك فَإِنَّهُ يعلم أَن جَمِيع مَا فِي الْكتاب وَالسّنة حق وَصدق وَهدى وَنور وَأَنت لم تسْأَل إِلَّا عَن ذَلِك.

Supposing the one being questioned fell short in his research and he provides a verdict to you, for example, with a weak ḥadīth and left the authentic one, or with an abrogated *āyah* and left the un-abrogated (*muḥkam*) one, there will be no harm upon you in that. This is because you have done what is mandatory upon you and asked the people of knowledge regarding the pure Sharīʿah and not in regards to the personal opinion of men. It is not proper for a *muqallid* to say the like of this statement of yours and assume that his *imām* is the [only one] conscious enough of Allah [to prevent him from] uttering a baseless statement. This is because we stated that he has admitted to some of his views being wrong and he did not command you to follow him in his errors. Rather, he forbade you from making *taqlīd* of him and he forbade you from that (i.e. following him in an error), as previously mentioned from the *imāms* of the *madhhabs* and the rest of the Muslims. This is contrary to the one whom you ask in regards to the Book and the Sunnah and he gives you a verdict based upon it, as he knows that the entirety of what is in the Book and Sunnah is the truth, guidance and light and that you are only asking him about that.

ثمَّ نقُول لَك أَيهَا الْمُقَلّد مَا بالك تعترف فِي كل مَسْأَلَة من مسَائِل الْفُرُوع الَّتِي أَنْت مقلد فِيهَا بأنك لَا تَدْرِي مَا هُوَ الْحق فِيهَا ثمَّ لما أرشدناك إِلَى مَا أَنْت عَلَيْهِ من التَّقْلِيد غير جَائِز فِي دين الله أَقمت نَفسك مقَاما لَا تستحقه ونصبت نَفسك فِي منصب لم تتأهل لَهُ فَأخذت فِي الْمُخَاصمَة وَالِاسْتِدْلَال لجَوَاز التَّقْلِيد وَجئْت بِالشُّبْهَةِ الساقطة الَّتِي قد قدمنَا دَفعهَا

فِي هَذَا الْمُؤلف فَهلا نزلت نَفسك فِي هَذِه الْمَسْأَلَة الْأُصُولِيَّة الْعَظِيمَة المتشعبة تِلْكَ الْمنزلَة الَّتِي كنت تنزلها فِي مسَائِل الْفُرُوع فَمَا لَك وللنزول فِي منَازِل الفحول والسلوك فِي مسالك أهل الْأَيْدِي المتبالغة فِي الطول.

Furthermore, we say to you, O *muqallid*, why is it that you assert in every issue amongst the subsidiary issues[201] in which you are a blind follower that you do not know what is the truth therein. Then, when we direct to you that what you are upon of *al-taqlīd* is not permissible in Allah's religion, you place yourself at a level that you do not deserve and set for yourself a position that you are not competent for, taking to dispute and making inferences of the permissibility of *al-taqlīd*. You bring forth doubts which are null and void, which we have refuted earlier in this treatise. In this great and diverse fundamental issue, why not put yourself at the level that you assume for yourself in subsidiary issues. Why would you assume the level of the scholars (lit. stallions) and trespass upon the path of the people of authority who have reached the utmost degree [in power]?

فَمَا هلك أمرؤ عرف قدر نَفسه فَقل هَاهُنَا لَا أَدْرِي إِنَّمَا سَمِعت النَّاس يَقُولُونَ شَيْئا فقلته فَنَقُول هَكَذَا سَيكون جوابك لنَكِير ومنكر بعد أَن تقبر وَيُقَال لَك لَا دَريت وَلَا تليت كَمَا ثَبت بذلك النَّص الصَّحِيح وَإِذا كنت معترفا بأنك لَا تَدْرِي فشفاء العي السُّؤَال فاسأل من تثق بِدِينِهِ وَعلمه وإنصافه فِي مَسْأَلَة التَّقْلِيد حَتَّى تكون على بَصِيرَة وَلَو كَانَ إمامك الَّذِي تقلده حَيا لأرشدناك إِلَيْهِ وأمرناك بالتعويل عَلَيْهِ فَإِنَّهُ أول ناه لَك عَن التَّقْلِيد

201 See *al-Musawwadah* (458-460), *Tanqīḥ al-Fuṣūl* (p. 442) and *al-Kawkab al-Munīr*.

كَمَا عرفناك فِيمَا سبق وَلكنه قد صَار رهين البلى وَتَحْت أطباق الثرى.

An individual who knows his personal level will not perish. So, say here, "I do not know. I heard people saying something, so I said it." We say, this is how your response will be to Nakīr and Munkar after you have been buried and it will be said to you, "You neither knew nor did you follow," as is established in the authentic narration.[202] If you know that you do not know, then the cure for ignorance is to ask. So, ask the person whom you have trust in his religion, knowledge and fairness about the issue of *al-taqlīd* so that you will be upon sure knowledge. If your *imām* whom you are blindly follow-

202 He is referring to the ḥadīth recorded by Abu Dāwūd (no. 4751) from Anas bin Mālik who said: The Prophet ﷺ entered the garden of the palm tree of Banu al-Najjār. He heard a voice and was terrified. He asked, "Who are the people buried in these graves?" The people replied, "O Messenger of Allah! These are some people who died during the pre-Islamic times." He said, "Seek refuge in Allah from the punishment of the fire, and the trial of al-Dajjāl." They asked, "Why is that, O Messenger of Allah?" He said, "When a faithful believer is placed in his grave, an angel comes to him and says to him, 'Whom did you worship?' Allah then guides him and he says, 'I worshipped Allah.' He is then asked, 'What was your opinion of this man?' He replies, 'He is Allah's servant and Messenger.' He will not be asked about anything further and will then be taken to his abode in Hell and will be told, 'This was your abode in Hell, but Allah protected you and had mercy on you and substituted for you an abode in Paradise for it.' He will say, 'Leave me so that I may go and give glad tidings to my family.' He will be told, 'Dwell.' When an infidel is placed in his grave, an angel comes to him, reprimands him and asks him, 'Whom did you worship?' He replies, 'I do not know.' He will be told, 'You neither knew nor did you follow.' He is then asked, 'What was your opinion on this man?' He replies, "I held the opinion that the other people held." He will then give him a blow between his ears with an iron hammer and will utter a shout which will be heard by all the creatures (near him) with the exception of men and Jinn." It is a *saḥīḥ* ḥadīth.

ing were to be alive, we would have directed you to him and ordered you to have trust in him, for he was the first person who forbade you from *al-taqlīd*—as we have made clear earlier in the book. However, he has become confined to decomposition under layers of earth.

فاسأل غيره من الْعلمَاء الْمَوْجُودين وهم بِحَمْد الله فِي كل صقع من بِلَاد الْإِسْلَام فَالله سُبْحَانَهُ حَافظ دينه بهم وحجته قَائِمَة على عباده بوجودهم، وَإِن كتموا الْحق فِي بعض الْأَحْوَال إما لتقية مسوغة كَمَا قَالَ تَعَالَى ﴿إِلَّا أَن تَتَّقُوا مِنْهُمْ تُقَاةً﴾ أَو بمداهنة أَو طمع فِي جاه أَو مَال، وَلَكنهُمْ على كل حَال إِذا عرفُوا من هُوَ طَالب للحق رَاغِب فِيهِ سَائل عَن دينه سالك مسالك الصَّحَابَة وَالتَّابِعِينَ وتابعيهم لم يكتموا عَلَيْهِ الْحق وَلَا زاغوا عَنْهُ فَإِن كنت لَا تثق بِأحد من الْعلمَاء وثوقك بإمامك الَّذِي نشأت على مذْهبه فَارْجِع إِلَى نصوصه الَّتِي قدمنَا لك الْإِشَارَة إِلَى بَعْضهَا وفيهَا مَا ينقع الْغلَّة ويشفي الْعلَّة.

So, ask others among the scholars that are present, whom—and all praise is due to Allah—are in every region of the lands of Islam. Allah—glory be to Him—safeguards His religion through them and His proof is established upon His slaves with their presence. This is the case even if they conceal the truth in some situations due to a justified fear of danger, as stated by the most High: **{...Except if you indeed fear a danger from them.}**[203] Or due to sycophancy (seeking favour) or the lust for status or wealth. However, if they find that someone is seeking the truth, desirous of it, asking about his religion, whilst following the path of the companions, their succes-

---

203 Āli 'Imrān: 28

sors and their successors, they will not conceal the truth from him nor turn away from him. And if you do not trust anyone amongst the scholars and you trust your *imām* whose *madhhab* you were nurtured upon, refer to his texts—of which we have presented some to you—for they contain that which will quench the burning thirst and cure the illness.

[نصيحة نافعة لمن يتصدر للفتيا وَالْقَضَاء من المقلدين]

[Beneficial Advise to Those Who Issue *Fatwa* and Judgements Amongst the *Muqallids*]

وَاعْلَم أرشدك الله أَيهَا الْمُقَلّد أَنَّك إِن أنصفت من نَفسك وخليت بَين عقلك وفهمك وَبَين مَا حررناه فِي هَذَا الْمُؤلف لم يبْق مَعَك شكّ فِي أَنَّك على خطر عَظِيم هَذَا إِن كنت مُقْتَصرا فِي التَّقْلِيد على مَا تَدْعُو إِلَيْهِ حَاجَتك مِمَّا يتَعَلَّق بِهِ أَمر عبادتك ومعاملتك، أمَّا إِذا كنت مَعَ كونك فِي هَذِه الرُّتْبَة الساقطة مرشحا نَفسك لفتيا السَّائِلين وللقضاء على المتخاصمين فَاعْلَم أَنَّك ممتحن وممتحن بك، ومبتلى ومتبلى بك، لِأَنَّك تريق الدِّمَاء بأحكامك وتنقل الْأَمْلَاك والحقوق من أَهلهَا وتحلل الْحَرَام لَهُم وَتحرم الْحَلَال وَتقول على الله مَا لم يقل غير مُسْتَند إِلَى كتاب الله وَسنة رَسُوله.

Know—may Allah guide you O *muqallid*—that if you are just with yourself and remove the barrier between your intellect and understanding and what we have documented in this work, there will be no doubt left in you that you are upon [a way entailing] great danger. This is if your blind following is limited to what you are in need of amongst that which is related to the issues of your acts of worship and dealings. However, if in spite of being at this degraded level, you prop yourself up as being competent to issue verdicts to questioners and judge between contending parties, know that you are tested and people are being tested through you; you are afflicted and people will be afflicted through you. This is because you will spill blood with your rulings and transfer ownership and rights from their owners [to others], legalise the unlawful for them and prohibit the lawful to them and say about Allah that which is not supported by the Book of Allah nor the Sunnah of His Messenger.

بل بِشَيْء لَا تَدْرِي أَحَق هُوَ أم بَاطِل باعترافك على نَفسك بأنك كَذَلِك، فَمَاذَا يكون جوابك بَين يَدي الله فَإِن الله إِنَّمَا أَمر حكام الْعباد أَن يحكموا بَينهم بِمَا أنزل الله وَأَنت لَا تعرف مَا أنزل الله على الْوَجْه الَّذِي يُرَاد بِهِ وَأمرهمْ أَن يحكموا بِالْحَقِّ وَأَنت لَا تَدْرِي بالْحق وَإِنَّمَا سَمِعت النَّاس يَقُولُونَ شَيْئا فقلته وَأمرهمْ أَن يحكموا بَينهم بالْعدْل وَأَنت لَا تَدْرِي بالْعدْل من الْجور، لِأَن الْعدْل هُوَ مَا وَافق مَا شَرعه الله والجور مَا خَالفه.

Rather, [you will support such statements with] that which you are unaware as to whether it is right or false, based upon your acknowledgment that you are like that (i.e. lacking understanding). What will be your response before Allah, for Allah has only ordered the judges of the slaves to judge amongst them with what Allah has revealed, whilst you do not know what Allah has revealed in the manner that it is intended. And He commanded them to judge in accordance with the truth, whilst you do not know the truth. Rather, you only heard the people saying something and you said the same. He commanded them to judge amongst them with justice, whilst you do not know justice from injustice. This is because justice is what conforms to what Allah has ordained and injustice is what opposes it.

فَهَذِهِ الْأَوَامِر لم تتنَاوَل مثلك بل الْمَأْمُور بهَا غَيْرك فكيف تلبست بشَيْء لم تُؤمر بِهِ وَلَا ندبت إِلَيْهِ وَكَيف أقدمت على الدخول فِي الحكم بِغَيْر مَا أنزل الله حَتَّى تكون مِمَّن قَالَ فِيهِ ﴿وَمَن لَّمْ يَحْكُم بِمَآ أَنزَلَ اللَّهُ فَأُولَٰئِكَ هُمُ الظَّالِمُونَ﴾، ﴿وَمَن لَّمْ يَحْكُم بِمَآ أَنزَلَ اللَّهُ فَأُولَٰئِكَ هُمُ الْفَاسِقُونَ﴾، ﴿وَمَن لَّمْ يَحْكُم بِمَآ أَنزَلَ اللَّهُ فَأُولَٰئِكَ هُمُ الْكَافِرُونَ﴾.

Therefore, such commands are not addressed to your like; rather those charged with them are individuals other than you. So why would you engage in something that you were not enjoined nor assigned to do? Why would you delve into judging with other than what Allah has revealed so that you would fall amongst those whom Allah states about: **{And whosoever does not judge by that which Allah has revealed, such are the wrongdoers}**,[204] **{And whosoever does not judge by what Allah has revealed, such are the obstinate sinners}**,[205] and: **{And whosoever does not judge by what Allah has revealed, such are the disbelievers.}**[206]?

فَهَذِهِ الْآيَات الْكَرِيمَة متناولة لكل من لم يحكم بِمَا انْزِلْ الله، وأنت لَا تَدعِي أَنَّك حكمت بِمَا أنزل الله. بل تقر أنك حكمت بقول الْعَالم الْفُلَانِيّ وَلَا تَدْرِي هَل ذَلِك الحكم الَّذِي حكم بِهِ هُوَ من مَحْض رَأْيه أم من الْمسَائِل الَّتِي اسْتدلَّ عَلَيْهَا بِالدَّلِيلِ ثمَّ لَا يدْرِي أهوَ أصَاب فِي الِاسْتِدْلَال أم أَخطَأ وَهل أَخذ بِالدَّلِيلِ الْقوي أم الضَّعِيف فَانْظُر يَا مِسْكين

204 Al-Māʾidah: 45
205 Al-Māʾidah: 47
206 Al-Māʾidah: 44

مَا صنعت بِنَفْسِك فَإِنَّك لم يكن جهلك مَقْصُورا عَلَيْك بل جهلت على عباد الله فأرقت الدِّمَاء وأقمت الْحُدُود وهتكت الْحرم بِمَا لَا تَدْرِي فقبح الله الْجَهْل وَلَا سِيمَا إِذا جعله صَاحبه شرعا ودينا لَهُ وللمسلمين فَإِنَّهُ طاغوت عِنْد التَّحْقِيق وَإِن ستر من التلبيس بستر رَقِيق.

These noble *āyāt* encompass anyone who does not judge with what Allah has revealed. Do not claim that you have judged with what Allah has revealed; rather concede that you have judged with the statement of such and such scholar; and you do not know whether that judgement which you have passed is mere opinion or from amongst the issues which were deduced through evidence. In addition, you do not know whether he was correct in his deduction or wrong; and whether he used a strong proof or weak one. So, O pauper, look at what you have done to yourself, because your ignorance is not limited to yourself, rather you have behaved foolishly towards the slaves of Allah. You have shed blood, established prescribed punishments and comprimised the inviolable through what you do not know. May Allah shame ignorance, especially when its possessor makes it a law and religion to himself and to the Muslims; indeed he is actually a false deity even if he is covered with a tiny screen on account of deception.

فيا أَيهَا القَاضِي الْمُقَلّد أخبرنَا أَي الْقُضَاة الثَّلَاثَة أَنْت الَّذين قَالَ فيهم رَسُول الله صلى الله عَلَيْهِ وَآله وَسلم: ((الْقُضَاة ثَلَاثَة قاضيان فِي النَّار وقاض فِي الْجنَّة)). فالقاضيان اللَّذَان فِي النَّار قَاض قضى بِغَيْر الْحق وقاض قضى بِالْحَقِّ وَهُوَ لَا يعلم أَنه الْحق وَالَّذِي فِي الْجنَّة قَاض قضى بِالْحَقِّ وَهُوَ يعلم أَنه الْحق فبالله عَلَيْك هَل قضيت بِالْحَقِّ وَأَنت تعلم أَنه

الْحق؟ إِن قلت نعم فَأَنت وَسَائِر أهل الْعلم تشْهدُونَ بأنك كَاذِب لِأَنَّك معترف بأنك لَا تعلم بِالْحَقِّ وَكَذَلِكَ سَائِر النَّاس يحكمون عَلَيْك بِهَذَا من غير فرق بَين مُجْتَهد ومقلد.

So, O you *muqallid* judge, inform us which of the three judges you are, from those whom the Messenger of Allah ﷺ said about, "Judges are of three types: Two will go to the Hell fire and one will go to Paradise."[207] The two judges who will go to Hell are the judge who judged without [following] the truth and the judge who judged in accordance to the truth but he did not know that it was the truth. The one who will go to Paradise is the judge who judged in accordance with the truth and he knew it to be the truth. I ask you by Allah, did you judge in accordance to the truth whilst you knew it to be the truth? If you say, yes, then you and all the people of knowl-

207 Reported by Abu Dāwūd (no. 3573), al-Tirmidhī (1322), Ibn Mājah (2315) al-Nasā'ī in *al-Sunan al-Kubrā* (3/461, no. 5922/1), al-Ḥākim in *al-Mustadrak* (4/90) and he said, "The *isnād* is *ṣaḥīḥ*." Al-Dhahabī refuted him, saying, "I say: Ibn Kathīr al-Ghanawī is *munkar al-ḥadīth*."

Al-Albānī said in *al-Irwā* (8/236): His *shaykh* Ḥakīm ibn Jabīr is similar to him or worse than him. Al-Dāraquṭnī said about him: "*matrūk*." No one considers him reliable except al-Baghawī. Al-Sājī said, "He is amongst the people of truthfulness but he is not strong. Ibn 'Adī attributed some *munkar* reports to him, and this is all that he has been criticised with. Ibn Hibbān mentioned him in *al-Thiqāt*."

It is a *ṣaḥīḥ* ḥadīth. Buraydah said: The Messenger of Allah ﷺ said: "Judges are of three types: two will go to Hell and one will go to Paradise. The one who will go to Paradise is a man who knows what is right and gives judgement accordingly; but a man who knows what is right and acts tyrannically in his judgment will go to Hell; and a man who does not know what is right and gives judgement to the people whilst he is ignorant will go to Hell."

edge bear witness that you are a liar because you admitted that you do not know the truth. Likewise all of the people will pass a verdict upon you with this fact, without distinction between the *mujtahid* and the *muqallid*.

وَإِن قلت بل قضيت بِمَا قَالَه إمامك وَلَا تَدْرِي أَحَق هُوَ أم بَاطِل كَمَا هُوَ شَأْن كل مقلد على وَجه الأَرْض فَأَنت بإقرارك هَذَا أحد رجلَيْنِ: إِمَّا قضيت بِالْحَقِّ وَلَا تعلم بِأَنَّهُ الْحق أَو قضيت بِغَيْر الْحق لِأَن ذَلِك الحكم الَّذِي حكمت بِهِ هُوَ لَا يَخْلُو عَن أحد الْأَمريْنِ: إِمَّا أَن يكون حَقًا وَإِمَّا أَن يكون غير حق وعَلى كلا التَّقْدِيرَيْنِ فَأَنت من قُضَاة النَّار بنَص الْمُخْتَار.

If you say that you judged with what your *imām* said without knowing whether it is the truth or falsehood—as is the case of every *muqallid* on the surface of the earth; with your confession, you are one of these two men: It is either that you have judged with the truth without knowing that it is the truth or you have judged without following the truth. This is because the judgement you pass is either of two: (i) the truth or (ii) other than the truth. On the basis of both possibilities, you are amongst the judges of Hell, as mentioned in the text.

وَهَذَا مَا أَظن بتردد فِيهِ أحد من أهل الْفَهم لأمرين: أَحدهمَا: أَن النَّبِي صلى الله عَلَيْهِ وَآله وَسلم قد جعل الْقُضَاة ثَلَاثَة وَبَين صفة كل وَاحِد مِنْهُم بَيَانا يفهمهُ المقصر والكامل والعالم وَالْجَاهِل الثَّانِي: أَن الْمُقَلّد لَا يَدعِي أَنه يعلم بِمَا هُوَ حق من كَلَام إِمَامه وَلَا بِمَا هُوَ بَاطِل بل يقر على نَفسه أَنه يقبل قَول الْغَيْر وَلَا يُطَالِبهُ بِحجَّة ويقر على نَفسه أَنه لَا يعقل

الْحجَّة إِذا جَاءَتْهُ.

I do not think that anyone amongst the people of understanding will doubt this due to two issues: One: The Prophet ﷺ classified judges into three and he explained the characteristics of each of them. He provided an explanation that the deficient and the complete, the scholar and the ignorant would understand. Two: A *muqallid* does not claim to know what the truth is from the statements of his *imām* nor what the invalid is. Rather, he concedes that he accepts the statement of others without seeking proof and he acknowledges that he would not understand the proof if it came to him.

فَأَفَاد هَذَا أَنه حكم بِشَيْء لَا يدْرِي مَا هُوَ فَإِن وَافق الْحق فَهُوَ قضى بالحق وَلا يدري أنه الحق وَإِن لم يُوَافق الحق فَهُوَ قضى بِغَيْر الْحق وَهَذَانِ هما القاضيان اللَّذَان فِي النَّار فَالْقَاضِي الْمُقَلّد على كلا حالتيه يتقلب فِي نَار جَهَنَّم فَهُوَ كَمَا قَالَ الشَّاعِر.

It can be deduced from this that he passed judgement with something he does not know about. Thus, if it conforms to the truth, he has judged in accordance with the truth but he did not know that it is the truth; and if it does not conform to the truth, he has judged with other than the truth. These are the two judges who will go to the Hell fire. A *muqallid* judge in both scenarios will be wallowing in the fire of Hell. He is as stated by the poet:

خذا بطن هرشي أو قفاها فَإِنَّهُ كلا جَانِبي هرشي لَهُنَّ طَرِيق

Take the interior part of Harsha (a mountain pass close to Makkah) or its rear part, for each side of Harsha is a

way.[208]

وكما تَقول الْعَرَب فِي الشَّرّ خِيَار وَلَقَد خَابَ وخسر من لَا ينجو على كل حَال من النَّار، فيا أَيهَا القَاضِي الْمُقَلّد مَا الَّذِي أوقعك فِي هَذِه الورطة وألجأك إِلَى هَذِه الْعهْدَة الَّتِي صرت فِيهَا على كل حَال من أهل النَّار؟ إِذا دمت على قضائك وَلم تتب فَإِن أهل الْمعاصِي والبطالة على اخْتِلَاف أنواعهم هم أَرْجَى لله مِنْك وأخوف لَهُ.

Just as the Arabs say: In evil there is an option. Indeed, he has failed and attained loss whomever is not saved from the fire in every situation. So, O *muqallid* judge, what caused you to fall into this dilemma and led you to this responsibility which has included you amongst the people of Hell in every situation? If you stay upon your judgement and do not repent, then the sinful and the bone idle—in spite of their variant types—are more hopeful and fearful of Allah than you.

لأَنهم يقدمُونَ على الْمعاصِي وهم على عزم التَّوْبَة والإقلاع وَالرُّجُوع وكل وَاحِد مِنْهُم يسْأَل الله الْمَغْفِرَة وَالتَّوْبَة وَيلُوم نَفسه على مَا فرط مِنْهُ وَيُحب أَن لَا يَأْتِيهِ الْمَوْت إِلَّا بعد أَن يطهر نَفسه من أدران كل مَعْصِيّة، وَلَو دَعَا لَهُ دَاع بِأَن الله يبقيه على مَا هُوَ متلبس بِهِ من البطالة وَالْمَعْصِيَة إِلَى الْمَوْت ليعلم هُوَ وكل سامع أَنه يَدْعُو عَلَيْهِ لَا لَهُ.

This is because they engage in sin whilst they have the resolve to repent, halt the sin and return [to righteousness.] Each one of them

208 Mentioned by the author of *al-Lisān* (15/76).

asks Allah for forgiveness, turns to Him in repentance and blames himself over the wrong he has committed; and he would love that death not come upon him except after he has purified himself from the filth of every sin. And if a supplicant were to pray for him that Allah make him remain upon what he is guilty of—such as idleness and sin—until death, he and everyone who hears it would know that he is supplicating against him and not for him.

وَلَو علم أَنه يبْقى على مَا هُوَ عَلَيْهِ إِلَى الْمَوْت ويلقى الله وَهُوَ متلبس بِهِ لضاقت عَلَيْهِ الأَرْض بِمَا رَحبَتْ لِأَنَّهُ يعلم أَن هَذَا الْبَقَاء هُوَ من مُوجبَات النَّار بِخِلَاف هَذَا القَاضِي الْمِسْكِين فَإِنَّهُ رُبمَا دَعَا الله فِي خلواته وَبعد صلواته أَن يديم عَلَيْهِ تِلْكَ النِّعْمَة ويحرسها عَن الزَّوَال وَيصرف عَنهُ كيد الكائدين وحسد الحاسدين حَتَّى لَا يقدروا على عَزله وَلَا يتمكنوا من فَصله وَقد يبْذل المخذول فِي استمراره على ذَلِك نفائس الْأَمْوَال وَيدْفَع الرشا والبراطيل والرغائب لمن كَانَ لَهُ فِي أمره مدْخلا فَجمع بَين خسراني الدُّنْيَا وَالْآخِرَة وتسمح نَفسه بهَا جَمِيعًا فِي حُصُول ذَلِك فيشتري بهما النَّار.

If he were to know that he would remain upon what he is doing until death and meet Allah whilst he is guilty of it, the earth would feel constricting to him despite its vastness, as he knows that this continuance is amongst that which necessitates Hell. This is contrary to this hapless judge, for he may call upon Allah in privacy and after his prayers that He should make these "blessings" last upon him; safeguard them from going away, and protect him from the machinations of the plotters and the envy of the envious, so that they will not be able to remove him nor be able to sack him. In order to continue upon that [i.e. his position], the forsaken may expend expensive wealth and offer bribes to one who can provide furtherance in his affair, thereby combining between the loss of this world and the Hereafter. He granted his entire life generously in the attaining of this but purchased naught but the fire.

وَالْعلَّة الغائبة الْمَقْصد الْأَسْنَى وَالْمطلب الْأَبْعَد لهَذَا المغبون لَيْسَ إِلَّا اجْتِمَاع الْعَامَّة عليه وصراخهم بَين يَدَيْهِ وَلَو عقل لعلم أَنه لم يكن فِي رياسة عالية وَلَا فِي مَكَان رفيع وَلَا فِي مرتبَة جليلة فَإِنَّهُ يُشَارِكهُ فِي اجْتِمَاع هَؤُلَاءِ الْعَوام وتطاولهم إِلَيْهِ وتزاحمهم عَلَيْهِ كل من يُرَاد إهانته إِمَّا بِإِقَامَة حد عَلَيْهِ أَو قصاص أَو تَعْزِير فَإِنَّهُ يجتمع على وَاحِد من هَؤُلَاءِ مَا لَا يجْتَمع على القَاضِي عشر معشاره بل يجْتَمع على أهل اللّعب والمجون والسخرية وَأهل الزمر والرقص وَالضَّرْب بالطبل أضعاف أَضْعَاف من يجْتَمع على ذالك القَاضِي.

The conclusive cause, grandest destination and utmost quest for this deluded person is nothing but the gathering of the common people and their yelling in front of him. Were he to be rational, he would have known that he is neither in a high position, a lofty place nor at a noble level, for he will share in this gathering of common people, the stretching of their necks to see him and crowding around him with all those who are to be humiliated through the establishment of a prescribed punishment, retaliation or discretionary punishment upon him. One tenth of those who gather around such an individual (i.e. the one to be humiliated) do not gather around the judge. In fact, droves of people gather around the people of entertainment, joking, jesting, and the people of song, dance and drum playing, far more than they gather around that judge.

وَهُوَ إذا زهى بركوب دَابَّة أَو مشي خَادِم أَو خادمين فِي ركابه فَليعلم أَن العَبْد الْمَمْلُوك والجندي الْجَاهِل وَالمولد من أَبنَاء الْيَهُود وَالنَّصَارَى يركب دَوَاب أفره من دَابَّته وَيَمْشي مَعَه من الخدم أَكثر مِمَّن يمشي مَعَه، وَإِذا كَانَ وُقُوعه فِي هَذَا الْعَمَل الَّذِي هُوَ من أَسبَاب النَّار على كل حَال طلب المعاش واستدرار مَا يدْفع إِلَيْهِ من الجراية من السُّحت فَليعلم أَن أهل المهن الدنيوية كالحائك والحجام والجزار والإسكافي أنعم مِنْهُ عَيْشًا وأسكن مِنْهُ قلبا لأَنهم آمنُون من مرَارَة الْعَزْل غير مهتمين بتحويل الْحَال.

If the judge becomes prideful of riding animals or having one or two servants walking along with him when he rides, he should know that a slave under the possession of another, the ignorant soldier and the *muwallad* from the sons of the Jews and Christians ride animals finer than his and have more servants walking with them than him. If his involvement in this job, which is one of the means to Hell in every situation, is to seek for livelihood and draw forth to himself a salary from the ill-gotten; then he should know that the people of worldly professions like the weaver, cupper, butcher and cobbler are more blessed than him in livelihood and have more peace of mind than him, because they are saved from the lingering threat of removal [from office] and the changing of circumstance.

فهم يتلذذون بدنياهم ويتمتعون بنفوسهم ويتقلبون فِي تنعمهم هَذَا بِاعْتِبَار الْحَيَاة الدُّنْيَا وَأما بِاعْتِبَار الْآخِرَة فخواطرهم مطمئنة لأَنهم لَا يَخْشون الْعقُوبَة بِسَبَب من الْأَسْبَاب الَّتِي هِيَ قوام المعاش ونظام الْحَيَاة لِأَن

مكسبهم حَلَال وأيديهم مَكْفُوفَة عَن الظُّلم فَلَا يخَافُونَ السُّؤَال عَن دم أَو مَال بل قُلُوبهم مُتَعَلقَة بالرجاء كل وَاحِد مِنْهُم يَرْجُو الِانْتِقَال من دَار شقوة وكدر إِلَى دَار نعْمَة وتفضل.

They are relishing life, amusing themselves and basking in enjoyment. This is with regard to the life of this world. As regards to the life of the Hereafter, their minds are tranquil as they do not fear the torment resulting from the means of earning one's livelihood and system of life one undertakes. This is because their earnings are lawful and their hands are bare of injustice. Thus, they do not fear questioning in regards to [the spilling of] blood or wealth [on the Day of Resurrection]. In fact, their hearts are connected to hope. Every one amongst them hopes to move from the abode of toil and struggle to the abode of blessing and favour.

وَأما ذَلِك القَاضِي الْمُقَلّد فَهُوَ منغص الْعَيْش منكد النِّعْمَة مكدر اللَّذَّة لِأَنَّهُ - لما يرد عَلَيْهِ من خُصُومَة الْخُصُوم ومعارضة المعارضين ومصادرة المتمنعين من قبُول أَحْكَامه وامتثال حلّه وإبرامه - فِي هموم وغموم ومكابدة ومناهدة ومجاهدة وَمَعَ هَذَا فَهُوَ متوقع لتحول الْحَال والاستبدال بِهِ وغروب شمسه وركود رِيحه وَذَهَاب سعده عَنْ نفسه وشماتة أعدائه ومساءة أوليائه فَلَا تصفو لَهُ رَاحَة وَلَا تخلص لَهُ نعْمَة، بل هُوَ مَا دَامَ فِي الْحَيَاة فِي أَشد الْغم وَأعظم النكد كَمَا قَالَ المتنبي:

As for this *muqallid* judge, he has a troubled life, miserable "blessing" and joyless enjoyment, for—due to what he is charged with in the litigations of litigants, dissent of dissenting parties and seizure of those who refuse to accept his rulings and comply with his solutions and settlements—he is embroiled in worry, distress, suffering, resistance and tension; and in addition, he foresees a reverse in his condition and his replacement, the setting of his sun, stagnation of his profit, departure of his happiness, gloating of his enemies and vile actions by his supporters. So, comfort will not be completely given to him nor will blessings. Rather, as long as he is alive, he is in severe distress and misery, as stated by al-Mutanabbi:

أَشد الْغم عِنْدِي فِي سرُور   تيقن عَنهُ صَاحبه انتقالا

The worst distress to me is in happiness, of which its companion is certain of reversion.[209]

وَلَا سِيمَا إِذا كَانَ محسودا مُعَارضا من أَمْثَاله فَإِنَّهُ لَا يطْرق سَمعه إِلَّا مَا يكمده، فحينا يُقَال لَهُ: النَّاس يتحدثون أَنَّك غَلطت وجهلت وحينا يُقَال لَهُ قد خالفك القَاضِي الْفُلَانِيّ أَو الْمُفْتِي الْفُلَانِيّ فنقض حكمك وَهدم علمك وغض من قدرك وَحط من رتبتك وَقد يَأْتِيهِ الْمَحْكُوم له منه فَيَقُول لَهُ جهارا وكفاحا فلان قال لَا عمل على حكمك وَنَحْو ذَلِك من الْعبارَات الخشنة فَإِن قَامَ وناضل عَن حكمه ودافع فَهِيَ قومة جَاهِلِيَّة ومدافعة شيطانية طاغوتية قد تكون لحراسة المنصب وَحفظ الْمرتبَة والفرار من انحطاط الْقدر وَسُقُوط الجاه.

[This is the case] especially if he is envied and seen as an adversary amongst his likes, nothing will reach his ears except that which will

209 See his *Dīwān* (3/224) with the commentary of Abu al-Baqā' al-'Ukbarī. Dār al-Ma'rifah edition.

trouble him. Sometimes it will be said to him, "The people are saying that you erred and were ignorant." And at times it would be said to him, "Such and such judge or such and such *muftī* has contradicted you and your judgement was invalidated; your knowledge was demolished, competence was questioned and your rank was lowered." The person the judgement was in favour of may come to him and say to him publicly and to his face, "So-and-so said that your judgement is not to be acted upon" or similar uncouth expressions. If he rises and defends his judgement, he takes a stand in an ignorant manner, and his defence is of a devilish nature. It could be to protect his position, safeguard his rank and due to scurrying to avoid the reduction of his worth and status.

وَمَعَ ذَلِك فَهُوَ لَا يدْرِي هَل الْحق بِيَدِهِ أم بيد من نقض عَلَيْهِ حكمه لِأَن الْمِسْكِين لَا يدْرِي بِالْحَقِّ بِإِقْرَارِهِ وَجَمِيع المتخاصمين إِلَيْهِ بَين متسرع إِلَى ذمَّة والتشكي مِنْهُ وَهُوَ الْمَحْكُوم عَلَيْهِ يَدعِي أَنه حكم عليه بَاطِل وارتشى من خَصمه أَو داهنه ويتقرر هَذَا عِنْده بِمَا يلقيه إِلَيْهِ من ينافس هَذَا الْمُقَلّد من أَبنَاء جنسه من المقلدة الطامعين فِي منصبه أَو الراجين لرفده أَو النِّيَابَة عَنهُ فِي بعض مَا يتَصَرَّف فِيهِ فَإِنَّهُ يذهب يستفتيهم ويشكو عَلَيْهِم فيطلبون غرائب الْوُجُوه ونوادر الْخلاف ويكتبون له خطوطهم بمخالفة مَا حكم بِهِ الْقَاضِي وَقد يعبرون فِي مكاتبتهم بعبارات تؤلم الْقَاضِي وتوحشه فَيَزْدَاد لذَلِك أَلمه وَيكثر عِنْده همه وغمه. هَذَا يَفْعَله أَبنَاء جنسه من المقلدين.

In spite of this, he does not know whether the truth is in his hand or in the hand of the one who invalidated his judgement, because the hapless does not know the truth based upon his acknowledgment (i.e. the acknowledgment of why he performs *al-taqlīd*). The nature of those who bring disputes to him is that they hastily condemn him and complain about him; and the person the judgement was against will claim that he judged against him with falsehood or he accepted a bribe from his opponent or showed sycophancy. He will affirm this upon him by bringing forth a rival of this *muqallid* from his fellow *muqallids* who craves his position, longs for his share or to substitute him in part of his duties, for he will go to them to seek rulings and to complain. Then they would seek for strange views and instances of difference, and write their thoughts for him so as to oppose what the judge ruled. They may utilise some expressions in their writings that would hurt the judge and alienate him. This would increase his pain, and cause his distress and worry to multiply. And this is what would occur to him from his fellow *muqallids*.

وَأما الْعلمَاء المجتهدون فهم يَعْتَقِدُونَ أَنه مُبْطل فِي جَمِيع مَا يَأْتِي بِهِ لِأَنَّهُ من قُضَاة النَّار فَلَا يرفعون لما يصدر عَنهُ من الْأَحْكَام رَأْسا وَلَا يَعْتَقِدُون أَنه قَاض لِأَنَّهُ قد قَامَ الدَّلِيل عِنْدهم على أَن القَاضِي لَا يكون إِلَّا مُجْتَهدا وَأَن الْمُقَلّد وَإِن بلغ فِي الْوَرع والعفاف وَالتَّقوى إِلَى مبلغ الْأَوْلِيَاء فَهُوَ عِنْدهم بِنَفس استمراره على الْقَضَاء مصر على الْمعْصِيَة وينزلون جَمِيع مَا يصدر عَنهُ منزلَة مَا يصدر عَن الْعَامَّة الَّذين لَيْسُوا بقضاة وَلَا مفتين فَجَمِيع سجلاته الَّتِي يكْتب عَلَيْهَا اسْمه ويحلل فِيهَا الْحَرَام وَيحرم الْحَلَال بَاطِلَة لَا تعد شَيْئا بل لَو كَانَت مُوَافقَة للصَّوَاب لم تعد عِنْدهم شَيْئا لِأَنَّهَا صادرة من قَاض حكم بِالْحَقِّ وَهُوَ لَا يعلم بِهِ فَهُوَ من أهل النَّار فِي الْآخِرَة وَمِمَّنْ لَا يسْتَحق اسْم الْقَضَاء فِي الدُّنْيَا وَلَا يحل تَنْزِيله منزلَة الْقُضَاة الْمُجْتَهدين فِي شَيْء.

As for the *mujtahid* scholars, they believe him to be a liar in all he comes with, as he falls amongst the judges of Hell. They do not raise their heads to what emanates from him in rulings, nor do they believe that he is a judge. This is because the proof is established with them that only a *mujtahid* can be a judge.[210] And even if a *muqallid* reaches the level of the *awliyā* in piety, chastity and fear of Allah, according to them (i.e. the *mujtahid* scholars), in his persistence in passing judgement he is persisting upon sin. They consider everything that emanates from him similar to what emanates from the laity who are not judges or *muftīs*. So all of his official record books upon which he writes his name, legalises the unlawful therein and prohibits the lawful are null and void. In fact, even if they conform to the truth, they will not consider it as bearing any substance. This is because the correct ruling here emanated from a judge who passed a judgement in accordance with the truth without knowing it; so he is amongst the inhabitants of Hell in the Hereafter and amongst those who do not deserve to be a judge in this world. Therefore, it is not permissible to ever appoint him to the status of the *mujtahid* judge.

وَبعد هَذَا كُله فَهَذَا القَاضِي المشؤوم يحْتَاج إِلَى مداهنة السُّلْطَان وأعوانه المقبولين لَدَيْهِ ويهين نَفسه لَهُم ويخضع لَهُم ويتردد إِلَى أَبْوَابهم ويتمرغ على عتباتهم، وَإِذا لم يفعل ذَلِك على الدَّوَام والاستمرار ناكدوه مناكدة

210 Ash-Shayrāzī said in *al-Muhadhab* (20/128), "Chapter: It is not permissible to tie the appointment of a judge to the condition that he should judge with a particular *madhhab* due to the statement of Allah: **{...So judge between men in truth [and justice]...}** [Ṣad: 26]. The truth is that which the proof denotes; and this is not specific to any particular *madhhab*. Thus, if he is appointed based upon this condition, the appointment is null and void because it is dependent upon a condition; and since the condition is void, the appointment is also void."

تجرح صدره وتوهن قدره.

After all of this, this hapless judge will be in need of flattering the ruler and his receptive aides; humbling and lowering himself to them, frequenting their doorsteps and wallowing over their chastisements. If he does not do that continuously and persistently, they will cause him troubles that will pierce his soul and weaken his worth.

وَمَعَ هَذَا فأعوانه الَّذين هم مستدرون لفوائده والمقتنصون للأموال على يَده وَإِن عظموه وفخموه وَقَامُوا بقيامه وقعدوا بقعوده فهم أضرّ عَلَيْهِ من أعدائه، لأَنهم يتكالبون على أَمْوَال النَّاس وَيتم لَهُم ذَلِك بِقُوَّة يَده وَلَا سِيمَا إِذا كَانَ مغفلا غير حَازِم وَلَا متطلع للأمور فتعظم الْقَالة على القَاضِي وينسب ذنبهم إِلَيْهِ وَيحمل جَوْرهمْ عَلَيْهِ فتَارَة ينْسب إِلَى التَّقْصِير فِي الْبَحْث وَتارَة إِلَى التغفيل وَعدم التيقظ وَتارَة إِلَى أَن مَا أَخذه الأعوان فَلهُ فيه مَنْفَعَة تعود إِلَيْهِ لَوْلَا ذَلِك لم يُطلق لَهُم الرشا ولا خلى بَينهم وَبَين النَّاس.

In addition to this, even if his aides who enlist for his benefits and to take the wealth [of others] under the cover of his authority exalt him and honour him, support and endorse him; they are more harmful to him than his enemies. This because they are covetous of people's wealth and they will accomplish this through the power he wields, especially if he is a dullard and not prudent or abreast with the issues. Then the aspersions against the judge will become enormous and the aides' sins and oppression will be ascribed to him. Sometimes it is attributed to a shortcoming in his capabilities of investigation, sometimes to inattention and lack of alertness, and sometimes it is said that he has some personal gain in whatever the aides collected, as were it not for that, he would not have given them free rein to [take] bribes and deal with the people howsoever they like.

وَأَيْضًا أعظم من يذمه ويستحل عرضه هَؤُلَاءِ الأعوان فَإِن كل وَاحِد مِنْهُم يطْمع فِي أَن تكون كل الْفَوَائِد له فَإِذا عرضت فَائِدَة فِيهَا نفع لَهُم من قسْمَة تَرِكَة أَو نظر مَكَان مشتجر فِيهِ فَالْقَاضِي الْمِسْكِين لَا بُد أَن يصيره إِلَى أحدهم فيوغر بذلك صُدُور جَمِيعهم وَيخرجُونَ وصدورهم قد ملئت غيظا فينطقون بذمه فِي المحافل وَلَا سِيمَا بَين أعدائه والمنافسين لَهُ وينعون عَلَيْهِ مَا قضى فِيهِ من الْخُصُومَات الْوَاقِعَة لَدَيْهِ بمحضرهم ويحرفون الْكَلَام وينسبونه إِلَى الْغَلَط تَارَة وَالْجهل أُخْرَى، والتكالب على المَال حينا والمداهنة حينا.

Moreover, the greatest from his condemners and violators of his honour are these aides. This is because each one of them is covetous of every benefit. Thus, when a benefit arises wherein there is potential gain, such as from the share of a bequest or the emergence of a land wherein there is dispute, it is inevitable for this unfortunate judge to give it to one of them (i.e. those covetous of it), and the hearts of the rest of them will be filled with spite because of this. This will cause them to come out whilst their hearts are consumed with rage. They will openly condemn him in gatherings, especially amongst his enemies and those competing with him. In their assembly, they will seek help against him for the judgements he passed in current disputes put before him, and they will alter [his] speech and attribute it (i.e. his speech) to error sometimes and ignorance at other times, to covetousness for wealth sometimes and sycophancy at other times.

وَبِالْجُمْلَةِ فَإِنَّهُ لَا يقدر على إرضاء الْجَمِيع بل لَابد لَهُم من ثلبه على كل حَال وَهو لا يَسْتَغْنِي عَنْهُم فيناله مِنْهُم محن وبلايا.

In brief, he cannot please everyone. Rather, it is inevitable for him to have one who will find fault in him in every situation and he cannot be free of them. He will receive trials and misfortune from them.

هَذَا وهم أهل مودته وبطانته والمستفيدون بأَمْره وَنَهْيه والمنتفعون بِقَضَائِهِ وَمَا أحقهم بِمَا كَانَ يَقُوله بعض الْقُضَاة الْمُتَقَدِّمين فَإِنَّهُ كَانَ لَا يسميهم لأمناء بل يسميهم الكمناء، وَلَا يخرج عن هَذِه الْأَوْصَاف إِلَّا الْقَلِيل النَّادِر مِنْهُم فَإِن الزَّمن قد يتنفس فِي بعض الْأَحْوَال بِمن لَا يتِّصف بِهَذِهِ الصّفة.

These are the people who are his supposed friends, inner circle and the beneficiaries of his orders, prohibitions and his judgements. They are more deserving of what was stated by one of the past judges, that they are not called *amnā'* (trustworthy, loyal), rather they are called *kumanā'* (clandestine [enemies]). None fall outside this description except very few amongst them, for a period of time may find relief of bearing anyone characterised with such traits in some situations.

فَهَذَا حَال القَاضِي الْمُقَلّد فِي دُنْيَاهُ وَأما حَاله فِي أخراه فقد عرفت أَنه أحد القاضيين اللَّذين فِي النَّار وَلَا مخرج لَهُ عَن ذَلِك بِحَال من الْأَحْوَال كَمَا سبق تَحْقِيقه وَتَقْرِيره فَهُوَ فِي الدُّنْيَا مَعَ مَا ذَكرْنَاهُ سَابِقًا من القلاقل

والزلازل فِي نعمه بِاعْتِبَار مَا يخافه من الآخرة من أَحْكَامه فِي دِمَاء الْعباد وَأَمْوَالهمْ بِلَا برهَان وَلَا قرآن وَلَا سنة بل بمُجَرّد جهل وتقليد وَعدم بَصِيرَة فِي جَمِيع مَا يَأْتِي ويذر ويصدر ويورد مَعَ وُرُود الْقُرْآن الصَّحِيح الصَّرِيح بالنَّهْي عَن الْعَمَل بِمَا لَيْسَ بِعلم كَقَوْلِه تَعَالَى: ﴿وَلَا تَقْفُ مَا لَيْسَ لَكَ بِهِ عِلْمٌ﴾ والآيات فِي هَذَا الْمَعْنى وَفِي النَّهْي عَن إتباع الظَّن كَثِيرَة جدا والمقلد لَا علم لَهُ وَلَا ظن صَحِيح.

This is the condition of the *muqallid* judge in his worldly life. As for his condition in the other world, you have seen that he is one of the two judges who will go to Hell; and there is no way out for him from that in any situation, as earlier affirmed and established. In this world, all that he faces from the unrest and troubles which we mentioned previously will be like heaven compared to what he fears for himself in the Hereafter due to his rulings regarding the blood and properties of Muslims which emanated without evidence nor [text from the] Qur'ān or Sunnah. Rather, [they emanated] through pure ignorance, blind following and lack of insight in all facets. He disseminates, discharges, and adduces in spite of the fact that the authentic and clear Qur'ān has mentioned the prohibition of acting upon a state besides knowledge, such as in the statement of the Most High: **{And do not pursue that of which you have no knowledge...}**[211] The *āyāt* with this meaning and which prohibit following speculation (*al-ẓan*) are extremely numerous. The *muqallid* has no knowledge nor the capability of making valid speculation.

وَلَو لم يكن من الزواجر عن هذا إِلَّا مَا قدمنَا من الْآيَات القرآنية فِي

211 Al-Isrā: 36

قَوْله ﴿وَمَن لَّمْ يَحْكُم بِمَآ أَنزَلَ اللّهُ فَأُوْلَئِكَ هُمُ الْكَافِرُونَ﴾، ﴿وَمَن لَّمْ يَحْكُم بِمَآ أَنزَلَ اللّهُ فَأُوْلَئِكَ هُمُ الْفَاسِقُونَ﴾، ﴿وَمَن لَّمْ يَحْكُم بِمَآ أَنزَلَ اللّهُ فَأُوْلَئِكَ هُمُ الظَّالِمُونَ﴾ مَعَ مَا فِي الْآيَاتِ الْأُخْرَى مِنَ الْأَمْرِ بِالحكم بِمَا أنزل الله وبالحق وبالعدل وَمَعَ مَا ثَبَتَ من أن من حكم بِغَيْرِ الْحق أَوْ بِالْحَقِّ وَهُوَ لَا يعلم أَنه الْحق أَنه من قُضَاة النَّارِ.

And if there were no deterrents except these *āyāt* of the Qur'ān which we presented, [it would have sufficed to cite]: {**And whosoever does not judge by what Allah has revealed, such are the disbelievers.**}[212] {**And whosoever does not judge by what Allah has revealed, such are the defiantly disobedient,**}[213] {**And whosoever does not judge by that which Allah has revealed, such are the wrongdoers).**}[214] Additional to this is that which is found in other *āyāt* in regards to the command to judge with what Allah has revealed; and in accordance with the truth and justice. Furthermore, in addition to this there is the established [narration] that whoever judges with other than the truth, or in accordance to the truth whilst not knowing it to be so, he is amongst the judges of Hell.

فَإِن قلت إِذَا كَانَ الْمُقَلّد لَا يصلح لِلْقَضَاءِ وَلَا يحل لَهُ أَن يتَوَلَّى ذَلِك وَلَا لغيره أَو يوليه فَمَا تَقول فِي الْمُفْتِي الْمُقَلّد؟

If the readers asks: If the *muqallid* is not suitable to pass judgements and it is not permissible for him to take charge of this, nor for some-

---

212 Al-Mā'idah: 44
213 Al-Mā'idah: 47
214 Al-Mā'idah: 45

one else to appoint him, what do you say about a *muqallid muftī*?[215]

أَقُول: إن كنت تسْأَل عَن القيل والقال ومذاهب الرِّجَال فَالْكَلَام فِي شُرُوط الْمُفْتِي وَمَا يعْتَبر فِيهِ مَبْسُوط فِي كتب الْأُصُول وَالْفِقْه، وَإِن كنت تسْأَل عَن الَّذِي أعتقده وَأرَاهُ صَوَابا فعندي أَن الْمُفْتِي الْمُقَلّد لَا يحل لَهُ أَن يُفْتِي من سَأَلَه عَن حكم الله أَو حكم رَسُوله أَو عَن الْحق أَو عَن الثَّابِت فِي الشَّرِيعَة أَو عَمَّا يحل لَهُ أَو يحرم له أو يحرم عَلَيْهِ لِأَن الْمُقَلّد لَا يدْرِي بِوَاحِد من هَذِه الْأُمُور على التَّحْقِيق بل لَا يعرفهَا إِلَّا الْمُجْتَهد.

I say: If you are asking about irrelevant talk and the *madhhabs* of men, then the discussion concerning the conditions of being a *muftī* and what is given consideration regarding it is contained in the books of *al-uṣūl*[216] and *al-fiqh*. But if you are asking about that which I believe and hold to be correct, then my view is that it is not permissible for a *muqallid muftī* to issue a *fatwā* to whoever asks him about the ruling of Allah, the ruling of His Messenger, the truth, what is established in the Sharīʿah, what is lawful to him or what is prohibited to him. This is because the *muqallid* does not in actuality know any of these issues. In fact, none knows them except a *mujtahid*.

---

215 Ibn al-Qayyim said in *I'lām al-Muwaqqi'īn* (4/195): It is not permissible for the *muqallid* to issue verdicts in Allah's religion with what he is a blind follower in and he is not upon sure knowledge in it. This is regardless of whether it is the statement of one whom he blind follows in his religion. This is the consensus of all the pious predecessors. And the *imāms* Aḥmad, al-Shāfi'ī and others explicitly declared it so." See the other views in *al-Kawkab al-Munīr* (4/557).

216 See *al-Kawkab al-Munīr* (4/550-553), *al-Musawwadah* (p. 545) and *I'lām al-Muwaqqi'īn* (4/254).

هَكَذَا إِذا سَأَلَهُ السَّائِل سؤالا مُطلقًا من غير أَن يُقَيِّدهُ بِأحد الْأُمُور الْمُتَقَدّمَة فَلَا يحل للمقلد أَن يفتيه بِشَيْء من ذَلِك لِأَن السُّؤَال الْمُطلق ينْصَرف إِلَى الشَّرِيعَة المطهرة لَا إِلَى قَول قَائِل أَو رَأْي صَاحب رَأْي. وَأما إِذا سَأَلَهُ سَائل عَن قَول فلَان أَو رَأْي فلَان أَو مَا ذكره فلَان فَلَا بَأْس بِأَن ينْقل لَهُ الْمُقَلّد ذَلِك وَيَرْوِيه لَهُ إِن كَانَ عَارِفًا بِمذهب الْعَالم الَّذِي وَقع السُّؤَال عَن قَوْله أَو رَأْيه أَو مذْهبه، لِأَنَّهُ سُئِلَ عَن أَمر يُمكنهُ نَقله وَلَيْسَ ذَلِك من التقول على الله بِمَا لم يقل وَلَا من التَّعْرِيف بِالْكتاب وَالسّنة، وَهَذَا التَّفْصِيل هُوَ الصَّوَاب الَّذِي لَا يُنكره منصف.

As such, if a questioner asks him an unrestricted question without limiting it to one of the previous issues, it is not permissible for a *muqallid* to issue a *fatwā* to him as regards to anything of that. This is because a general question should be directed to the pure Sharīʿah and not to the statement of a person or the personal view of a *ṣāḥib raʾyin* (lit. holder of an opinion). But if the questioner asks him about the statement of so and so, the personal opinion of so and so,[217] or what so and so said, then there is no harm for the *muqallid* to mention it to him and narrate it to him. This is if he is learned about the *madhhab* of the scholar of which the inquiry is in regards to his statement, opinion or *madhhab*. This is because he was asked about an issue which is possible for him respond to. And this is not considered to be from stating about Allah what He did not state, or from explaining the Qurʾān and Sunnah. This clarification of the matter is the correct view, which a just person will not reject.

217 See *Iʿlām al-Muwaqqiʿīn* (4/253-273).

فَإِن قلت هَل يجوز للمجتهد أَن يُفْتِي من سَأَلَهُ عَن مَذْهَب رجل معِين وينقله لَهُ.

If the reader asks: Is it permissible for a *mujtahid*[218] to give a verdict to someone who asks him about the *madhhab* of a particular person and transmit it to him?

قلت يجوز ذَلِك بِشَرْط أَن يَقُول بعد نقل ذَلِك الرَّأْي أَو الْمَذْهَب إِذا كَانَا على غير الصَّوَاب مقَالا يُصَرح بِهِ أَو يلوح أَن الْحق خلاف ذَلِك فَإِن الله أَخذ على الْعلمَاء الْبَيَان للنَّاس وَهَذَا مِنْهُ لَا سِيمَا إِذا كَانَ يعرف أَن السَّائِل سيعتقد ذَلِك الرَّأْي الْمُخَالف للصَّوَاب.

I say: It is permissible, upon the condition that he should say after transmitting that opinion or *madhhab*—if it is not correct—a statement that would declare explicitly or indicate indirectly that the truth is contrary to it. This is because Allah has charged the scholars to explain the truth to the people and this is a part of it, especially if he knows that the questioner will believe that the contradicting opinion [or *madhhab*] is correct.

وَأَيْضًا فِي نقل هَذَا الْعَالم لذَلِك الْمَذْهَب الْمُخَالف للصَّوَاب وسكوته عَن اعتراضه إِيهَام للمقصرين بِأَنَّهُ حق وَفِي هَذَا مفْسدَة عَظِيمَة فَإِن كَانَ يخْشَى على نَفسه من بَيَان فَسَاد ذَلِك الْمَذْهَب فَليدع الْجَواب ويحيل على غَيره، فَإِنَّهُ لم يسْأَل عَن شَيْء يجب عَلَيْهِ بَيَانه فَإِن أَلجأته الضَّرُورَة وَلم يتَمَكَّن من التَّصْرِيح بِالصَّوَابِ فعَلَيهِ أَن يُصَرح تَصْرِيحًا لَا يبْقى فِيهِ

218 See *I'lām al-Muwaqqi'īn* (4/261-266).

شكّ لمن يقف عَلَيْهِ أن هَذَا مَذْهَب فلَان أَو رَأْي فلَان الَّذِي سَأَلَ عَنهُ السَّائِل وَلم يسْأَل عَن غيره.

Similarly, in this scholar's transmitting of this *madhhab* that is contrary to the truth, his silence over opposing it would give the illusion to the negligent ones that it is the truth, and this contains great evil. If he fears for himself in explaining the invalidity of this *madhhab*, he should avoid responding and move to other than it, for he was not asked about something that is obligatory upon him to explain. However, if he is forced to do so by necessity and he is unable to explicitly declare the correct position, he is duty bond to state explicitly, leaving no doubt to the one who seeks this information from him, that this is the *madhhab* of so-and-so or opinion of so-and-so whom the questioner asked about specifically.

انتهى ما أردت تحريره بقلم مؤلفه محمد بن علي الشوكاني غفر الله له.

This ends what I wished to compose. From the pen of the author, Muḥammad ibn ʿAlī al-Shawkānī. May Allah grant him forgiveness.